Walter Benjamin

Walter Benjamin

by
Julian Roberts

Humanities Press

Atlantic Highlands, N. J.

First published in 1983 in the United States of America by
HUMANITIES PRESS INC.
Atlantic Highlands
N.J. 07716

ISBN 0-391-02796-4

Printed in Hong Kong

Library of Congress Cataloging in Publication Data

Roberts, Julian.
  Walter Benjamin.

  (Contemporary social theory)
  Includes bibliographical references and index.
  1. Benjamin, Walter, 1982–1940.   I. Title.
II. Series.
B3209.B584R62   1982   838′.91209   82–18713
ISBN 0–391–02796–4 (pbk.)

Gang leaders
Stride about like statesmen. The peoples
Are no longer visible under the armaments.

So the future lies in darkness, and the forces for good
Are weak. All this you saw . . .

BRECHT, 'On the suicide of the refugee W. B.' (1941)

Contents

viii   *Contents*

Preface

I owe many thanks to those who read and commented on this book as it took shape. They include John Ashton, Chloe Chard, Tony Giddens, David Held, Charles Lewis and John Winckler. I am particularly indebted to the deep scholarship and unfailing support of James Bradley.

I am very grateful to my colleagues at the Cambridgeshire College of Arts and Technology for making it possible for me to take a year off to write this, and also to the German Academic Exchange Service for their financial help.

I owe perhaps most to the learning and loyalty of my parents, Mark Roberts and Rosalind Depas, and to the affectionate forebearance of Philippa Bush.

Cambridgeshire College of Arts and Technology   JULIAN ROBERTS
October 1981

Introduction

The highly respected enigma

Since his death in 1940 Walter Benjamin has become recognised as one of the major figures of modern philosophy. For a man who during his life had no proper career and published little except short articles and book reviews, the acclaim he has now received in the academic world and among publishers is remarkable. The 'Benjamin renaissance' started in 1955 with the publication of a slim selection of pieces. Since then output has multiplied enormously, and we are at present half way through the massive *Collected Works* which have, to date, produced nine substantial volumes. This project is a monument of editorial skill and innovation.[1]

The upsurge of interest in Benjamin was also accompanied, as might have been expected, by extensive contributions from academic researchers. A rich body of commentary accumulated throughout the 1970s – most of it in the form of doctoral dissertations and scholarly articles. A great deal of this has appeared outside Germany.[2]

At the same time the assimilation of Benjamin's work among a wider public is less conspicuous. Despite the enormous attention paid to him by specialists, it is noticeable that Benjamin still has no generally recognised theoretical identity. There is nothing which people would commonly acknowledge as 'Benjaminian' in the same way that they might locate 'Brechtian' or 'Lacanian' motifs in a theoretical text. It is almost unthinkable that anyone might be described as 'a Benjaminian'; or at least it would be entirely obscure what that might signify. Similarly, Benjamin does not reap the citations which might be felt appropriate to a thinker of his stature. While other, lesser writers supply the counters of learned debate, Benjamin's endorsement is rarely sought. After a spate of citations in the 1970s, reference to Benjamin is no longer *de rigeur* among writers on cultural theory. Equally, it is very noticeable that nobody has so far attempted a general account of Benjamin. To some extent, this reflects the fact that the final volume of the main part of the *Collected Works* only appeared in 1977, and indeed some important manuscript material has still not been published at all. But the two principal non-specialist accounts which have been published since then – the books by Werner Fuld and Terry Eagleton – both explicitly avoid tackling Benjamin as a completed corpus of theory. Fuld's book, which is in the first instance biography rather than theoretical analysis, declares itself to be 'provisional'.[3] And Eagleton, although his book is entirely theoretical, disclaims any attempt to provide a 'critical account' of Benjamin's texts and says, disarmingly enough, that he is 'trying rather to manhandle them for my own purposes'.[4]

The trouble with Benjamin is that nobody knows whose side he is on. Writers about Benjamin tend to affect a tone of high moral indignation; but it is often unclear who the targets of this indignation might appropriately be. Benjamin's polemical relevance in the modern world seems to remain deeply obscure and controversial. Does his work give support to Marxist iconoclasts and cultural saboteurs? Or is it a slap in the face for academic mandarins who, as George Steiner would have it, have no understanding for 'abstruse thought and scholarship'? The perennial Aunt Sally is the Weimar university administration which failed to give Benjamin a job. But the interpretation of this event among Benjamin's commentators is as varied as their interpretations of the work itself.

To a large extent this uncertainty reflects the situation of Benjamin's own work. From 1925 onwards, after the failure of his attempt to start a university career, Benjamin was constantly caught between opposing groups of friends or associates. From his youth he retained Gerhard Scholem, the Israeli religious historian. Among his new friends in the late 1920s were Bertolt Brecht and the Bolshevik producer Asja Lacis. And during the 1930s he was associated with the Hegelian Marxism of the 'Frankfurt School' – Theodor Adorno and Max Horkheimer. All these people had widely differing political and religious commitments. But since Benjamin, the unemployed academic, was to a large degree financially dependent on their goodwill, it was important not to offend any of them by seeming to endorse any of the others too whole-heartedly.

This was a matter of some pain and doubt for Benjamin during his life. The whole problem was brought into sharp focus again during the Student Movement in the late 1960s, when the Marxist magazine *Alternative* vigorously attacked those members of the Frankfurt School who had undertaken the re-publication of Benjamin's work. The flames were fanned by the intervention of scholars from East Germany, which possesses documents of Benjamin's which had so far not been made available to scholars from elsewhere.[5]

Alternative's accusation – that Benjamin's editors were suppressing 'Marxist' material from the selections and from the 1966 *Briefe* – has now largely been met by the exhaustively documented *Collected Works* and other publications. But it can hardly be said that the additional material has made the picture much clearer. Indeed, it seemed only to confirm that Benjamin was a forbiddingly obscure writer. Habermas's 1972 essay on Benjamin, which announced 'a body of Benjamin criticism that treats its material in scholarly fashion, and . . . gives notice to the imprudent that this is no longer unfamiliar terrain',[6] heralded a decade of commentary which has perhaps been distinguished by too much scholarly prudence. It is interesting to compare the early Benjamin issues of *Alternative* with the recent one (1980), which does not stray an inch beyond the limits of scholarly tact. And, as I have mentioned, the many special issues, article collections, and doctoral dissertations on Benjamin are still not matched by any attempt, specialist or general, to set out the overall co-ordinates of Benjamin's work. The desire to avoid unseemly controversy or over-hasty interpretation has not had very desirable consequences for the understanding of Benjamin, who is probably now even more obscure and misunderstood a figure than he ever was.

This book is an attempt to provide a general critical account of Benjamin's work. It certainly does not claim to be exhaustive; but it does propose a general introductory framework for the interpretation of his texts.

Benjamin is undeniably a difficult figure, partly because much of his writing is itself extremely concise and opaque, and partly because his opinions do not always appear to be consistent. I have tried to follow certain principles in order to overcome these difficulties.

Benjamin's writing was his livelihood, and that livelihood depended intimately on the institutions and organisations he worked for. At the same time, these institutions were themselves complex and bound up with wider historical determinants. The person of Benjamin is a motif which appears to unite a variety of different acts and experiences. But a historically adequate account must recognise that the true unity is only given by the institutions and functional structures that enabled Benjamin to work. This principle of material contextualisation seems to me to have three implications.

First, it is necessary to attend to the question of 'background'. Benjamin, like all writers, wrote within a set of influences and traditions. In order to make sense of what he was saying, it is necessary to identify those influences with reasonable precision, especially when they are no longer familiar to modern readers. This is simple spadework, but important particularly in the case of Benjamin. Modern commentators sometimes attempt to harness Benjamin before the cart of Derrida and de-construction, belabouring him with an anachronistic terminology which rapidly brings the entire vehicle to a halt. 'Symbol', as one example, did not mean the same to Benjamin as it means to French interpreters of Freud; for him it was a term in late nineteenth-century theology. Mixing the two simply leads to a conceptual Babel. Harnack and Klages are more effective – and simpler – instruments for understanding Benjamin than any modern French writer.

Second, the influences on Benjamin were not just the ethereal vapours of pure theory. Benjamin wrote for an audience, and he wrote for a living. His ideas had to be suited to those purposes; they had to do the job demanded of them. And while an individual writer may, in principle, be isolated from the rest of the world, an audience is something that is intimately connected with the political and social conditions of the time. That is true of any writer, however unearthly or lyrical the content of the writing itself. As Benjamin said, 'Commentary has a duty to expose the political content precisely of the purely lyrical parts.'[7] This need do no violence to the integrity of the work, as is evident from the work of Benjamin or indeed other materialist intellectual historians like Kautsky.[8] Accordingly, I have tried to point up the political implications of Benjamin's own work: not so much the explicitly political statements, as the general sense in which his writings address themselves to political tasks. Ultimately this is an influence, or determinant, much more important than the question of theoretical sources.

Third, I have tried to avoid any kind of biographical hero-worship. The person of Benjamin is in the last resort a hook on which to hang a fully historical topic of discussion. The discussion, I would suggest, is the still urgent one of the function of cultural labour in an era of political crisis. The success or failure of 'Benjamin's life', whatever that is, is in the last resort a fable to give narrative continuity to this discussion. Benjamin himself worked for different organisations, and at a time when the progressive intelligentsia were in even greater disarray than they are now. It is hardly surprising that his work, which always attempted to engage in the immediately practical, shows certain inconsistencies. But ultimately we must take the historical and political lesson from the fate of those organisations and Benjamin's work in them, not the purely *moral* one of Benjamin's personal existence. The attempt to extract single-minded purpose from a biographical subject is only a reflection of what Benjamin himself attacked as the intellectuals' mythology of 'creative personality'.

In this sense there is not really any 'conclusion' to draw about Benjamin: his career mirrors the continuing struggle between socialism and the vast ideological resources of monopoly capitalism. None the less, a few specific points may be made here in summary of my own position in relation to other work on Benjamin.

In the first place, it seems to me that Benjamin's sister-in-law was right when she characterised him as 'on the road to Marxism and socialism, albeit with many diversions and dead ends'.[9] The view of Adorno and Scholem, that Benjamin's Marxism was only the result of the malign influence of Brecht, seems to me entirely untenable, unless one is to dismiss the greater part of his work after 1925. (It seems to me also to rest on a strange misunderstanding of the 1924 book on tragedy.) This applies also to the many interpreters since Habermas who suggest that Benjamin was 'above' the Communist Party and its politics. In reality, Benjamin was struggling to make Marxist-Leninism work, for him, against the most advanced positions of bourgeois cultural philosophy. This was a lonely fight, but by no means an apolitical one.

The weakness of Benjamin's later position, after his conversion to Communism, lies in his failure ever to re-examine its metaphysical foundations. He recognised that there were problems in his move to dialectical materialism, and initially, at least, he regarded its metaphysics as 'inapposite' (*unzutreffend*).[10] Later he expressed the view that his long-held philosophy of language was in fact compatible with materialism.[11] But despite such incidental comments, and a passing plan to take systematic issue with the quintessential idealism of Heidegger, Benjamin never did attempt a thorough reconstruction.

This weakness finally showed itself, as I shall argue in the last chapter of this book, in the famous 'Theses on History'. The Theses, largely on the initiative of Theodor Adorno, have long been regarded as the centrepiece of Benjamin's work. They are not in any orthodox sense Marxist and, accordingly, have frequently been used as a stick with which to beat would-be Marxist interpreters. I am not so foolish as to suggest that 'not being Marxist' is the weakness of the Theses; what I would most strongly argue, however, is that the Theses do not stand up even from the point of view of commentators like Adorno. The Theses, in great part, are a bizarre recapitulation of the views of Heidegger and Klages, skimpily dressed in the language of revolution. The Theses do not give much comfort to Communism, it is true; but then neither do they give it to *anyone* of good faith. Benjamin's greatest work lies elsewhere; whatever our assessment of his politics, we do him a disservice by holding too fast to the Theses.

Benjamin's greatest work is on cultural practice. The striking originality of this work seems to me confirmed by the difficulty with which it has been assimilated in Britain. Benjamin's ideas are not just another model for the analysis of texts; they are an immensely sophisticated set of propositions about the function and impact of ideological labour. In that sense, they affect not only the way historians describe historical phenomena, but the way in which they organise their own labours. Benjamin's attempts to determine what class consciousness means in the context of academic work are far superior to the scholasticism with which many cultural theorists try nowadays to buttress their activities.

Contrary to what many commentators seem to think, the essence of Benjamin's work is that it is *not* sceptical or pessimistic. It is addressed to the possibilities of immediate implementation, and the realities of practical politics. Benjamin acclaimed the notion of 'destructive' work. This destructiveness, however, was not the sour reaction of those who claim that things are bad, but that ideas of improvement are illusory. The destructive character might have little interest in knowing exactly what would follow destruction.[12] But something will follow, and it can only be an improvement. Meanwhile, in the words of the architect Adolf Loos, 'When human labour consists only of destruction, then it will be really human, natural and noble labour.'[13] The scepticism of those who exclude any possibility of progress, particularly if they claim to be left-wing radicals, was characterised by Benjamin as:

> precisely that stance which corresponds to a complete cessation of political activity. He [the 'radical'] stands not to the left of this or that faction, but quite simply to the left of anything possible. But then after all, he never did have anything else in view except to enjoy himself in peaceful negativity.[14]

This is the hypocrisy of those who use scepticism to undermine attacks on the institutions from which they draw their sustenance, while satisfying their consciences by seeming to agree with the attacker. Benjamin's dictum about 'standing to the left of anything possible' has been used, with some justification, about the 'Negative Dialectics' of the Frankfurt School.[15] It is important to remember that it is not part of Benjamin's own thought, however 'destructive'.

Finally, a practical point must be made. Benjamin's style of writing is in itself not always easy to follow. Beyond this, it is frequently difficult on first acquaintance to understand which positions he is attacking and which ones he is defending. Benjamin does not usually refute directly his opponents or those with whom he disagrees; he carefully takes them in and instals them on mounts, the beautiful and delicate trophies of the collector. The problem for the reader is recognising that these are indeed trophies, dead despite their beauty. To the collector, the fact that a particular beautiful specimen is one of a species nearing extinction, or a cruel parasite, is sufficiently obvious to be hardly worth mentioning. The unprepared reader, however, may not be so fortunate, and emerge quite uncertain whether the object so lovingly described by the specialist is alive or dead, estimable or abhorrent. The immediate task of a commentary is to prevent such misunderstanding.

Instructions for use

This book was conceived and written as an introduction to the work of Walter Benjamin. Some of his thought, however, is unusually difficult, and this is inevitably reflected by the level at which I have been forced to conduct some of the discussion. Ultimately, it is important that the book be read as a unity, and that the difficult passages should be taken along with the more accessible ones. But it is possible to obtain a general view without necessarily ploughing at once through the entire book.

The most accessible passages are Part I, and the first two sections of Part II, 'Context and Background'. They will provide the general biographical and historical data indispensable to an understanding of Benjamin. Next, the second section of Part III, entitled 'Historical Materialism', is a straightforward thematic exposition of the views for which Benjamin is probably best known. Taken together, these passages will give an approachable and reasonably comprehensive account of Benjamin's work during his mature years.

That is all that such a reading can achieve, however. It would leave out two very important areas. The first is the work Benjamin did before his mature period (that is, before 1925), in particular the extraordinary piece on Goethe's novel *Die Wahlverwandtschaften* and the book on Baroque drama. Second, it would omit any discussion of Benjamin's place in the intellectual landscape of the twentieth century, whether in his own immediate context or for us now.

But these objectives are very much more challenging than the historical materialism of Benjamin's maturity taken in isolation. That can be followed with only a rudimentary understanding of Marxism. But the role of this Marxism within Benjamin's own thought, and its position in relation to the many other theoretical traditions that he confronted, is something that can only be understood with a great deal more effort. Without this understanding it is not possible to do justice to Benjamin's work, and in particular the fact that his polemic is frequently directed *against* many of those same positions with which commentators try to associate him. Part of Benjamin's significance is his very sophisticated adaptation of Marxism to cultural criticism. But a greater part of it is his assault on the bankrupt avant-gardism of groups whose theoretical descendants still survive today.

So, the remaining parts of the book are devoted to the difficult task of critical contextualisation. The third section of Part II, 'The Intellectual Background', is an attempt to give a summary of the outstanding ideological tension of the time (Benjamin's and our own) – namely, the confrontation between a rich and elaborate philosophical idealism, supplied in particular with a very compelling theory of culture, and an apparently somewhat threadbare materialism. This section describes the background against which all of Benjamin's theoretical moves have to be seen. It is difficult to the extent that neo-Kantian and Heideggerian logic are not always entirely simple.

This section is followed by the first part of my commentary on Benjamin's own work, entitled 'From Ethics to Politics'. This is the theoretical heart of the book. Unfortunately it also contains the most difficult passages. The difficulty arises largely from the fact that Benjamin's early work leans heavily on theology as a theoretical resource. For a post-war Anglo-Saxon reader this is likely to be a somewhat daunting prospect. I have, however, persisted in my attempt to clarify the theological dimensions of Benjamin's progress. That is because, as Benjamin recognised, Christian theology offers an immensely powerful repository of philosophical instruments which have nothing in the first instance to do with any specific faith. Secondly, Christian theology offers a range of *political* commitments; and although these are nowadays rarely made explicit, it is still true that some of the greatest ideological battles of the modern world have been fought – are being fought – within *theological* structures. It is not otiose that Heidegger was brought up a Catholic. And Benjamin's lifelong critique of Catholicism is in important respects as crucial as his embrace of Marxism. His earlier writings, especially the Goethe essay and the book on Baroque *Trauerspiel*, are the first advances in a campaign which only later settled on a mainly Marxist tactic.

Theologies are philosophical structures with an explicit or implied religious commitment. From the viewpoint of the historian, such structures supply refined and comprehensive accounts of earlier forms of social self-consciousness, and inevitably therefore lie at the heart of the history of ideas. The materialist, however, regards the religious commitment of theology as superseded; and from that viewpoint, what might once have been humane and enlightened can only appear as reactionary mystification if it sets itself against modern theories. This explains what may seem to be an inconsistency in Benjamin's evaluation of theological issues.

The final section of the book, 'Revolution – Utopia or Plan?', is an attempt at an overall critical assessment. I have applied myself both to Benjamin and to the many critics who have fought over his legacy. In certain ways this is the essential message of the book. But it is not a message that will be understood without negotiating the paths that lead to it.

All the translations from Benjamin's work are my own. I cannot unreservedly recommend any of the English translations currently available. Translators inevitably interpret; and many of the interpretations that have resulted rest on a quite inadequate critical framework. One problem is that central technical terms can be lost or obscured. I have marked some of the worst clashes between my reading and that of the translators by adding an asterisk to the English reference. Readers with any German at all would be well advised to acquire the German collected works, now available in cheap format for around £30.

My text is heavily and perhaps intrusively referenced. This is because Benjamin's prose is so very dense – so much so that I did consider using line numbers as well. I have given references to the German collected works and to the major English translations currently available. (I have used the British editions – pagination in the American editions is not always uniform with them.) Where the piece has not appeared in one of these major selections I have simply given a short English title. It is worth noting that other translations of pieces by Benjamin occasionally appear in magazines such as *Screen*.

I have used a form of shorthand for referring to the titles of Benjamin's books which is based on the way he himself referred to them. 'The Goethe essay' is the article, 'Goethes Wahlverwandtschaften'. 'The *Trauerspiel* book' is the 1924 Habilitation dissertation on Baroque drama, *Ursprung des deutschen Trauerspiels*. 'The Reproduction Essay' is the article commonly translated into English as 'The Work of Art in the Age of Mechanical Reproduction'. 'The first Baudelaire essay' is 'The Paris of the Second Empire in Baudelaire', and 'the second Baudelaire essay' is 'Some Motifs in Baudelaire'. Any other titles are self-explanatory. Beyond this, it should be emphasised that by Benjamin's 'mature' work I mean the work of his historical materialist period between about 1925 and 1939. Before that comes 'early' Benjamin; after it come the 'Theses on the Philosophy of History'. This schematisation is clarified at a number of points in the book.

I

Benjamin's Life

Benjamin's working life may be divided into four periods: his years as a student before and during the First World War; the years of growing political awareness between 1919 and 1925; the mature work as a professional writer between 1925 and 1939; and the brief coda of refugee existence in 1939 and 1940, which concluded with his suicide in September of that year. The forty-eight years of Benjamin's life passed through a distinct sequence of organisational associations. This sequence was reflected in his work and its more or less explicit commitments.

Studentship

Walter Benjamin was born in Berlin on 15 July, 1892, the son of affluent Jewish parents. His father traded in antiques and oriental rugs; from 1918 onwards he seems to have concerned himself mainly with dealing on the stock exchange.[1] The family lived in Grunewald, which was then the patrician quarter of Berlin, full of large houses in secluded grounds. Benjamin kept the extravagant habits acquired in the parental villa for most of his life. Asja Lacis describes the first impression she had of him as an 'affluent intellectual'[2] who revealed himself to be an accomplished gourmet,[3] a munificent lover capable of profligate generosity,[4] and an impassioned collector of valuable books and other beautiful objects. Benjamin's collections stood him in good stead in later years of poverty as a source of ready cash.[5]

Benjamin was not intellectually close to his family, but retained personal links with them throughout his life. While he and his wife lived in Berlin they lived in the Grunewald villa. Even in his thirties, Benjamin was still sufficiently enmeshed with his parents to be having emotional rows with them[6] and negotiating with them for allowances.[7] Benjamin had a younger brother, Georg, who was a militant Communist Party member and worked as a doctor in a workers' district in Berlin.[8] One would have expected Benjamin to have taken an interest in his brother's affairs, particularly in the years in which he himself nearly joined the Communist Party. But even Asja Lacis never met Georg during the period she lived with Benjamin in Berlin.[9] Georg died in a Nazi concentration camp. His wife Hilde, also a communist and described by Benjamin as 'ein sympathisches junges Mädchen', became Minister of Justice in the GDR after the war.[10] Hilde was a friend of Benjamin's younger sister Dora, in whose Paris flat Benjamin lived for a period during the exile.

Benjamin's privileged background no doubt contributed towards his cavalier attitude to money and the means of existence. He enjoyed gambling for reckless stakes[11] and shocked his friend Scholem with his cynical expectations of parental support.[12] His attitude towards careers and an ordered lifestyle was always extremely casual. He married in 1917, long before he had completed an academic qualification or had any prospect of earning his own living; but he was able to rely on support from his own parents, those of his new wife,[13] and on the fact that his wife's previous and very affluent husband had settled property on her.[14]

Benjamin was already a prolific writer during this early period. Until 1914 his work was mainly associated with the German youth movement, of which he was an active member. He abandoned this after the outbreak of war, when the leader of the movement and many former members endorsed the call to arms. (Benjamin himself avoided conscription by feigning sciatica.)[15] His first work of real substance, a commentary on two poems by Hölderlin, was produced in reaction to this, and to the suicide of his poet friend C. F. Heinle, itself a response to the war.

Benjamin's university studies started in 1912 at Freiburg im Breisgau, and continued in Berlin. During the war he also studied at Munich, and in 1917 moved to Bern, where he stayed for two years before taking a D.Phil. in 1919. Much of Benjamin's work after 1914 was concerned with the development of a philosophical position which, as Gerhard Scholem noted, seemed to be taking on the features of a complete intellectual system.[16] This tendency was reflected in pieces such as 'On the programme of future philosophy'. Generally this work consisted in the exploration of a strongly religious Judaism against the background of the Neo-Kantianism of his first professors. The two 1916 essays on language are reflections of this. The doctoral dissertation itself, 'The Concept of Art Criticism in German Romanticism', was a relatively straightforward exposition of Fichte's metaphysics and Friedrich Schlegel's aesthetics. Its importance for the future lay in its analysis of intellectual *practice* as opposed to merely intellectual *theory*.

The move towards politics 1919-25

Until 1919 Benjamin enjoyed a comfortable existence, protected by his family and wife from the exigencies of the real world. The completion of the D.Phil. removed the justification for a life of pure study, however, and Benjamin soon came under pressure from his parents to find a job. This pressure was intensified by the difficulties his parents themselves faced after the 1923 inflation. Benjamin and his wife were forced to return to Berlin and to resign themselves among other things to living in his parents' house.

To escape this claustrophobic situation Benjamin embarked, rather half-heartedly, on preparation for the Habilitation examination, which would have guaranteed him a university post. But Benjamin's 'ironical' (Adorno) attitude towards the universities, and his failure to establish any real links with university life, eventually culminated in the traumatic failure of his 1925 Habilitation attempt at Frankfurt.

He was more successful as a free man of letters. An attempt to start a magazine of his own, the *Angelus Novus,* failed, but thereafter an introduction to the Austrian poet, Hugo von Hofmannsthal, gave him entry into a variety of intellectual circles. In 1923, Benjamin published a volume of translations from Baudelaire, and the major theoretical text, 'Goethes Wahl-verwandtschaften'. By 1925 he was well established as a contributor to journals in Berlin and elsewhere, and had particular responsibility for French aesthetic theory on the journal *Literarische Welt.*

The years after the war ended in 1918 were extremely turbulent in Germany, and this turbulence was reflected in the political radicalisation of many intellectuals. For Benjamin, political socialism began to merge with the ethical puritanism he had endorsed since his years in the youth movement. Although Benjamin's output during the early 1920s was relatively modest, it moved through three distinct stages. In 1921, under the influence of Bloch's messianic socialism, Benjamin produced the utopian texts 'Critique of Violence' and the 'Theologico-Political Fragment'. The following year he wrote the essay, 'Goethes Wahlverwandtschaften', which is in essence a theistic account of ethics. And finally the Habilitation dissertation itself, the *Ursprung des deutschen Trauerspiels,* took all the exploratory elements of the previous years and synthesised them into a magnificent critique of intellectual practice set against the ideological production of the German Baroque period. By this time Benjamin had read Lukács's *History and Class Consciousness,* and in his dissertation it was real history which provided the resolution of the conflicting elements of religious ethics and anarchist politics.

Maturity 1926-39

Ursprung des deutschen Trauerspiels was Benjamin's major theoretical achievement, but it did not bring him the professional security in pursuit of which it had originally been written. If anything, Benjamin's life became more and more bohemian as the 1920s progressed. His marriage had already started to founder in 1921, and the following years saw the love affairs with the sculptress Jula Cohn, and the Bolshevik producer Asja Lacis. Although Benjamin and his wife were soon to all intents and purposes separated (the divorce came in 1930), he never settled down again with anyone else, and from 1929 onwards Benjamin's liaisons were all more or less casual.

Despite their insecurity, Benjamin's circumstances as a journalist and writer during the late 1920s were reasonably affluent (he does not seem to have had any significant support from his parents after 1925). The articles and essays published during these years financed many extended trips abroad, in particular to Paris and the Mediterranean (repeatedly), and to Moscow (in the winter of 1926-7). In 1928 and 1929 an elaborate attempt by his friend Scholem to persuade Benjamin to come to Palestine, where he had excellent prospects of a post at the new Hebrew University, failed when he decided that he was better off in Berlin.

The happy years after 1925, when Benjamin published and broadcast prolifically and became an esteemed member of the circles around Brecht and the left-wing avant-garde, came to an abrupt end in 1933 with the Nazi takeover. Benjamin, along with most of his associates, was forced to flee the country. Life among the Berlin avant-garde suddenly turned into the desperate struggle to find a means of existence. What had once been leisured holidays became the wanderings of a man searching for the cheapest place to live. The elegant resorts of Ibiza, San Remo, Paris, and Skovsbostrand in Denmark were now the staging posts of an impoverished fugitive.

Apart from members of his family with whom he could stay (his ex-wife in San Remo, his sister in Paris), Benjamin did manage to retain a number of other sources of support during his exile. At one time or another, for example, he received funds from the Alliance Israelite[17] and from his old lover Jula Cohn (now Radt) and her husband.[18]. Kitty Marx-Steinschneider, whom Benjamin met shortly before leaving Berlin in 1933,[19] held open a permanent offer of the fare to Palestine: and the Adornos, as well, stressed their readiness to help. (Benjamin did not take up either offer.) He was able to continue with commissions from various German journals, albeit pseudonymously. He edited a collection of letters which was published in Switzerland. He contributed to a variety of emigré journals, and made efforts to develop links with the two Bolshevik German journals published in Moscow. This met with only limited success, despite the fact that his friend Brecht was on the editorial board of one of them.

But the mainstay of Benjamin's professional existence after 1933 was the Institute for Social Research, and its journal, the *Zeitschrift für Sozialforschung*. Benjamin received his first commissions from the *Zeitschrift* early in 1933, and a year later the Institute began to pay him a monthly allowance. This was gradually increased over the years until, by the end of 1937, Benjamin was considered a full member of the Institute and was receiving an inflation-proof US $80 per month.[20] At this point, Benjamin, who had spent the first two years of exile moving despondently around Europe and even hoping for a call from the Soviet Union,[21] was well established in Paris and considering an application for French citizenship.[22]

Benjamin's production was substantial during the years of his maturity, even though he did not complete any full-length books. His writing in Berlin was mainly journalistic. Many of the less technical essays of that time were published in the collection of aphorisms, *One-Way Street* (1928), which among other things chronicled Benjamin's turn to explicit Marxism. Specialist work appeared in the many reviews he wrote, all of which deepened his understanding of Marxism and of the role of intellectuals in the modern political arena. The series of reviews on contemporary literary history is particularly important, as are those on Jünger, Kracauer, Kästner and others. (Unfortunately few of these have been translated.)

During the 1930s, and especially as an aspect of his association with the Institute for Social Research, Benjamin's work again took on a more systematic and academic character. It had two sides. On the one hand were the monographic treatments of particular writers or groups of writers, such as the essays on Kraus, Kafka, Baudelaire, Jochmann, the Surrealists, and modern French writers ('On the Present Social Situation of the French Writer', 1933). The historical pieces all exemplify Benjamin's principle of depicting the modern world in history.[23] All scrupulously accurate in research, and powerful in historical scope, these essays nevertheless always make clear that the events described are directly connected with the historical processes the intelligentsia faces today.

The second major division of this 'academic' work during the 1930s was theoretical. To some degree, it may be inferred from his comments, this was an attempt to meet the need for a coherent historical-materialist account of culture.[24] Some of these writings, such as the pieces on Eduard Fuchs, on 'The Author as Producer', and on Brecht, revolved around common topics of contemporary Marxist interest. Others, particularly the essay on 'The Work of Art in the Age of Mechanical Reproduction', were more concerned with Benjamin's principal historical project for the Institute, the so-called 'Arcades' complex. This massive work, which never got beyond a huge collection of material and a number of preparatory methodological sketches, was intended to unfold the ideological panorama of nineteenth-century Paris. The short sketch, 'Paris, Capital of the XIX Century', was the project proposal that Benjamin elaborated for the Institute in 1935.

Coda 1939-40

In August 1939 the Soviet Union signed a non-aggression pact with Germany, freeing Hitler's hand for the invasion of Poland and thus ushering in the Second World War. This seemed treachery indeed against the European Left, who had for so long assumed that Stalin, at least, would stand up to Fascism.

Benjamin was caught out, like so many others who believed that Hitler's regime could not last long, and that even if it did come to war Hitler's ruin would only be accelerated. Benjamin, who believed that the next war would be fought with gas and bring the extinction of civilisation, was not as naive as some. But he was sufficiently sure of himself, at least after the consolidation of his relations with the Institute, to have settled down in Paris and did not make any serious attempts to leave.

So, the outbreak of war found Benjamin in Paris, and he spent the autumn of that year incarcerated in an internment camp in Nevers. Freed by the efforts of his friends and the PEN club, he finally threw himself into a belated struggle to obtain a US immigration visa. When the German troops flooded into France in June 1940 he was still in Paris and still had no visa. After fleeing south, he spent a desperate summer wondering whether he would be extradited under the Franco-German armistice agreements before his visa arrived from America. Eventually it did arrive (it is not entirely clear through whose agency), but by this time the closure of the border between France and Spain had put fresh obstacles in his path. He attempted with a group of other refugees to enter Spain by an unmarked route over the mountains. They were apprehended by border guards, who allowed them to spend the night in Spain, but told them they would be taken back across the border in the morning. During the night, Benjamin committed suicide by swallowing morphine tablets. Shaken by this, the guards allowed his companions to proceed.

Benjamin produced only one work of note after the summer of 1939, when he had completed the large Baudelaire project. That work however, the famous 'Theses on the Philosophy of History', is the focus of all the controversy that surrounds Benjamin. The work amounts to a repudiation, certainly of Benjamin's previous commitments to the Soviet Union and organised Communism, and arguably also of his work within the framework of historical materialism. Some commentators, led by Benjamin's associates Adorno and Scholem, have claimed that the work's continuity with early religious writings, and (supposedly) with fragments written during the mature period, establishes it as the crowning testament of the entire oeuvre. For others this is an unacceptable view. In what follows I shall attempt among other things to resolve this problem.

II
Context and Background

1
The Early Years

One reason for Benjamin's elusive image is the fact that he was never conspicuously part of any intellectual group. He was never a university professor, nor a member of the 'George circle'. He did not join the Communist Party, and he was not a Zionist. He associated with the Frankfurt school, but only while also consorting with quite different elements, like Bertolt Brecht and the German emigrés in Moscow. It is not always clear who his friends were: his professional allegiances were commonly even more obscure. Does this mean that he was a member of what Karl Mannheim termed the 'unaffiliated intelligentsia' (*freischwebende Intelligenz*) – that he was a vindication of those who claim that successful intellectual enquiry is only possible when insulated from the interference of class or professional interest? It is certainly tempting to regard Benjamin as a heroic outsider, misunderstood by friends and associates, and excluded from their baser interests by his own uncompromising pursuit of truth. This view is clearly manifested in much commentary on Benjamin, as in George Steiner's account of him as an esoteric visionary 'committed to abstruse thought and scholarship'.[1]

There are elements of truth in this view. The problem lies in its sentimental occlusion of the passage between thought and practice. It is undoubtedly the case that organised interests can seriously distort theoretical deliberation. In this sense, pursuit of a career is not always compatible with the maintenance of a high intellectual independence. But that does not mean that the reverse – maintenance of intellectual independence without any regard for career – is itself of any value. The choice is not between Parnassian isolation and sordid material interest, but between the critical and the uncritical selection of a working context. Benjamin neither sought nor believed in isolation; but he was highly conscious of the practical extensions his thought would acquire in any particular working organisation. Throughout his life, his reflections on his own personal situation were firmly anchored in his general understanding of theory and its practical application. And the story of his 'career' is the story of a struggle to exploit unsympathetic or refractory organisational structures for his own purposes. In this respect, Benjamin can indeed claim all the moral stature of a thinker in adversity; but that morality, however attractive, is very much less interesting to the historian that the tactical manoeuvres he employed to sustain his project. Benjamin's bravery is admirable, but his cunning is instructive.

The youth movement

As Adorno noted, with surprise, Benjamin's intellectual inclinations were from the first characterised by 'collectivism'.[2] Adorno felt that this was in paradoxical contrast to Benjamin's own 'nonconformism', which would, in his view, lead one to expect a more 'individualist' attitude. But the opposition of 'individualism' and 'collectivism' is a rather inadequate account of any intellectual project. It is not that Benjamin was unusually public in his thinking; it is rather that he chose to do this thinking within structures specifically designed for it. The schools and universities to which Adorno accommodated himself were no less 'collectivist' than Benjamin's discussion groups; it is only that their existing presence was uncritically accepted. And Adorno's argument that Benjamin's great genius inevitably alienated him from all his 'collectives' is an illegitimately sentimental account of Benjamin's progress through a series of organisations which, as we shall see, revealed themselves for quite practical reasons as unsuitable or inaccessible.

Benjamin's first intellectual collective was the youth movement of the early years of this century. This was the *Jugendbewegung* of the pre-war years which, in a development similar to that of the 1960s student movement, subsequently broke up into a variety of entrenched positions covering the entire political spectrum from anti-Semitism to Communism. Like its modern counterpart, the early years of the movement saw the birth of many more or less radical alternatives to the supposedly bankrupt traditional forms of social life. Benjamin's choice, the faction loyal to the ideas of the educational reformer Gustav Wyneken, was one of the most radical and the most notorious.[3]

In keeping with the general tendency of youth movements, however, this radicalism was rather more anti-political than political; certainly Benjamin himself saw freedom from pragmatic political aims as a precondition of the spiritual regeneration offered by the youth movement.[4] Wyneken himself, who taught Benjamin while the boy was spending two years away from Berlin at a rural boarding school,[5] inclined towards attitudes similar to those of the English public school. This involved, on a general level, dissolving specific partisan allegiances into a general commitment to the national, the social, the ethical and the religious – all understood in a rather diffuse sense.[6] Such interests were not to be guided by 'party or sect'. Wyneken's central principle, based on a rationalistic humanism, affirmed the primacy of individual experience over all traditional authority. As in the English public schools, authority was to be self-generated, and the principle of freedom was to be exploited in order to make the pupils educate themselves, rather than allowing precedent to do it for them.[7] In opposition to the traditional German model, in which state-run grammar schools transmitted a centrally determined curriculum, Wyneken's 'Free School Community' in Wickersdorf regarded the free development of its pupils as a supreme goal. Educational aims would be achieved naturally, by relying on the 'will to culture' *(Kulturwille)* of the pupils.

These principles, which were regarded as unacceptably radical by the educational establishment (Wyneken was forced to leave his newly founded school after only four years),[8] exercised a powerful influence on the young Benjamin. Benjamin's contact with Wyneken as a pupil was brief, but from 1910 onwards Wyneken was a full-time propagandist for his own ideas, and Benjamin became deeply involved in the movement between the time that he left school in 1912 and the outbreak of war in 1914. Benjamin's first move after his Abitur was to the university of Freiburg. There, at Wyneken's request, he sought to take over part of the work of the local 'Free Students' *(Freie Studentenschaft)*,[9] an organisation within the youth movement which set up in opposition to the dominant 'Fraternities' with their reactionary political orientation. In the following semesters he extended this activity both at Freiburg and in Berlin. For much of 1913 he was engaged in the production of the Wyneken group's magazine, *The Beginning (Der Anfang)*, for which he wrote numerous contributions.[10] By early 1914, he had become closely involved with the discussion groups set up by the movement throughout Germany to deepen the impact of the magazine.[11] Finally, in May 1914, Benjamin was elected president of the Berlin 'Free Students'.[12] All of these commitments demanded skill in dealing with large propagandistic organisations. His later rather distanced attitude towards similar organisations was not the genius's horror of the collective, but a clear vision of what they could and could not achieve for him.

Wyneken's principles received a considerable enrichment in the thought of the young Benjamin, who amalgamated them with elements derived from a variety of other thinkers, notably Kant, Plato, Hölderlin, Kierkegaard, Nietzsche and the George circle. There were three distinct elements in this early position: spiritualism, a theory of leadership, and the principle of Eros. Benjamin's early spiritualism was based on his understanding of a Platonic and Kantian idealism. In immediate terms, it meant a rejection of traditional religious authorities in favour of the guidance of spirit – *Geist*. Apealing to Kant, Benjamin contrasted the 'empirical' norms of a crudely partisan ethics with the transcendental purity of the categorical imperative.[13] Rejection of the simplistic demands of any movement or dogma, and absorption into the purer sources of morality, were for Benjamin a sufficient ground for his organisational work. This position also established his distance from Zionism, with which he was in close contact during his first summer as a student.[14] In a position closely akin to that of the assimilated Jewish philosopher Hermann Cohen, he declared that however valuable Judaism might be to him, it could never be as an end in itself, but only because it had shown itself to be 'a particularly eminent bearer of the spiritual' *(des Geistigen)*.[15] A nationalistic Zionism was necessarily quite alien to this view.

The young Benjamin's emphasis on the ideal and the spiritual made him into something of a prig. In a 1913 letter, notable for its pompous self-regard, he reported a quarrel between himself and a friend in the Berlin discussion group, describing with relish how the two recognised their difference to be 'stern and necessary', and

how they both withstood temptation – Benjamin's friend the
temptation to declare hostility, and Benjamin the temptation to
accept the offer of reconciliation which his friend made instead.
Benjamin characterises his own standpoint in this as perceiving
'the necessity of the Idea'; his friend believed that it was possible
to set about implementing this Idea, whereas Benjamin saw that it
was possible only piously to await the Idea's self-fulfilment.[16] He
expressed a similarly Calvinistic view of the elect: *Geist* was not
necessarily in league with the 'brothers' of the actually existing
movement, but rather with inspired individuals whether organised
or not, 'the friendship of friends who are strangers to one another'.
The grace of the spirit was bestowed in mysterious ways. Benjamin
could only be sure of his immediate duty: 'to eject Heinle [the
friend] from the movement and leave the rest to *Geist*'.

As we have seen, however, this attitude did not mean that
Benjamin disdained organisational involvement for himself. Nor
did it free him from the mystique of community and leadership
which characterised the youth movement at this time. Much of this
derived, at least for those with literary resources, from the work of
the circle around Stefan George, and, at a greater distance, from
Friedrich Hölderlin. Hölderlin, in an era still enormously affected
by the success of the French Revolution, produced in his novel
Hyperion (1799) a vision of secular regeneration implemented in
the passionate commitment of two idealistic youths. Legitimately
or not, this text stood throughout the nineteenth century as a
model of the nationalistic cultural revolution, by means of which
the Germans could achieve results comparable with the French.
Hölderlin was one of Benjamin's earliest interests. Another was
the poet Stefan George. Hölderlin's literary celebration of manly
friendship was carried a great deal further by Stefan George, who
assembled a well known circle of comrades and disciples. Like F.
R. Leavis in England, George was immensely influential through
his 'circle' even while himself standing rather to one side of the
things he influenced. Benjamin's own career encountered persons
associated with George at a number of points. The most important
of these was the Austrian Jewish poet, Hugo von Hofmannsthal;
other figures significant for Benjamin's work were Ludwig Klages,
whom he met in 1914,[17] the critic Friedrich Gundolf, who was
associated with Benjamin's lover Jula Cohn, the historian Kurt
Breysig, whom Benjamin described in 1914 as 'the only man of

research in this whole university [Berlin]',[18] and, rather more tenuously, Georg Simmel the cultural philosopher.

Despite his extensive influence George was no intriguer or string-puller; his attractions for a generation of German intellectuals lay rather in his uncompromising rejection of the norms of bourgeois behaviour in favour of a prophetic vision of spiritual riches. Like Nietzsche, to whom he was much indebted, this revolved around rejection of a slavish Christianity, and celebration of a reawakened sense of present power and present purpose. Much of this was based on the deeply emotional appeal of a spiritualised corporality – 'deifying the body and embodying the deity', as he expressed it in his programmatic poem 'The Knights Templar'. This, in turn, concentrated on the pathos of community and heroism experienced in a warlike manly group. Such groups alone, in George's eyes, were capable of the action and resilience (*jede eherne tat und nötige wende*) that could establish meaning and consistency in a chaotic world. The mysteries of community and leadership guaranteed a power that the disintegrating bourgeois world lacked. Such lyrical visions found wider currency and a political implementation in phenomena such as the youth movement.

Benjamin, it should be said, did not appropriate the militaristic aspects of George's writings. He did, however, attach considerable importance to the conceptions of leadership and community. Of Wyneken he wrote that through him the members of the movement had been privileged 'to grow up conscious of a leader'[19] and had experienced 'what leadership is'.[20] Benjamin speculated that the minimum quality of a leader was 'consciousness'[21] – the basis that made him, as Wyneken was, the 'bearer of the Idea'.[22] If this sounds a somewhat different emphasis from the robust physicality of George's heroes, the same may also be said of Benjamin's vision of community. *Gemeinschaft,* a term Benjamin frequently employed, indicated not so much physical togetherness as a form of simultaneous spiritual isolation. Benjamin's ethical pathos – this he derived from Kierkegaard – demanded that each individual feel the whole weight of personal responsibility for him or her self. An individual's highest ethical attainment was the experience of being alone with the absolute. Thus, community and loneliness were joined at the highest moment of ethical experience. 'I believe that a man can only be truly lonely . . . in the most intimate community of believers: in a loneliness in which his I raises itself towards the Idea in order to come to itself.'[23] Again, this had no practical consequences for Benjamin's behaviour towards organisations, except in so far as it gave his preciosity an outlet in episodes such as that with the unfortunate Heinle. But it was close to contemporary ideologies of the 'artist creator' familiar to literature students from books such as Mann's *Tonio Kröger*. The mystique of creative individuality, or of the small organic community, could serve as a refuge from and a feeble reproach to established political organisations. The blindness of such a view became obvious by the end of 1914, at the latest. The only advantage of Benjamin's attitude to leadership and community, as compared with George's, was that its idiocy was even more shamefully revealed. The pathos of manly solidarity, unfortunately, survived to be abused by later ideologues.

These theories were given cohesiveness and emotional appeal by the principle of Eros. Eros, or sexuality, was a valuable theme for many thinkers besides Freud in the first decades of the century. The classic text for intellectual debate on sex was Plato's *Symposium*, the dialogue that places physical attraction on a continuum of values ascending into the heaven of the most abstracted forms. This piece, which was highly esteemed by the young Benjamin, [24] is notable for us in two ways. In the first place, it attempts to account for the philosopher's trade by suggesting that love of knowledge is essentially the highest manifestation of the love of beauty, which is itself common to all human beings. This location of theoretical activity in a firmly non-instrumental context was clearly attractive to the young purist Benjamin. It meant that intellectual activities, or spirituality in general, could be regarded as universal, natural, and not dependent on particular motives or interests. Philosophy, being the highest and purest aspect of what was a universal inclination, justified itself.

The other point about the *Symposium* is that it effectively instals sexuality on the same scale as wisdom itself. Sex, at least when looked at in the right way, could be presented by modern Platonists as an activity as essentially humane and worthwhile as philosophy itself, albeit at a somewhat more humble level. The appreciation of beauty – and here it should be added that Plato preferred male beauty to the debased functionalism of the female sort – was part of the universal extent of Eros, the love of forms.

This inversion of previous sentiments of chastity and the sinfulness of the body was common in discussion during the period.
In Wyneken's educational thinking it yielded notions of the training of the whole man, body as well as soul, familiar from English
schools. The cult of masculine friendship issued for young men like
Benjamin in soulful nights of forest companionship, while for
Wyneken, and very much more blatantly for Stefan George, it
emerged in the practice of homosexuality.

For Benjamin, the whole question was posed most interestingly
by the problem of prostitution. Benjamin was a person of sensual
and amorous inclinations. His succession of relationships with
women was a determining feature of his career at least until 1933.
Scholem cites the opinion of 'several women' that Benjamin was
not sexually attractive;[25] but this view is somewhat discredited by
his references elsewhere to a plurality of girlfriends.[26] In any
event, it does not need to be pointed out that there is little correla-
tion between conventional physical attractiveness and sexual ac-
ceptability. In Benjamin's case the Platonic idea of Eros had a
certain immediate validity. From his first lover, Grete Radt, onwards, the women in his life were all to some degree connected
with his intellectual preoccupations. Grete Radt, and then his wife
Dora, were both in the youth movement; Jula Cohn, friend of
Gundolf, inspired Benjamin's break with conventional literary
criticism (in the *Wahlverwandtschaften* essay); and Asja Lacis led
Benjamin to the Marxism of his mature period. In all these cases,
love of the body was indeed a libidinous component of love of the
idea.

The same may be said of Benjamin's relations with prostitutes,
or at least of his own view of such relations. It is clear from
Benjamin's 1932 autobiography, *Berlin Chronicle,* that he was a
not inexperienced customer of prostitutes, at least during early
adult life.[27] Prostitution occupied Benjamin intellectually until
late works such as the essays on Baudelaire. In his early thinking it
played a nodal role. Because of his own intellectual honesty, and
because of the principle of Eros, which bulked large in his work at
this period,[28] Benjamin was strongly opposed to the hypocritical
and exploitative treatment of prostitutes by bourgeois society.
Rather than see this in socio-economic terms, however, he – at
this stage characteristically – construed the problem in quasi-religious terms. Employing a dichotomy from Kierkegaard's *Either/*

Or, the young Benjamin posed the ethical alternative of aestheticism or morality. Aestheticism, in Kierkegaard's text, is the cynical but morally bankrupt attitude of the seducer; morality, the responsibility and self-understanding offered to him as the higher solution. Rather dramatically, Benjamin attributed his own decision to leave Berlin for Freiburg in part to this ethical 'ultimatum'.[29] Doubtless the attractions of the capital city raised difficult problems for a nineteen-year-old anxious to concentrate on higher spiritual companionship. By the summer of 1913, however, Benjamin had resolved to tackle the problem head on. Back in Freiburg after a winter in Berlin he wrote to one of his no doubt startled friends a long letter on the 'morality of prostitutes'. Dismissing as stale aestheticism any position that conceded 'beauty' to the whore while reserving the sphere of 'dignity' for itself, Benjamin asserted that prostitutes were not ethically different from any other profession: 'Either all human beings are prostitutes or none are.' Modifying George's dictum about body and deity, Benjamin declared that the prostitute 'sexualised the spirit'. In that sense, prostitution was a major cultural advance, for it drove nature 'from its last sanctum, sexuality'. Eros was thereby made to serve culture. 'The whore represents the completed will to culture.'[30]

This was in a private letter; but Benjamin had no hesitation in developing the same standpoint in a long article published as 'Student Life'. There he argued that it was damaging to separate the spiritual from the physical. As far as the student movement was concerned, the availability of prostitutes had merely succeeded in 'neutralising Eros in the universities'. The radical separation of organisations such as the intellectually creative student corps on the one hand, and prostitutes on the other, had left a 'distorted and dismembered torso of the one spiritual Eros'. Sexuality fell to one side as an 'unmastered force of nature', while relations between male and female students were characterised by a feeble aestheticism.[31]

So, either whores should be recognised as being part of the domain of culture and morality, or female students should be seen to be part of the domain of Eros, or preferably both. The separation of the 'aesthetic' from the wholeness of the ethical life was a hypocrisy Benjamin could not tolerate; and the principle of Eros, love of forms, was the theoretical basis of his demand for integration. Emotionally, it was a longing for the unity of personal love and professional commitment, which could be seen also in the homoerotic allegiances of the George circle.

Benjamin's position in the first years of his undergraduate career had strengths and weaknesses. His view of Eros showed considerable moral integrity; sex was not merely to be exploited in remote 'aesthetic' corners, but to be integrated into the deliberate and purposeful levels of 'culture' and morality. This was not merely a steamy mystification of lust; it was a practical implementation of one of Benjamin's central beliefs, namely that 'nature' should wherever possible be supplanted by clarity and reason.

Benjamin's high principles of intellectual purity also, despite lapses into priggishness like the Heinle affair, gave him a sense of the vices and virtues of existing intellectual institutions. Set beside his noble vision of the youth movement as bearer of 'spirit', no mere terrestial university could cut a very estimable figure. It is noticeable that Benjamin, unlike most of his later associates, never acquired a professor as 'teacher'. His later ironical self-description as a pupil of Rickert's underlines this.[32] Benjamin's more considered critiques of the university during the late 1920s had their roots in an early rejection of it as an establishment inimical to the needs of the spirit.[33] We shall discuss this further in the next section.

But Benjamin's spirituality had its glaring weaknesses, and nowhere more obviously than in his linking of prostitution with the theory of Eros. However hypocritical the conventional view he was attacking, his own idealised visions of morality were scarcely any better. Celebration of whorish ethics made no difference whatever to the material position of people compelled to their labours by bitter economic necessity. Benjamin's graciously condescending reformulation of the problem, like indeed the whole theory of Eros, entirely passed over the material context of prostitution, as it did also that of intellectual labour. Benjamin's belief in the autonomy of 'moral' acts and of intellectual contemplation led him to the conclusion that they were indifferent to the context in which they were practised. But the practice of prostitution is no more separable from the relations of social exchange than are the contemplations of intellectuals. Whores and intellectuals are indeed similar, as Benjamin later came to realise, but not by virtue of high purity of their trades.

The crisis came to Benjamin's ideas of Eros with the outbreak of war in 1914. We shall see his reaction to the mobilisation of professorial support behind the dismal illusion of 'national interest'. But not only the professors, from whom Benjamin doubtless expected it, proved to be susceptible to the base charms of the partisan. Much worse than this, the one person whom he *had* regarded as his 'teacher',[34] Gustav Wyneken, declared his patriotic support for the war effort. This, together with the despairing suicide of Heinle and his fiancée, a week after the outbreak of war, was the shock that drove from Benjamin's mind any naive faith in the self-sufficiency of spirit. From 1915 onwards Benjamin had nothing more to do with the youth movement, now largely gone to war with martial intoxication in its heart. And the whole theory of community, leadership, loneliness and Eros collapsed back into Benjamin's mind to await rebirth, ten years later, as a theory of partisan political intervention. The spiritualists had been unmasked for the muddy reactionaries they were. And the sufferings of the war years, and those that followed, revealed to the cosseted bourgeois son which elements in his thought were high principle and which were merely shabby self-deception.

Benjamin took his leave of Wyneken and all that he had represented in a dignified letter at the beginning of 1915: 'You have committed the most repulsive betrayal . . . To the state which had taken everything from you, you finally sacrificed the young.'[35] With George he had had no personal connection; but his revulsion at what George now represented was equally clear.[36] And while his former associates marched off to war, Benjamin feigned sciatica to persuade the military physicians that he was unfit for active service.[37]

Benjamin's verdict on this period of his life, and his involvement with the youth movement, was implied in much of his subsequent more theoretical work on bourgeois cultural forms. It was fairly directly stated, however, in two pieces he wrote shortly before and shortly after the collapse of the Weimar republic. They were a review of two books on Stefan George (1933) and the autobiographical fragments *Berlin Chronicle* (1932). In both of these pieces Benjamin clearly stated his rejection of any attempt to achieve cultural reform on the basis of a subjective, individualist platform. His words reflected his own experience of the introverted debates of small circles forever frustrated by the narrowness of their base. 'That "spiritual movement" which worked for a renewal of human life without taking into account public life was reduced to the reproduction of social contradictions in those unresolvable and tragic struggles and tensions which are characteristic of the life of small conventicles.'[38] Memories of his battle with Heinle no doubt echo in Benjamin's words. Such struggles were inevitably unresolvable and without issue. Their outcome was the exasperated gesture of 'sabotage and anarchism' which only makes things worse, and even more difficult 'for the intellectual to come to any insight into things.'[39]

Even given honest good will on the part of the reformer, spiritual reform was condemned to consolidate the rule of the bourgeois system it claimed to detest. Benjamin conceded that George was indeed a 'reformer', but as a leader he was only capable of producing 'feeble and unwordly rules' of conduct. All the discipline he had to offer collapsed inwards upon the subjective formalism of his art. It alone, in George's conception of the 'seventh ring', was to do the duty of holding together a social order which was already bursting asunder. 'There is no doubt that this art has shown itself to be apposite and finely wrought, and the ring to be tight and precious. But what it embraced was the same order as that which the old powers, albeit with very much less noble means, were also committed to preserving.'[40] George's work was part of the vacuous and sterile Art Nouveau, known in German as 'youth style' *(Jugendstil)* – 'that style with which the old bourgeoisie disguises the presentiment of its own weakness by affecting a cosmic enthusiasm in every sphere, and, intoxicated by its fantasy of the future, abusing the word "youth" as an incantation'.[41] George's only surviving issue had been the 'priestly science' of his academic acolytes; those who had most honestly embraced his false precepts were those who had perished on the battlefields of the First World War. But for those, wrote Benjamin, George no longer had an ear.[42]

The ultimate reason for the inadequacy of such movements was their insensitivity to social and economic determinants – factors that circumscribed their sphere of action to a degree they were unable to appreciate. 'Associations of bourgeois intellectuals', commented Benjamin, 'were very much more common then' – before the war – 'because they had not yet recognised their limitations.'[43] The radical bourgeoisie had no conception of the organisational preconditions for any successful implementation of their radicalism. Themselves protected by the upper levels of capitalist systems of exchange, their only model for organisation was the random association of the market place, together with the individualistic idiosyncrasies of consumerism which it encouraged. The mythologies of 'loneliness' and 'community' were a vapid reflection of this. This was a theme Benjamin developed in more theoretical and historical detail in the Baudelaire work, as we shall see. In *Berlin Chronicle,* however, he characterised it in terms of two images from his schooldays. One was his distaste for the 'mass of schoolchildren' pressed into the corridors and stairways of his school. Faced by this, he remembered, being alone 'seemed the only condition worthy of a human being' – 'for such a mass of schoolchildren is one of the most shapeless and unworthy sorts of mass, and betrays its bourgeois character simply by being the most rudimentary of all organisational forms, just like every assembly of this social class in our era'.[44]

The other remembered image was that of his walks with his mother, during which, as he recalled, he seemed incapable of walking together with her but always followed at some distance behind. This 'failure to form a united front' is compared, only half ironically, with the failure of anarchistic bourgeois intellectuals to establish realistic forms of intervention.[45]

Adorno also cites this latter image, but as evidence for Benjamin's innate incapacity for organisation.[46] It is quite clear that Benjamin intended to convey precisely the opposite. The failure of the youth movement in which he had played a part, and his own abandonment of that movement, had nothing to do with lone-wolf traits in his character. The movement was simply a naively bourgeois organisation trapped within its own inability to see beyond subjective and individualist horizons. In the end, Benjamin's personal talents as an organiser are irrelevant. What matters is his practical experience, articulated here in the principle that random associations of individuals, as on school staircases, are both uncongenial and irredeemably weak. Benjamin's references to 'being alone' were not a precept of his own life, but simply the only worthy response to the feeble shapelessness of bourgeois organisations. Adorno's attempts to force Benjamin into the mould of a Tonio Kröger only illuminate his own very different commitments. In reality, the problem of effective organisations was one of the central concerns of Benjamin's mature work.

Universities

Benjamin's involvement with the youth movement started while he was still at school and continued until 1914. By this time he had already been a student for two years. His links with the academic world lasted for longer and were in certain respects a stronger influence than the youth movement.

Between 1912, when he left school, and 1919, Benjamin studied philosophy at Freiburg im Breisgau, Berlin, Munich and Bern. Freiburg, Benjamin's first university, was an ancient foundation where he could enjoy the privileged and decorative life of traditional studentship. Philosophy was one of the major attractions of the university, which had increased its student enrolment eightfold since 1871.[47] The outstanding figures of pre-war Freiburg philosophy were the neo-Kantians Heinrich Rickert, Jonas Cohn and Emil Lask. Another notable talent attracted to Freiburg by this array of luminaries was Martin Heidegger, who, three years older than Benjamin, took his higher doctorate under Rickert in 1915.

None of the other universities visited by Benjamin seems to have been able to match the heady metaphysics in which Benjamin was absorbed at Freiburg. In fact Benjamin never took any examination there, or indeed at any of the German universities he attended. But in 1917 he moved to Bern, in Switzerland, where he started work on a D.Phil. The dissertation was 'The Concept of Art Criticism in German Romanticism' and concerned itself mainly with Novalis and Friedrich Schlegel. One of the purposes of taking a D.Phil. was to enable Benjamin to extract continuing support from his parents for what they would otherwise have regarded as a life of feckless idleness. Once he had the doctorate, in the summer of 1919, he delayed telling his parents in order to postpone the day of reckoning.[48] When he did tell them, they insisted on his return (now with wife and child) to Berlin, where he could be supported more cheaply.[49]

For a determined academic, the next step would have been to start work for the 'Habilitation', or higher doctorate, which in German universities has generally been necessary for a start in university teaching. This was in Benjamin's mind soon after the D.Phil.[50] But he seems to have been no more serious about the higher doctorate than he had been about the first. The problem, however, is that a higher doctorate is a very much more demanding enterprise than an ordinary D.Phil., and carries with it the *'venia legendi'*, or licence to lecture. This means that the doctor has the right to announce lecture courses at a university, and in practice would usually be expected to start lecturing at the university of his or her candidature. In other words, receiving the *'venia legendi'* was much like being given a job, except that (in those days) it carried no salary. As a result, the Habilitation candidate is subject, explicitly or not, to the same personal scrutiny as the applicant for a job. In a competitive and exclusive institution like a university, this could give rise to all sorts of obstacles. One of those, in Benjamin's case, was his Jewishness; a difficulty he could not fail to be aware of.[51]

Whatever the reasons, Benjamin does not appear to have put as much effort into gaining the higher doctorate as the institution demanded. Three years passed before he found a university, Frankfurt, and a supervisor, Franz Schultz, and it was another year before they gave their agreement to examine Benjamin (in December 1923).[52] During those years, Benjamin had seemingly at first abandoned the idea of a Habilitation once his initial plan to carry on in Bern had been crushed by his financial situation.[53] He only took up these plans again because of pressure from his parents, for whose benefit, as he said sarcastically, he needed 'a certificate of public approval'.[54] Benjamin's dilatoriness is perhaps in part explained by his reluctance to devote himself to a career, and his contentment with life as it was. Despite shrill complaints about his parents' meanness, he was able, with their support and that of Dora, who had a job,[55] to continue to lead a life of free intellectual enquiry. Before quarrels with his parents finally forced him to take up the Habilitation idea once more, his only concession to the idea of earning an independent living had been to take in commissions for the analysis of handwriting[56] and to speculate about the possibility of starting an antiquarian business.[57] Both of these were hobbies of his. As soon as his parents were sufficiently convinced of his Habilitation plans (for which they had already financed a term in Frankfurt)[58] to give him an allowance,[59] he left for Capri, where he impressed Asja Lacis with his air of affluence.

The young Benjamin obviously enjoyed a relatively protected life, protests notwithstanding.[60] But this does not sufficiently explain his evident lack of interest in a university career. A further aspect is that he was probably temperamentally unsuited to teaching, and he spoke with dislike of the prospect of giving lectures and looking after students.[61] It was also the case that Benjamin did not depend on university status to be able to publish his work; although he in fact hardly published anything in the early 1920s, by 1922 he had established promising contacts with publishers,[62] and, most important, his major essay on Goethe's *Wahlverwandtschaften* had been accepted for publication in Hugo v. Hofmannsthal's *Neue deutsche Beiträge*.

In fact, Benjamin's diffidence towards the university also had more constructive grounds, grounds that became more definite as the Frankfurt examination dragged on. Even while he had been writing his first doctorate, Benjamin lamented 'the hopeless situation of the university at present'.[63] By the time he was involved with the Habilitation he was declaring that he could 'see through the mechanism of this institution'[64] and that the philosophers in particular (his own submission was in aesthetics) were the 'lackeys of the bourgeoisie'.[65]

The roots of this view went back some ten years, to the autumn of 1914. At that time, he wrote that he had found only one true man of research in the whole university of Berlin – and that man's position there was 'only excused (perhaps) by his complete seclusion and his contempt for such things'.[66] The university itself had poisoned the springs of the mind. Why? Because the war had just broken out and because the professors of Berlin, in particular, had been competing against one another to produce bellicose patriotic homilies.[67]

Benjamin's resistance to the war, and to the part intellectuals played in whipping up war fever, is not attributable to pacifism. He felt, at this stage at least, that it was a betrayal of the high principles of *Geist* and, more concretely, that it was a 'sacrifice to the state'.[68] What Benjamin saw as the disgrace of the universities in 1914, and, as it turned out, even more so after the war, was their sacrifice of intellectual principle to the base interests of the state. This was the result of a combination of factors more or less unique to German higher education of that period. Benjamin himself never attempted a systematic critique of the German universities.[69] But in order to understand his own professional background it is necessary to recognise the extent to which the universities formed a group with a very distinct ideological and political identity. This can be followed in three areas: the role of the universities in professional training; their class composition; and their autonomy in relation to other power structures.

At the end of the nineteenth century the German universities still retained, or had achieved, a strong hold over professional training.[70] The universities, in origin, were part of the medieval ecclesiastical superstructure. After the Reformation, universities throughout Europe went into decline, and in countries where bourgeois revolutions took place they were pushed even further to one side by the development of alternative institutions of professional training. In Britain, the progress of the modern bourgeois state had practically eclipsed the universities entirely by the end of the eighteenth century; and in the same period, the French bourgeois revolution was followed by the setting up of a completely reformed system of higher education. Only in Germany, where social development had been disastrously inhibited by the wars of the sixteenth and seventeenth centuries, did the universities remain as virtually the only source of advanced professional training.[71] Education for all the professions of a modern society was in the hands of these medieval ecclesiastical foundations. There were no arrangements outside the universities for producing lawyers, civil servants, priests, physicians or teachers.

When, largely under the impact of the Napoleonic occupation, the German states began at last to wake up to the modern era, governments found they had a usefully concentrated system of higher education and training ready to hand. All that needed to be done was to drive out from the existing institutions the vestiges of medieval autonomy and ecclesiasticism, and to harness them firmly to the secular government. This process of secularisation reached an early high point in the educational reforms in Prussia, where Berlin University was founded in 1810. Such a process, it is worth noting, would have been impossible in a country like Britain, where a more rapid bourgeois revolution 'from below' had already consolidated the autonomy of institutions like the Inns of Court as non-governmental centres of training. But the extremely fast state-led development of Germany during the nineteenth century meant that governments could everywhere take the initiative in founding superstructural institutions to meet their needs. There is also no doubt that Germany's educational centralisation enabled her, particularly after 1871, to plan a coherent educational system which responded rapidly to changing requirements, and soon outstripped the lamentably reactionary British universities crouching behind their ancient privileges. Germany's superiority in science and technology was directly attributable to this flexibility in organising higher education inside and outside the universities.

On the other hand, of course, it is clear that such a system could make only very circumscribed concessions to notions of academic freedom. It is true that many of the remarkable men involved in Prussia's early educational reforms – Humboldt, Schleiermacher, Fichte – held strong views about the necessity of freedom in research and teaching. But it is a symptom of the naivete of their thinking that they imagined such abstract concepts to be sufficient to determine the very practical and complex issues involved in institutional autonomy. Thus, after an early period of liberalism which culminated in the fiasco of the 1848 parliament (the so-called 'professors' parliament'), the political position of the universities gradually became evident. After the unification of the empire in 1871 the state used its control more and more to ensure the priority of its own interests, mainly by seeking to achieve a homogeneity of class, ideology and political orientation. To a large extent these overlapped. Class homogeneity was achieved by the simple measure of financial constraint. In the absence of a proper system of grants, only students with some degree of financial independence could afford to take courses lasting four years and upwards. Entry into the university teaching profession itself was even more difficult for those of slender means; assistant lecturers *(Privatdozenten)* received no salary, although by Benjamin's time there was a minimal grant. Financial exclusiveness bred social exclusiveness; by the late nineteenth century the universities were not merely a necessary precondition for a professional career, but also the source of an indispensable social cachet. The propertied classes dominated German universities during the Wilhelminian period.[72]

Ideological homogeneity was a principal concern of the Prussian authorities from 1871 onwards. A major focus of this was the *Kulturkampf* of the early empire, devoted towards extending Prussian hegemony over the Catholics newly incorporated into the Reich. The Jews were the other main ideological minority in the new Empire. They were initially seen as allies; only in 1871 were they assured of the chance to enter the civil service, and so to become university teachers. After the end of the *Kulturkampf,* however, they increasingly replaced the Catholics as the main targets of ideological vilification. Neither group, Catholics or Jews, suffered formal discrimination in universities; but they could be and were made to suffer the indignities of a socially exclusive system.

Political intervention by state authorities had been practised as early as 1837, when the King of Hanover, in a celebrated case, sacked seven Göttingen professors for protesting against the suspension of the constitution. By the time of the Empire, with a much larger and more influential university system, smooth regulation of such questions was obviously very important. This was not difficult, since all professors, as civil servants, were in the direct employment of the state and under oath to preserve its interests. Assistant lecturers, who had no civil-servant grade, were beyond the direct reach of such measures, but additional legislation (such as the 1899 'Lex Arons') could be introduced to cover this area as well. The unfortunate Arons was a social democrat; his case was part of a systematic campaign from 1878 onwards to combat social democracy within areas accessible to the state.[73]

The universities were a powerful and in their own way very progressive instrument of the imperial German state. As educational institutions there is no question of their excellence in all fields. Their fault was not that they did not live up to the academic ideal, for that is an ideal that has never had any substance anywhere. Admittedly, they served interests that by 1914, and certainly by 1918, were appearing unacceptably class-orientated. But by means of generous funding and the discreet granting of privileges, the imperial government had by 1914 assured itself of a contented and loyal professorial body, whose vanities were copiously flattered by the state's deferential attitude towards 'culture'. Within the limits of their structurally determined aims, the universities did a good job conscientiously. There is nothing startling about their patriotic turn-out in Autumn 1914.[74]

But the universities were not such as to convince intellectual purists like Walter Benjamin. The troubles he ran into with his attempt at Habilitation were almost inevitable given his attitude. His somewhat casual search for a supervisor ended with Franz Schultz, a man for whose intellectual abilities Benjamin had no regard,[75] and who on his part felt little commitment to this recently appeared candidate who was 'not his student'.[76] When the literary historian Schultz was actually confronted with Benjamin's dissertation, *Ursprung des deutschen Trauerspiels,* he became alarmed, insisted that the candidature be transferred from literature to aesthetics, and in this way effectively washed his hands of the proceedings. Benjamin submitted the final version of his dissertation together with a formal application in May 1925. Two months later Schultz wrote suggesting that he should withdraw the application; the professor in charge of aesthetics had written a damning assessment.[77] After wondering whether to force the university into a formal rejection, Benjamin finally agreed to withdraw. The professor who wrote the assessment was Hans Cornelius, whose own student Theodor Adorno successfully took the Habilitation with him five years later.

The actual reasons why Frankfurt rejected Benjamin's Habilitation candidature are a compound of relatively trivial practical issues. The dissertation itself was only one element. Moral indignation, as Benjamin himself said, was an entirely inappropriate reaction. The dissertation is without doubt an extraordinarily brilliant piece of work. But at the same time parts of it, particularly the 'epistemological prologue', are perhaps unnecessarily obscure, and require enormous efforts of concentration even from a sympathetic reader. The fact that Benjamin had not assured himself in advance of sympathetic and prepared readers among the faculty meant that even a clear and orthodox piece of work might have faced obstacles. His own highly esoteric submission, under the circumstances, really stood no chance of success.

The decisive factor, ultimately, was Benjamin's lack of integration into the academic community. And this, in turn, reflected his antipathy towards what the community, as an organisation, represented – towards the 'mechanisms' he later claimed to have seen through. Benjamin's rejection was not a political issue in any direct sense; but it did raise the whole question of what the academic world, as a functional organisation, was doing. It was not that Benjamin was anxious to reform the universities; it was more that their structure prevented them from achieving the goals they claimed to have set themselves – or, as Benjamin put it, they were 'sullying the purity of their sources'.[78] But where was the alternative? In 1925 Benjamin still felt that there was 'certainly not yet any effective locus of activity outside the universities'. However, this identification of the problem was a significant step towards its resolution. The exploration of alternative organisations of intellectural activity was a major concern for the rest of Benjamin's life.

Zionism

Benjamin's failure to obtain an academic post, and with it the disappearance of parental support, forced him to look around for other organisations which would be professionally congenial and also provide real material support. One clear option was Zionism, which by the mid-1920s was actively and successfully colonising the traditional Jewish territories in Palestine. Benjamin's friend Gerhard Scholem had already emigrated to Palestine in 1923.

Zionism was one of the responses of the German-Jewish community to increasing anti-Semitism.[79] The Jewish Diaspora in Europe, a set of communities that could easily be isolated by the societies within which they lived, had always been targets for the working-out of social tensions. 'The Jew' was a widely available, clearly identifiable and usually unprotesting object of blame for a wide variety of evils.

The Jewish community in Germany, after a period of conciliation during the liberal and expansionary regime of Bismarck, resumed this position of scapegoat during the growing tensions and conflicts of the end of the century. There was a danger in fighting social disaffection by tackling the growth of working-class organisation head-on, as the government found from the failure of its anti-Socialist laws. The Jews, on the other hand, offered a good diversionary target for the resentments of the less educated. As a highly dynamic social group, little constrained by conservative influence such as the prizes of public office – which were only partly open to them – the Jews offered useful instances of both successful capitalism and active left-wing militancy. The two could be used as propaganda instruments either separately, or linked in the spectre of 'international Jewry'.

There were two possible reactions to this. Jews could, in the first instance, cease to be conspicuous as Jews, thus removing their value as a visible target of manipulated prejudice. This could be achieved by assimilation to dominant cultural norms, something that initially demanded also that Jews submit to Christian baptism, at least if they were to attain professional and civil acceptance. By the end of the nineteenth century, the demand of baptism had largely been dropped in the German territories, and side by side with this, Jews were themselves taking a more active part in assimilating themselves to German social expectations. By the time that anti-Semitism again became a conspicuous element of social control many Jews had effectively committed themselves to a policy of assimilation. Prominent Jews made considerable – and successful – efforts to be absorbed into the social life of the ruling classes. Certain areas of public life were still barred to them, but in those which were open – the old areas of finance and commerce, and the newer ones of the professions and education – they were notable for their progress.

The other reaction to prejudice and discrimination was defensive and assertive. Assimilation was most attractive to those who had something to gain from the social openings offered to them. For the working classes, the petty-bourgeoisie, and the rural Jews of Eastern Europe, who had to compete with Gentiles in similarly unpromising economic circumstances, the abandonment of the support they received from the traditional group identities could hold no attractions whatever. It is against this background of poverty and deprivation – although not necessarily within that social group – that Zionism as a political movement began to acquire significance in the late nineteenth century.

The term 'Zionism' originated with the Viennese Nathan Birnbaum, but came into wide use as part of a political programme with Theodor Herzl (1860-1904), a teacher and journalist. It was not in the first instance a religious movement so much as a late upsurge of nineteenth-century nationalism. The achievement of a territory for the establishment, or re-establishment, of the Jewish national interest was always a central element of this movement. This did not necessarily have to be Palestine – Uganda was a possibility at one point – but increasingly the idea of a return to the ancient Jewish lands came to play a central part in the ideological appeal of Zionism.

By the post war period Zionism was a much more practical option than ever before. Until 1918 Palestine had been under Turkish jurisdiction. With the defeat of Turkey during the war it came under British jurisdiction, and the British government was happy to use colonisation by amenable Jewish settlers as an easy way of consolidating its own position against the indigenous population.

Within Germany, the two options facing Jews after about 1918 – further assimilation, or retrenchment and possibly emigration – were reflected in ideological positions. The assimilationist position was adopted by, among others, the philosopher Hermann Cohen, an eminent thinker who became a professor at Marburg soon after Bismarck's liberalising measures. Cohen fought the reappearance of anti-Semitism in a celebrated controversy with the Prussian historian Treitschke, in which he maintained that German Jews were first Germans, and Jews only second. At this period his account of the religious and cultural content of Jewish tradition was so abstracted and watered-down as to incur the hostility of many more orthodox Jews.[80] Cohen also warmly welcomed the outbreak of war in 1914, which, as a patriot, he saw as a just vindication of Germany's abused rights. Cohen's philosophy was a neo-Kantian rationalism which emphasised the universality of ethical norms and eschewed any ethnocentric or cultural relativism.

At the same time, Cohen was far from being politically blind or timid. He was first appointed to a chair under F. A. Lange, the radical author of a *History of Materialism*, and he himself had social-democratic leanings. When it became clear that the war was not a campaign of injured innocence, but had been provoked by Germany in the interests of commercial expansionism, his views changed entirely.[81] In despair at the apparently hopeless barbarity of the Gentile world – which by this stage was expressing itself in a fresh upsurge of anti-Semitism – he spent the last years before his death in 1918 writing an elaborate defence of the humane and progressive character of Judaism.[82]

Cohen's return to a more orthodox Judaism, and the radicalisation of his political viewpoint, were characteristic of the general shift of opinion among younger Jews during and after the First World War. Many Jews, traumatised by the collapse of pre-war anti-militarism and by the experience of the war itself, turned to the revolutionary Left, abandoning Wilhelmine assimilationism for a radically socialist variety. Others, meanwhile, intensified their attempts to solve the 'Jewish question' once and for all by means of a determined recourse to Jewish tradition. The most prominent theorist of this group during the war decade was Martin Buber (1878-1965), with his book *Drei Reden über das Judentum* (1911) and his magazine *Der Jude*[83] (1916-26). Buber took much of his argument from the nationalistic existentialism of the time, and applied it to the Jewish situation. The ideal of moral purpose, in such a scheme, was to cultivate 'inwardness' and maintain it against a hostile and distortive environment.[84] 'Inwardness' in these terms was largely a function of 'blood', itself the incarnation of tradition, the unbroken community of those who have lived and those yet to come.[85] At the basic level, therefore, authentic living demanded the recognition of this blood-borne tradition and its clear implementation. Beyond this, it involved the perception that such a tradition could only successfully be implemented when the inner and the outer were harmonised – when the expectations of the 'blood' were matched by the environment. In the case of the Jew this could really only happen when the Jewish people were reunited with their traditional environment, in other words the Palestinian lands.[86]

Benjamin was the son of wealthy, assimilated *haut-bourgeois* parents, and perhaps tended more naturally towards the cultured universalism of the Cohen tradition, rather than towards the 'blood' nationalism of the Buber camp, which demanded a feeling for the pathos of impoverished Judaism which Benjamin did not have. The first organisation towards which Benjamin felt attracted was, as we have seen, the somewhat highbrow youth movement, with its devotion to *Geist* and the upper reaches of the intellect. Although Benjamin's group contained many young Jews, they were, as Scholem commented, the sort 'who made little or no use of this fact'.[87] Indeed the first time Scholem ever saw Benjamin was at a joint meeting with a Zionist group, at which Benjamin was speaking, characteristically, against Zionism.

Benjamin's attitude to Zionism and things Jewish was not always obvious. He did, however, express a persistent antipathy towards Buber himself.[88] Buber asked Benjamin to contribute to the magazine *Der Jude* when he started it in 1916; Benjamin replied that partisan journalism of the kind envisaged by Buber degraded 'the word' to the status of a mere instrument, and refused.[89] This perhaps slightly precious viewpoint actually concealed a more substantial position. Benjamin strongly objected to the fact that Buber had, initially at least, greeted the war as a means of a greater purity and immediacy of experience.[90] Also, there could be no real meeting-point between Buber's rhetoric of blood and nationalism, and Benjamin's almost mystical respect for the clear rationality of the 'word'.[91]

It is important to identify the polarity exemplified by Buber and Cohen, because Scholem, in particular, has tended to associate Benjamin with Judaism in a very undifferentiated way. But in the first place it is doubtful whether Judaism was any more homogeneous a phenomenon than Christianity at that time; and like Christianity, the divergent currents in Judaism probably had more to do with politics than with spiritual truth. Cohen's rationalism moved naturally towards social democracy and the revolutionary Left; Buber's nationalism moved towards what Brecht rightly characterised as 'Jewish Fascism'.[92] Second, it is clear that Scholem's own position within Judaism had distinct tactical commitments. While he rejected the bellicose politics of Zionism[93] he none the less inclined strongly towards the traditionalist interpretation of the Jewish situation which was affirmed so strongly by Buber.[94] His insistence on using Hebrew,[95] his scholarly concern with the more esoteric dimensions of Jewish mysticism,[96] and indeed his own emigration to Palestine, all bear this out. None of these invalidates Scholem's own position; but they do make it important to recognise the difference between him and Benjamin. Benjamin had immense respect for Scholem as a historian of theology, and he recognised in this a valuable resource for his own work. But he is strictly a 'rationalist' and 'free spirit' in matters of religion;[97] and as we shall see, any thinker like Buber who sank into the murky waters of tradition and ancestor cult was assured of a hostile reception from Benjamin.

The real test of a Zionist was whether he or she emigrated to Palestine. Buber and Scholem both did; Benjamin did not. This is not to say that he did not actively consider moving to Palestine, particularly in the later 1920s. Scholem himself had emigrated in the autumn of 1923, without, at that stage, any clear idea of what lay before him. In 1925, however, the Hebrew University of Jerusalem was opened and Scholem was appointed to lecture on religious history.[98] This may have encouraged Benjamin, whose attempts at the Habilitation were failing at the same time. At all events, when Scholem next saw Benjamin in Paris in 1927, he introduced him to Judah Magnes, who was an influential member of the new Hebrew University.[99] Benjamin succeeded in making a considerable impression on Magnes with, as Scholem describes it, his clear and pragmatic endorsement of the need to build up a new state in Palestine.[100] As a result, plans were developed for a possible teaching post at Jerusalem in the area of German or French.[101] The problem was that Benjamin, despite desultory attempts to learn it in the early 1920s, had no real command of Hebrew. Magnes, however, was ready to support Benjamin in learning the language, and sent Benjamin a bursary for this purpose at the end of 1928.[102] This, it might be said, was contrary to the plan laid by Scholem, who had intended to bring Benjamin to Palestine to learn under his own watchful eye. Scholem's forebodings were indeed justified. Benjamin took the money and used it to support himself in Berlin, comforting Scholem throughout 1929 with regular letters about his industrious concern with Hebrew, and the imminence of his arrival in Palestine. This culminated in the announcement, by telegram, of his disembarkation in Palestine on 4 November 1929 – an event which, as might have been expected, never took place. Thenceforth the plans for Benjamin to learn Hebrew and teach in Palestine lapsed.

Despite the precarious nature of Benjamin's professional existence, particularly after the Frankfurt debacle, it is not easy to believe that he could ever have viewed the practice of Zionism very seriously. As he commented after Scholem had emigrated, from his own point of view there was 'neither the practical possibility nor the theoretical necessity for going'.[103] Benjamin's rejection of the 'blood' conception of tradition, and on the other side his very Cohenesque embrace of the theoretical possibilities of Western Europe, meant that Israel could represent only intellectual isolation and inconvenience. Even when the 'practical possibility' of his emigration became a reality, its continuing 'theoretical' irrelevance remained a total block. Benjamin was prepared to woo his Zionist connections to flatter them, to believe in them a little, and to take money off them. But he was not prepared to join them. Benjamin's consciousness of the organisations appropriate to his own enterprise was uncompromising.

There was, however, one organisation which he very nearly did join and which, in 1929, was the immediate cause of his failure to set out for Palestine. At the same time that he was telling Scholem of his last-minute preparations for emigration, he had already agreed to set in train arrangements for a radically different move – to Moscow, with his Bolshevik mistress Asja Lacis.[104]

2
Socialism and the Writer

Bejamin as a young student had condemned the universities for their debasement of *Geist* to the functional purposes of acquiring a profession. 'There are evil consequences when institutions which offer titles, qualifications and openings into a career and a profession are allowed to call themselves places of science', he had roundly declared.[1] But, as he later recalled at the age of forty, he too had been obliged to seek a career, and had not noticed in his failure any of the high-minded compensations his early attitude might have led him to expect.[2] His failure to achieve the Habilitation, and his father's fairly brutal insistence that his son had to earn a living just like anyone else, concentrated his mind firmly on the realities of practical employment.

The German universities really could not be an option for Benjamin, for the various reasons we have already considered. But his rejection of the academic world, and its rejection of him, raised the pressing question of how he was to survive as a writer when his kind of work seemed naturally to assume an academic readership. The question of readership had occupied Benjamin even at the time of his work for *Der Anfang*. Seeing a schoolboy on the street, he had thought how remote this potential reader seemed to him, and how impersonal their link was.[3] At that time this was not a serious problem, since Benjamin was supported by his father and it did not matter that the magazine had a circulation of only some 1,000 copies.[4]

But by the middle 1920s Benjamin's readers were not merely potential proselytes of the spirit; they were critical and paying customers, readers on whose collective approval Benjamin depended both for his living and for his work to be worthwhile at all.

'But for *whom* are we writing? Do you know the answer?', Benjamin wrote in a letter from Moscow, repeating the words of his correspondent Siegfried Kracauer, and incidentally raising the question that is faced by any genuinely progressive writing.[5] The second half of the 1920s, from the failure of the Habilitation, through the flirtations with Palestine and with Moscow, to Benjamin's final embrace of friendship with Brecht, were years of doubt and difficulty. In them we can trace the deliberations of an avant-garde intellectual searching for the right professional context.

In effect, Benjamin's options lay on a scale ranging from the established institutions at one end to provisional or revolutionary organisations at the other. The problem was that while established institutions like the German universities guaranteed a livelihood and a ready-ordered field of activity – a constituted readership – they also, precisely by virtue of their pre-existing organisation, severely restricted any potentially revolutionary activity. At the other end of the scale, institutionalised restrictions could be minimal, but the difficulties of material livelihood were that much more conspicuous. These material difficulties were not even principally those of staying alive; rather, they were the issues of partisanship and group allegiance, which were much closer to the surface in the precarious existence of new or revolutionary organisations. This was particularly evident in Benjamin's dealings with the Bolsheviks.

Leftism and the literary avant-garde

Bolshevism – revolutionary Leninism – appeared in Benjamin's thinking in 1924, the year he spent a summer on Capri with Ernst Bloch and other friends.[6] Capri, like Ibiza where he later also spent time, was in these days a place of recuperation for avant-garde intellectuals, among them Brecht, Gorky and Marinetti.[7] Benjamin did not make contact with any of these, but he did meet a woman who was to become one of the great loves of his life – Asja Lacis. Lacis was a Latvian theatrical producer who worked with important left-wing dramatists such as Piscator and Brecht, and was herself particularly interested in didactic and proletarian forms. By the time she met Benjamin, who started talking to her in a shop on Capri, she was thirty-three, and on holiday with her daughter Daga. Her lover, the German producer Bernhard Reich, was also intermittently with her on Capri.[8]

The six months that Benjamin spent on Capri that summer were a turning-point in his life. Asja Lacis awakened his interest in art as a form of political action, and Bloch, a friend and admirer of George Lukács, helped supply a new philosophical framework to incorporate these insights. Lukács's collection of essays, *History and Class Consciousness,* had appeared the previous year, and for Benjamin, as for many thinkers at this time, the book offered a radical and decisive reorientation. It is perhaps worth pointing out that Lukács, a Hungarian aristocrat, had gone through a development similar to that now experienced by Benjamin. His early work in literary criticism was a brilliant extension of the critical modes dominant at the time, and was, fittingly, published in such highly established organs as *Logos,* a magazine that might be described as the German universities' contribution to the class war. In 1918, on the general wave of disgust with the war and its conclusion, he joined the Hungarian communist party and was a member of Bela Kun's Council Republic. *History and Class Consciousness* documents the conversion of an avant-garde neo-Hegelian, once strongly influenced by thinkers such as Rickert and Lask, to a practice-oriented Marxism. It was, in fact, only the first part of his conversion. The essay of the following year on Lenin brought Lukács to a Bolshevism only partially anticipated in *History and Class Consciousness.* Benjamin was familiar with this later text as well.[9]

Benjamin's experiences on Capri, and particularly the new intellectual perspectives he found there, set the orientation of most of his subsequent work. He had, it seems, discovered what he needed. As he wrote, looking back on 1924, it had been 'a happy year' – a highly uncharacteristic declaration for him, but a confirmation of the contented and determined air that entered his work at this time and continued until the disasters of 1932.[10]

Benjamin's 1924 move towards a Bolshevik Marxism was not a sudden conversion on the spiritual road. Nor, indeed, was it simply a function of his affections for Lacis. It was a response to external historical conditions. As Scholem points out, Benjamin rarely, either in his work or even in private communications, discussed political events directly.[11] But there was obviously no way he could escape them or their intellectual reverberations.

Benjamin had first met Bloch in 1919 while working on his D.Phil., at which point his politics, if they can be described as such, were a kind of Dostoyevskian nihilism.[12] Bloch, however, had recently published *Geist der Utopie*, a text which, rather like Lukács's early Hegelian revolutionism, expressed the digust and outrage of a wartime observer equipped only with the blunt weapons of traditional cultural criticism. It mentioned Marx, but can hardly be described as Marxist. But it did indicate that intellectuals had a direct and active role to play in political affairs, and this, one must assume (Benjamin's long review of the book is lost), contributed significantly to Benjamin's interest.[13] One product of this early and rather abstracted interest in politics was the essay 'Critique of Violence' which argued, from a position of Sorelian anarchism, that force was a legitimate political weapon. But this was the fruit of a period in which probably only a minority of Western intellectuals were capable of more than romantic reaction to the confused situation of post war Europe.

By 1924 the political situation appeared very much clearer. In Germany, the previous year had seen the crisis of inflation, a disruption that had shattered the security of the greater part of the population while immensely strengthening monopoly capital. It was the overture to a period during which the concessions won by organised labour at the beginning of the Weimar Republic were gradually eroded by falling wages, lengthening hours of work, rising unemployment, and the dismantling of social-security provision. The disbanding of the trade unions in 1933, Hitler's first major piece of social legislation, was only the final act of a drama that had started ten years earlier. It also conclusively illuminated the concentration of financial and industrial power which had remained unbroken, if disconcerted, by the 1918 revolution, and which eventually took up Hitler as the most convenient instrument for quick revenge.[14]

The imminent horror of this situation was not yet clear in the early 1920s. Hitler's Bavarian putsch of late 1923 seemed a local disturbance at the time. On the other side, the left wing appeared to have been forced by a conspicuous failure into salutary reorganisation. At the end of 1923 the Social-Democrat federal government had sent in troops to dissolve the state governments of Thuringia and Saxony, both of which had had the temerity to include – quite legitimately – communist ministers. The Communist Party leadership of the time, anxious to preserve the policy of a 'united front' with the Social Democrats, dragged its feet and failed to mobilise the strongly sympathetic workers not only of the KPD but also of the left wing of the SPD. Only in isolated areas such as Hamburg did it come to bitter fighting between insurgent workers and government troops. To the left generally, this only seemed to confirm what many had felt since 1914. The SPD, a supposedly socialist party, would always opt for the central power in preference to the genuine interests of the workers. At the beginning of the First World War an SPD-controlled Reichstag had voted finance for 'defence'; and now, after frequent bloody repressions from 1918 onwards, it had shown the full extent of its cynicism by overthrowing legitimate representative government. At the same time, the Communist leadership itself had clearly failed, and it was, in consequence, quickly replaced by a 'Left' group strongly opposed to alliances with the SPD or its supposed supporters in the Trade Union movement. One member of this group, it is interesting to note, was Gerhard Scholem's brother Werner who, along with other intellectuals such as Ruth Fischer, Arkadi Maslow and Karl Korsch set the tone of the Communist Party in the mid-1920s.[15]

However, all this came too late, and the new sectarianism of the KPD arguably undermined its own objections.[16] The Communist Party had missed its chance of a successful revolution. Conservative interests were able to consolidate their hold continuously from 1923 onwards, and the KPD was never again in a position to rely on the assistance of significant numbers of workers outside the party. The left Leninism initiated by the 1924 group gradually degenerated into a narrow-minded rivalry with the SPD, and thus fatally weakened whatever defensive strength a 'united front' might still have had in 1933.

This was to a large extent the fault of Soviet intervention, particularly as guided by Stalin. As Soviet Russia, during the later 1920s, transformed itself into an introverted and regimented monolith, its attitude towards foreign revolutionaries changed. The emphasis was on domestic consolidation and defence to ensure that the anticipated next onslaught from the capitalist nations could be adequately met. This was to be a priority even at the expense of foreign socialists. This was revealed in 1926 by the discovery, intensely embarrassing to the KPD, that the Reichswehr was engaging in arms deals with the Red Army. At the same time, Stalin's elimination of opposition within Russia led also to the rejection of foreign party members who were considered sympathetic to it. Among other things, this meant that the resourceful intellectuals who took over the KPD in 1924 were soon replaced by people like Thälmann, who would toe Moscow's line and not insist on the distinct conditions of Germany's road to socialism. Stalin's hostility to intellectuals, and to the threat of a 'Western' form of Bolshevism, was one of the most debilitating influences on foreign parties trying to fight for revolutions which only partly matched Soviet needs and expectations.

These developments, and their catastrophic consequences not only for the KPD but for Germany were not yet apparent in the mid-1920s. But it is an ironical coincidence that Benjamin was in Moscow in late 1926 investigating his chances of joining the Bolshevik apparatus at the same time that Werner Scholem was also there – being expelled from the party. Benjamin had previously proclaimed his own 'elective affinity' with Werner Scholem.[17] In fact, Benjamin's progress from 1923 onwards had been resolutely towards the political left. His present for Gerhard Scholem, emigrating to Palestine that autumn, had, appropriately enough, been the 'Journey through German Inflation', an essay that subsequently appeared in his first 'Marxist' book, *One-Way Street*.[18] In 1924 he was with Bloch and Lacis on Capri. The following year, after the Habilitation episode, he was already considering whether to join the Party.[19] And that autumn he went on a surprise visit to Riga to watch Asja Lacis running political theatre in the left Trade Unions' club.[20] He spent most of 1926 in Paris working on books consisting 'mainly of a few communist things', including important writings by Bodganov.[21] At the same time he was also preparing to write an article on Goethe for the Soviet Encyclopaedia,[22] and defending himself against reproaches from Gerhard Scholem who could not accept his turn to the left.[23]

Benjamin's attitude to the German Communist Party and the possibility of becoming a member was always straightforwardly pragmatic and, as he put it, 'experimental'[24] – if it suited his purposes as a form of employment he would join, but not for any other reason. Initially, indeed, Benjamin was extremely sceptical about Communism, both as a political philosophy[25] and as a metaphysics.[26] But as a circle of active commitments, and even as the possible basis for a career, membership of the KPD seemed increasingly attractive, particularly in view of his fading academic prospects. During 1925 this project stood in direct relation to the success or failure of other plans; if his publishing ventures came to naught, as he told Scholem in May 1925, he would intensify his political involvements and join the KPD immediately, although that was something he expected to do sooner or later anyway.[27] Such a step would also give him a chance of going to Moscow, this being more or less a precondition of any paid employment in Bolshevik organisations.

Benjamin eventually made his journey to Moscow some eighteen months after this. He had still not joined the KPD, no doubt partly because his affairs as a writer were not going badly. Benjamin's visit to Russia was a tour of inspection, during which he weighed the pros and cons of joining the Party. The advantages, as he set them out in his diary, were as follows. The overriding consideration was that of organisation. As a 'left-wing outsider' he lacked any 'framework' for his activities.[28] Membership of the party, on the other hand, would have 'decisive advantages: an established position, and a mandate, even if only by implication. Organised and guaranteed contact with people.'[29] And beyond that, party membership would give him the 'massive advantage of being able to project one's own thinking into a force-field which had already been set up'. The Party's intellectual apparatus could match the German academic system and had the advantage that the Party was operating in a direction Benjamin endorsed, whereas the German universities clearly were not.

The lively and purposeful nature of Russian intellectual organisation was a major factor in Benjamin's deliberations. German traditional intellectual circles were not merely reactionary, in his eyes, but in comparison with what was happening in Russia they were quite moribund. Benjamin was enormously impressed by the dynamic collectivism of Soviet film production. On a more day-to-day basis, he several times in his diary remarked on the quality of debate and organisation in Moscow, and the comparative apathy of Western intellectuals.[30] On his return to Berlin he noted: 'Berlin is a dead city for anyone coming from Moscow. The people on the street seem quite miserably isolated, everyone is at a distance from the others and is lonely in the middle of a great area of street.'[31] Benjamin's very negative assessment of this 'loneliness' is not by chance in opposition to his youthful glorification of such a state. The other element of his youth-movement thinking which appeared in a different light after the radicalising experience of Moscow was Eros. Focus on love and the private realm as a medium of film was regarded by Soviet film makers as profoundly reactionary, Benjamin noted with interest.[32] For himself, he was convinced, the next period of his life would differ from the previous one by virtue of the fact that it would be less determined by 'the erotic'.[33] This was not puritanism – Benjamin, a married man, was after all in Moscow in pursuit of another man's mistress – but it did underline his deliberate turn from romantic subjectivism towards practical concern for a livelihood and an effective occupation.

But there were also, of course, notable disadvantages in any attempt at a Party career. In the first place, Benjamin's main area of competence was, as he conceded, somewhat 'specialised' and unlikely to meet with many openings within the existing apparatus.[34] At the time of his Moscow visit this particular issue does not seem to have weighed very heavily with Benjamin, who was no doubt only too ready to forget his Habilitation work and the ensuing traumas.[35] Four years later he defended the resumption of his literary-critical and, from a Party point of view, even 'counter-revolutionary' interests by claiming that he was rendering them unusable for bourgeois historians.[36] But at the time of his visit to Moscow Benjamin apparently viewed with equanimity the prospect of abandoning that whole area of concern.

The more significant obstacles to Benjamin's projected career as a party functionary seem to have been practical. The problem was that there were inevitable differences between the Party apparatus in Moscow, an established Bolshevik state, and in Germany, which was still in the foothills of the revolutionary ascent. The Soviet Union needed an ideological and educational superstructure, and put considerable effort into forming one. For the German Party, however, this was a rather remote consideration. As a result, the German left-wing intelligentsia either had to fend for themselves, or be more or less directly dependent on Moscow. As a case in point, the Communist literary magazine *Linkskurve* was not supported by the KPD, which felt little interest in such projects, but by Ludwig Renn with the aid of funds from the Comintern.[37] But even this institution would not have supported any of

its German contributors. Really the only option for German intellectuals who wished to devote themselves to, and live by, the Party
was to go to Russia. This was what the director Bernhard Reich,
Asja Lacis's lover, had done. And as Benjamin learned during his
stay in Moscow, Reich had not had a particularly easy time of it.
To Benjamin it seemed that Reich's position was now strong, after
six months of considerable hardship.[38] But even so he did not
expect to have a job before a further six months had elapsed. (He
was in fact a professor of drama by the time Brecht visited him in
1932.)[39] And in his first six months Reich had managed to learn
Russian, something in which Benjamin apparently made no progress whatever during his eight weeks in Moscow. To Scholem,
Benjamin claimed that it was possible to 'make a relatively good
living' if one knew a little Russian;[40] but even this seems rather
doubtful given the dispiriting encounters Benjamin had with Party
functionaries, such as those in charge of the Soviet Encyclopaedia
who had commissioned the article on Goethe from him.[41] As
Benjamin had in fact recognised in the beginning of his stay, his
chances in Moscow were 'minimally small'.[42]

The fact was that language really stood for a range of cultural
and social obstacles. Moving to Moscow and learning Russian,
whatever Benjamin's theoretical assessment of the idea, had to
mean a great deal more than that in practice. This was clear to
Benjamin by 1931 at the latest:

> Where is my productive base? [he wrote to Scholem in that
> year]. It is in W. Berlin. W.W., if you like. [The western part of
> the city contained the chic residential areas.] The most highly
> developed civilisation and the most 'modern' culture are not
> only part of my private comforts, but they are also in part
> directly a means of my production. That implies: it is not in my
> power to move my productive base to E. or N. Berlin. (I could
> move house to E. or N. Berlin but I would then be doing
> something different there from what I do here.)[43]

In 1926 Benjamin thought he was prepared to do that – to move
his base and to change his production accordingly – but he was
perhaps overestimating his own adaptability and the willingness of
his prospective new neighbours to receive him.

So Benjamin stayed where he was in Berlin, moving neither to Moscow nor, as we have seen, to Palestine. He only spoke the 'language' of the most sophisticated Western European communities: he had to remain in that context if he was to work at all. This was at least as clear to his friend Scholem as it was to Benjamin himself. Despite repeated attempts to encourage Benjamin to come to Palestine, Scholem never concealed the difficulties posed by Benjamin's 'so pronouncedly European' leanings.[44] If Benjamin was to be accepted by the Jews in Palestine, he would have to feel 'completely bound to the country and to the cause of Judaism'. Learning Hebrew was an inescapable precondition of such an involvement; and as with Russian, and later also English, this was an enterprise to which Benjamin regularly turned with some fanfare but little visible progress. Without Hebrew, however, Benjamin would have suffered the fate of those other German-Jewish immigrants to Palestine, from whom Scholem and his Hebrew-speaking friends turned away disdainfully.[45] Benjamin's concern to retain a readership, however small, which would accept his own 'advanced standpoint',[46] prevented his emigration in this period, and lay at the heart of the difficulties that he later encountered even in France.

Staying in Berlin, however, posed its own problems. Benjamin was working, as he saw it, with an 'illegal incognito among the bourgeois authors'; his particular version of the history of ideas associated him superficially with the bourgeois ideological machine while allowing him, 'incognito', to pursue his destructive projects within it. The problem, however, was whether this was any more than a comfortable, if not dangerous, excuse for apathy. Was it possible for Benjamin to be an 'outsider' without defecting to the bourgeois camp or damaging his own work?[47] Would Benjamin's remote field of specialisation be firm enough to take account of the 'rhythm' of his 'convictions', and to 'organise his existence'?[48]

Under the pressure of external circumstances, and perhaps encouraged by his own growing success as an independent writer during these years, Benjamin answered these questions affirmatively. Until 1932, at least, he seems to have been right. Benjamin's most fruitful contact during the 1920s was the Austrian poet Hugo von Hofmannsthal, who in 1923 accepted a long essay on Goethe for publication in his *Neue Deutsche Beiträge*.[49] This was an important success for Benjamin: Hofmannsthal, who was introduced to Benjamin through a mutual friend, Florens Christian Rang, was enthusiastic about the essay, and subsequently showed himself very willing to assist Benjamin in his search for publishing outlets elsewhere.[50] Benjamin made major steps forward during 1925, when Willy Haas, a friend of Hofmannsthal's,[51] hired Benjamin to review French art theory books in a new Rowohlt journal, *Die Literarische Welt,* which he was editing.[52] By 1926 Benjamin was an established contributor to that periodical, and also to the books section of the *Frankfurter Zeitung* and the journal *Querschnitt.* At the same time, Rowohlt also commissioned him, together with Franz Hessel, to translate Proust's *A la recherche du temps perdu.*[53] Since late 1924, Ernst Schoen, a schoolfriend of Benjamin's and at one stage his wife's lover, had been working in production at the Frankfurt radio station, and Benjamin was able to obtain broadcasting work through and with him.[54] Collaborative work of this sort, which Benjamin also carried out with his editor Haas,[55] with Bernhard Reich,[56] and with Asja Lacis,[57] helped establish him among important circles of the progressive German intelligentsia during the declining years of the Weimar Republic.

None the less, it is obvious that this was very much the loose bourgeois form of association of which Benjamin did not really approve. There was no sense in which there could be a productive working-out of differences within an agreed overall framework – something that might have been a positive aspect of the party apparatus.[58] Hofmannsthal himself was not a left-winger, and Benjamin seems to have regarded him more as a remote and benevolent patron than as an immediate associate. Certainly he could not consider him as an intellectual ally.[59] Benjamin seems to have been even less happy with Willy Haas, despite the fact that Haas facilitated the production of a stream of brilliant and deeply committed articles in the *Literarische Welt.* In 1932, soon after Haas and Benjamin had together produced the very striking '*Vom Weltbürger zum Grossbürger*' issue of the journal, Haas wrote to Benjamin, now on holiday in Ibiza, to tell him that his services were no longer required. The political climate was already getting uncomfortable, and, as Benjamin commented, there seemed little basis for preserving a group solidarity. 'The "intellectuals" among our "co-religionaries" are the first ones to offer sacrifices from their own ranks to the oppressors, simply in order to be spared themselves.'[60]

But in fact, Benjamin's commitment to 'Berlin W.W.' did not confine him to the high culture of Haas or Hofmannsthal. After his return from Moscow in 1927 he had continued to pursue the options offered by organised communism. At the end of 1928 Asja Lacis came to Berlin for a year. She and Benjamin lived together for some of that time,[61] and while she was there she introduced him to Bertolt Brecht and to the Communist 'Federation of Proletarian Revolutionary Writers'. Brecht, as we shall see, was to be Benjamin's most important associate from 1930 onwards; and the Writers' Federation (the BPRS) set the context for much of Benjamin's outstanding work.

The BPRS, a Communist organisation which regarded bourgeois leftists like Haas with contempt,[62] was an attempt to direct the efforts of German writers committed to a Bolshevik line. Founded in late 1928, it was an aspect of the 'left' orientation of official German communism during the decade leading up to Hitler's takeover. In stressing the need for a specifically proletarian culture it was opposing the previous Party tendency to denigrate proletarian experimentation in favour of the traditional products of bourgeois progressives. This had been an aspect of the Soviet desire to present a familiar and 'respectable' face to the world. In the early 1920s, the Soviet Government had stressed the value of the existing cultural tradition, and attacked the attempts of avant-garde writers and artists to match the political revolution with a cultural one. One of the leaders of this avant-garde was Bogdanov, whose 'Proletkult' conceptions of the proletarian takeover of culture were immensely influential both in Russia and abroad. Bogdanov's work on the 'organisational task of ideology' and on art's function in 'organising thoughts and feelings' was one of Benjamin's concerns in Paris in 1926.[63]

In the Soviet Union itself the 'Proletkult' and associated movements had been largely discredited by the late 1920s, and supplanted by the reasonably amenable RAPP (the Russian Association of Proletarian Writers). The BPRS was set up in 1928 under the wing of RAPP, but had a more radical public image in line with the leftist trend in German Communism. Perhaps as a consequence, the organisation was a focus of rather more fruitful debates than RAPP itself, despite the fact that Johannes R. Becher, the BPRS's Moscow-supported leader, tried to impose a very moderate line.[64] These debates, in which men like Brecht and Benjamin occupied the corner of the leftist opposition, centred around the question of the legitimacy of a radically proletarian break from traditional or bourgeois culture, and around the implications of modern technology and the socialisation of production for art. The leaders of the BPRS were extremely wary of participation by Brecht and Benjamin.[65] Despite more than one attempt, Benjamin was never accepted by Becher or the KPD's literary establishment.[66]

The BPRS and its magazine *Die Linkskurve* were the high point of leftist intellectual organisation in Weimar Germany; when it became clear that the revolution was not imminent, and particularly after the disasters of 1932 and 1933, the atmosphere changed radically. In emigration, the German left-wing writers no longer had a realistic base for their activities, and those under the protection of Moscow had to realise that their only options were to adapt fully to the Moscow line or abandon the position entirely. This was one of the more painful aspects of the emigration, especially for writers like Brecht and Benjamin, both of whom continued with an entirely unambiguous commitment to Bolshevism. After 1933 there was no longer an active KPD to join, so that was not an issue. But co-operation with the committed Russian camp was made more and more difficult by the increasing suspicions and insularity of the Russians, and by their demands for seemingly quite unnecessary conformity from workers in the field of culture. Brecht's controversy with Lukács at the end of the 1930s was only the culmination of several years of frustration in which even his co-editors on *Das Wort,* a journal published in Moscow, were refractory about accepting his articles.[67]

Benjamin was in a much weaker position than Brecht over this kind of issue, but he tried persistently until at least 1937 to have his work published in Bolshevik journals.[68] Despite Brecht's assistance, his success was minimal, and it is an index of his commitment to the Bolshevik cause that he persisted as he did. At least until 1935 he also continued to hope that Lacis might be able to find him a job in Moscow, thus enabling him to move there.[69] It was not until 1938 that he seems finally to have lost patience with the Soviet Union, partly as a result of Stalin's apparently shameful treatment of the non-Communist left in the Spanish Civil War.[70]

This was not the only reason for the accusation of 'Macchiavellism' which he flung at the Soviet leadership, for in this year, 1938, Asja Lacis was arrested and put in a Soviet prison camp – where she remained for the next ten years.[71] Such was the end of Benjamin's commitment to the Soviet regime. But it was not, even then, the end of his commitment to the kind of cultural Bolshevism he had worked out under the influence of Lacis and Brecht, and which was the key to his most important work.

Organised Communism may have failed Benjamin. But his own political and theoretical convictions remained, and indeed grew stronger throughout the 1930s. The most important figure in this was Bert Brecht.

In 1931, and from then on, Brecht was for Benjamin associated with a 'small, but very important avantgarde'; and 'solidarity with Brecht's production' became central to Benjamin's own pro-gramme.[72] The precise nature of Benjamin's relations with Brecht is still something of an enigma, and will doubtless remain so until the full contents of the Benjamin and Brecht archives are made publicly accessible. But by all available accounts, Brecht rep-resented, at least from a professional point of view, the only standpoint that Benjamin could embrace without reserve. Most of Benjamin's commentators with access to all the material have so far tended to take a different view, stressing, for example, Benja-min's personal reservations about Brecht, or Brecht's rude remark in a work diary about Benjamin's aura theory, or Brecht's alleged sabotage of Benjamin's attempts to publish in Moscow, or, as Adorno and Tiedemann would have it, Benjamin's supposed 'fear' of Brecht.[73] But these arguments, which recur in the big Benjamin edition and in the various writings of Adorno, Scholem and their followers, do not really add up to very much when compared with the undeniable differences between Benjamin and the positions of these men. We have already considered some of those differences, and in their most interesting aspect they are theoretical anyway, and so will be dealt with in more detail later. There is no reason to suppose that Benjamin was unreservedly committed to anyone's theoretical position. But at least he could say quite categorically of Brecht that there were no proposals in his work that were not worthy of consideration;[74] and indeed Benjamin's letters are full of praise which goes very much further than that.[75] That kind of endorsement cannot be mustered for either Scholem or Adorno.

The 'small avantgarde' Benjamin referred to probably included Brecht, Lacis and Reich. This was the group among whom his 'bourgeois incognito' was unnecessary. Later, in Paris, it may also have included Brecht's collaborator Margarete Steffin, through whom Benjamin conducted many of his negotiations with Moscow intellectuals; and the communist theologian Fritz Lieb, a pupil of Barth's, to whom Benjamin was close. But these associations are not easy to discern since Benjamin did not tell Scholem or Adorno much about them, and alternative sources are scarce.

At all events, Brecht was the principal figure in this avant-garde. It is important that Brecht's significance for Benjamin was in the first instance professional; Benjamin stressed solidarity with his production, rather than with his person. As far as can be judged from the available evidence, the two men were never particularly intimate, and always remained on *'Sie'* terms with one another. Brecht was six years younger than Benjamin, which may have contributed to this. Certainly it was the case that Brecht was never the senior partner in the relationship; if anything it was the other way round. Admittedly Lacis says that it was at Benjamin's request that she introduced him to Brecht in Berlin in 1929.[76] But Benjamin was at this stage not uncritical of the thirty-one-year-old Brecht who, beyond having written the popularly successful *Threepenny Opera,* had little to recommend him to a theorist and Bolshevik such as Benjamin.[77] Benjamin's estimation of Brecht grew gradually as he became more familiar with his work, and as Brecht came to substantiate his own position in publications such as the series of *Versuche,* where both dramatic and theoretical work appeared.

During the 1930s the relationship between Brecht and Benjamin was important to both of them. When Brecht had to leave Germany in 1933 he moved to a house in Denmark. He attempted to persuade Benjamin to move up there also.[78] Benjamin refused, but he did have his Berlin library sent up there,[79] and during the following years made three prolonged visits to where Brecht was living. As in most of his affairs during these years, Benjamin had to be guided by considerations of cost. He did not live with Brecht, and there is no reason to suppose that Brecht subsidised his visits. But the Danish countryside was cheaper than Paris. A disadvantage was that he had to cope with Brecht, who was not always an easy companion. It could be 'another way of being lonely', as he wrote in 1933.[80] None the less, he accepted this side of the relationship as part of Brecht's vivaciously polemical nature, and was even rather worried when the increasingly depressed Brecht, in 1938, became quite easy to get on with.[81]

One of the inevitable targets of Brecht's polemic was Benjamin's more theological vein of speculation. After hearing Benjamin's 'aura' theory, Brecht exclaimed in his diary: 'All mysticism, at the same time as an attitude attacking mysticism. So this is how the materialist theory of history is adapted! It's pretty horrible.'[82] These are strong words. But it is not something that would have disconcerted Benjamin, who was aware of the counter-revolutionary appearance of his specialisation, and doubtless did not mince his words either in discussions with Brecht. In any case, this isolated comment by Brecht seems out of character when set against his other respectful observations about Benjamin. Benjamin obviously represented for Brecht a crucial discussion partner, if one is to judge by their regular contacts in Denmark and Paris throughout the 1930s; by the fact that it was Brecht who invited Benjamin to Denmark in 1933 and again on each subsequent occasion;[83] and by the long memorandum on the Moscow Trials which Brecht apparently addressed to Benjamin,[84] and which is presumably representative of his input into the relationship.

Benjamin saw a great deal more of Brecht during the last decade of his life than he saw of either of the two men who have implied that their own influences were more important – Scholem and Adorno. Benjamin's thought reached its full power in the discussions with Brecht. As he made clear in a letter to Adorno, the encounter with Brecht's thinking was decisive for his development away from the 'rhapsodic naivete' of his early philosophy. The discussion with Horkheimer and Adorno had been a stage on this road, but Brecht was the *einschneidende Begegnung* ('epoch-making encounter') that had brought him to his conclusive position.[85] Ultimately, Brecht was the only other writer whose position was remotely comparable to that of Benjamin. Benjamin had chosen not to join the KPD and the Moscow apparatus, partly because it would not have been easy to do so for 'external' reasons, and partly because it would have involved abandonment of the field of study that was most directly his own. But in taking this decision he was also aware of the serious danger that he might simply be absorbed into an inappropriate organisation, and thus betray his work in a much more unfortunate way. The option he chose – staying as close as possible to the centres of his kind of civilised culture ('Berlin W.W.') and declining any commitment to organisations that would have demanded emigration – condemned him to a life of personal and professional isolation. Benjamin's letters during the 1930s were filled with the pain of this isolation. He was suffering a kind of double exile. Although a German, he was unable to live in the country where he had the easiest access to a readership. And although, as he said, his writing was most properly 'at the right address' *(zuständig)* in the Soviet Union,[86] even there a narrow conception of party discipline and a primitive attitude towards 'formalism' frustrated him.

But this was precisely what had happened to Brecht as well. Ejected from Germany, his intellectual compass pointed towards Moscow. But in Moscow, critics like Lukács (now) and Becher were making life difficult for him. Brecht's isolation was just as bad in Denmark as Benjamin's was in Paris. 'In his growing isolation', Benjamin commented, could be recognised 'the consequences of that faith to which we both hold'.[87]

Brecht did finally address Benjamin as *'Du'*, in the two very moving poems he wrote on Benjamin's suicide. It was a fitting conclusion to a strange but fruitful comradeship.

The Institute for Social Research

In the end Benjamin had to return to an academic milieu. Zionism and Bolshevism had both revealed themselves to be inappropriate, partly because of the need in each case to emigrate and partly because Benjamin could not muster the dogmatic loyalty required. And the association with Brecht, whatever its personal satisfactions, provided neither livelihood nor professional structure.

It is perhaps ironic that the institution to which Benjamin returned was the Institute for Social Research, often called the 'Frankfurt School' because of its association with Frankfurt University. Even more ironically, the two most famous members of the Institute, Max Horkheimer and Theodor Adorno, were both pupils of the same Hans Cornelius who condemned Benjamin's Habilitation to failure. But unfortunately this was not really the vindication that it might appear to be, for Benjamin's relationship with the Frankfurt School was in certain respects as unhappy as his relationship with the university itself had been.

The Institute for Social Research was a classic example of academic leftism. It had been founded in 1922 for the study of Marxism. That was its revolutionary aspect. On the other side it was closely linked with Frankfurt University, and its director had to be a full professor of the university. Frankfurt was generally regarded as progressive at this time; but even so, this provision would appear strangely inconsistent in the light of what we already know of the Weimar Republic's universities. The paradox of the situation was perhaps clearest in the fact that the foundation's money came from the heir to a trading fortune. Brecht contemplated using this in his satirical novel on the Weimar intelligentsia. 'A rich old man (the wheat speculator Weil) dies, disturbed at the misery in the world. In his will he devotes a large sum for the founding of an institute which will investigate the source of this misery. Of course he is himself the source.'[88]

The Institute's ambiguous position was reflected in its work. On the one hand its members made undoubted contributions towards the theoretical systematisation of Marxism and, in early years at least, towards its implementation in empirical work. But at the same time, their views of revolutionary agency were entirely sceptical; pragmatic political organisation seemed not to be envisaged in their scheme. As David Held has put it, 'they offer a theory of the importance of fundamental social transformation which has little basis in social struggle'.[89] This was nowhere clearer than in the work of Adorno himself. Harmut Scheible has recently identified this problem:

'For only that is true which does not fit into this world': this sentence from the *Aesthetic Theory* marks Adorno's critical attitude to society, but at the same time it shows the implied tendency in his thought to withdraw into an aesthetically mediated alternative world. This alternative world may indeed be irreconcilably opposed to the empirical world; but at the same time it is a world which exacts no obligations, just like the perfectly formed autonomous works of art whose complete lack of practical effect . . . Adorno himself had to concede.[90]

But theories which exact no obligations, and which make no specific demands on practice, in the end leave the empirical world how they find it. In Adorno's hands, Marxism was reduced to a rich and compelling description of the inevitable.

Benjamin's relations with the Institute were ambiguous, and, given the lack of any substantial biographical material on the main figures of the Institute, it is difficult always to be precise about their attitude towards, and treatment of, Benjamin. By the time Benjamin came to be associated with the Institute during the 1930s the original director, a Marxist historian of labour, had retired. With the replacement of Carl Grünberg by Max Horkheimer in 1931 the Institute began a change of emphasis towards a less orthodox and more philosophical version of Marxism. The change was reflected in a change of publications; the original *Archiv für die Geschichte des Sozialismus und der Arbeiterbewegung,* which Grünberg had started long before the Institute was founded, ceased to appear and was replaced by a new *Zeitschrift für Sozialforschung*, which was to become the principal organ of those Institute members later known as the 'Frankfurt School'.

Benjamin, who was three years older than Horkheimer, had met the new director some years previously. Horkheimer had taken his D.Phil. in 1922, and was himself completing the Habilitation at the same time as Benjamin's attempt in 1925. Horkheimer already knew Benjamin at this stage – Benjamin was spending much of his time in Frankfurt, both in connection with the Habilitation, and also in pursuit of journalistic plans.[91] Horkheimer claimed to have interceded with Cornelius for Benjamin,[92] although, himself a candidate, he can hardly have been in a very strong position.

Benjamin came to know Horkheimer better during the years after the Frankfurt debacle. In 1928 he visited Königstein near Frankfurt, where Horkheimer lived,[93] and when Asja Lacis came to stay with him later that year they both saw Horkheimer in nearby Cronberg, whose Hotel Frankfurter Hof was apparently favoured by Institute members.[94] At the end of 1930 Benjamin was invited to give a talk at the Institute; this was postponed, however, on account of his mother's death, and seemingly never did take place.[95]

Benjamin's relations with the Institute, hitherto entirely informal, became very much more significant towards the end of 1932, when he realised that his sources of income were being cut off by the increasing power of the Nazis. In the spring, the *Frankfurter Zeitung* and the *Literarische Welt* (in which most of Benjamin's work appeared) seemed about to be closed to him.[96] After a lonely and depressed summer in Ibiza and Nice Benjamin returned to Germany determined to do something about his bleak future. In January he was able to report that the *Frankfurter Zeitung* was in fact prepared to accept further work from him, and he had been able to establish new contacts in Berlin's *Vossische Zeitung,* which would also take some of his work.[97] Both, it should be said, did so, but after April 1933 the pieces only appeared anonymously or pseudonymously. Benjamin's other new contact was the *Zeitschrift für Sozialforschung,* Horkheimer's publication. Benjamin had visited Horkheimer in Frankfurt on his way back to Berlin, and Horkheimer had agreed to start sending him work.

The Institute was well prepared for the Nazi takeover in 1933, having transferred its endowment abroad two years before. The Nazis seized the Institute's library and building in Frankfurt, on the grounds of its 'tendencies hostile to the state', but Institute members were able to reconvene in Geneva and set up branch offices in Paris and London. In 1934 Horkheimer succeeded in affiliating the Institute to Columbia University, and from then on it was based in New York.[98]

During the course of the next six years – for the rest of his life, in fact – Benjamin supplied the *Zeitschrift für Sozialforschung* with one major essay every year, and an irregular series of reviews. The first essay, 'The Present Social Situation of the French Writer', was submitted in the summer of 1933 and appeared at the beginning of 1935. The topic was specified by the Institute,[99] as indeed were most of the subsequent ones. As a result, Benjamin generally had no difficulty persuading the Institute to accept his pieces. At the same time, it was true that Horkheimer exercised a fairly determined control over contributions, and was particularly careful to ensure that none appeared more 'political' than was good for the journal's academic image. Benjamin, more often than not, had to accept political softening of his contributions – not, it would seem from his reactions, something he was accustomed to.[100]

Despite this, Benjamin's relations with Horkheimer seem to

have been consistently good, and Horkheimer was probably the decisive instrument in bringing Benjamin into the Institute's narrower circle of members.[101] From 1935 or so, when German periodicals ceased to publish work by Benjamin even pseudonymously, he was almost entirely dependent on the support of the Institute. From the beginning of 1934 he had been receiving an allowance of 500 French francs per month. By early 1935 the situation seemed to be getting appreciably more difficult. Benjamin seems to have had some hope of joining the Institute in New York at this stage;[102] this failed, but the Institute did agree temporarily to increase their support to a level that was tantamount to a full subsistence allowance.[103] It would seem from the evidence available that the Institute then extended this, and effectively supported Benjamin entirely from this period onwards. In the spring of 1936, Friedrich Pollock, who was largely responsible for the Institute's finances, saw Benjamin in Paris and reached a satisfactory financial arrangement with him;[104] Benjamin was by this time regarded as a member of the Institute's 'inner circle'.[105] The franc was devalued later that year, which made Benjamin's position difficult again; but during the following summer he evidently felt sufficiently sure of his position to negotiate vigorously with the Institute for an increased allowance.[106] During September 1937 Horkheimer himself was in Paris, and came away sufficiently charmed and impressed by Benjamin[107] to place his finances on an entirely different footing. Thenceforth, Benjamin, now regarded as 'in the full sense' a member of the Institute,[108] was to be paid his monthly allowance in hard dollars. The upshot was that Benjamin could afford, at last, to rent a flat of his own in Paris.[109]

It was at this point that another figure began to play an influential role in Benjamin's relations with the Institute. Theodor Adorno, who was eleven years younger than Benjamin, had first met him in Frankfurt while Benjamin was taking a token semester at the University as part of his Habilitation application.[110] At this point – it was 1923 and Adorno was barely twenty – there was little contact between them. After Adorno had taken his D.Phil in 1924 he went to Vienna. When he returned, in 1928, he became part of the circle around Horkheimer and the Institute, and consequently also became closer to Benjamin.[111]

Adorno seems to have acted as Benjamin's contact within the Institute already from these early days. When Benjamin postponed his proposed talk in 1930, he wrote to Adorno.[112] And it is possible that Benjamin decided to tackle Horkheimer on the possibilities of contributing to the *Zeitschrift* after encouragement from Adorno.[113] Adorno did not play any direct role in the Institute's affairs in these early years, however. Both he and Horkheimer had to stop teaching in the spring of 1933 as a result of Hitler's 'Law for the reconstitution of the German Civil Service'. Horkheimer then moved, with the Institute, to Geneva and subsequently to New York. Adorno, however, wished to stay in Germany 'at any cost'[114] and attempted to survive as a journalist in Berlin. By the middle of 1934 this was already no longer possible, and so he decided to go to Oxford to do an English doctorate.

Adorno's motivation in staying in Germany, and then in attempting an Oxford D.Phil. (from which he anticipated an opening into an English academic career) was professional rather than material. He had independent means, and was less concerned to establish a means of subsistence than to maintain his '*Wirkungsmöglichkeiten* – in other words, his opportunities to publish and teach.[115] This raises the question of why he did not follow Horkheimer, since he would have been able to do so financially even without a full salary from the Institute. But he was not yet a full member; and in any case his future wife Gretel Karplus was still in Berlin.[116] Adorno stayed in Oxford for two years, during which time he travelled regularly to the Continent. In 1937 he travelled to New York, and on his return for a last year at Oxford was able to report that he now had a firm 'prospect of work with the Institute'.[117] That autumn he married Gretel Karplus, and the following spring he was established as a firm member of the Institute in New York.[118]

Adorno was one of Benjamin's closest links within the Institute, both before they became full members and in even more significant ways afterwards. But it is also clear that this was not a relationship without tensions, both personal and professional. Initially at least, Adorno was very much Benjamin's junior and to an important degree also his disciple. Adorno's Habilitation thesis, on Kierkegaard, drew heavily on Benjamin's work on the Baroque. Some of his early teaching at Frankfurt was on the *Trauerspiel* book.[119] His correspondence, at least until the mid-1930s, regularly cites Benjamin as authority.[120]

But Adorno's behaviour towards colleagues in areas close to his

own was marred by a curiously gratuitous assertiveness. This was
perhaps especially so with people who were a little ahead of
Adorno in their careers. Adorno's response to such people was to
overwhelm them with laudatory oratory in which, however, praise
was often mixed with what Ernst Bloch called the air of the
'professorial know-all'.[121] This hidden competitiveness, which
simultaneously tries to flatter and frighten possible rivals, is of
course not uncommon among academics. As Adorno applied the
technique, it took the form of enormously long and highly theoretical letters which left the correspondent at an apologetic loss. In
Benjamin's case, these lengthy critiques started arriving in 1930,
when he had to fend off criticism of a proposed lecture title for the
Institute.[122] For the next few years, including the first period of his
Zeitschrift contributions, Benjamin was dealing directly with
Horkheimer. His reluctance to involve Adorno in his writing was
demonstrated by his dilatoriness in sending him a copy of the
major essay on Kafka in 1934; Adorno eventually managed to
borrow someone else's.[123] Even then the result, as Benjamin had
perhaps anticipated, was an immensely long letter of criticism –
which Benjamin answered in one politely evasive paragraph.[124]
This was the pattern of their correspondence for the next few
years. Whenever Adorno saw any of Benjamin's work related to
the Institute he would respond with a massive letter of criticism
which Benjamin, in his turn, would answer briefly or not at all.
Benjamin's more Bolshevik work did not go to Adorno, and even
one *Zeitschrift* contribution, the famous 'Work of Art in the Age
of Mechanical Reproduction', only went to Adorno after he had
insistently requested it.[125]

This relationship became more difficult in 1938, when Adorno
had taken up residence in New York and started wielding direct
editorial control. Adorno was an important link between Benjamin and the Institute because of their close interests. Horkheimer,
although a philosopher, was basically a political theorist, whereas
Adorno was a musicologist and cultural critic; Horkheimer thus
inevitably accorded Adorno precedence in this area. That could
have been to Benjamin's advantage when he was first establishing
himself with the Institute, and when he was persuading them to
support his 'Arcades' project (the synopsis, 'Paris Capital of the
XIXth Century' was sent through Adorno). But as soon as Adorno
had free rein to intervene in the actual publication of the work,

matters became more difficult.

This may be seen from the amount of work by Benjamin that actually appeared in the *Zeitschrift* before and after Adorno's arrival in New York. In 1937 and early 1938 the *Zeitschrift* published Benjamin's long piece on 'Eduard Fuchs', together with five reviews; a further review was accepted. After Adorno joined, two reviews appeared in 1938, nothing in 1939, and then finally two articles and the previously accepted review early in 1940.[126] As Benjamin protested in May 1940, four reviews he had written the previous year had not appeared at all (and they never did).[127]

The real cause of his discontent at this point was not the suppression of a few short reviews, so much as the prolonged wrangle over part of what was supposed to be Benjamin's major project, the 'Arcades'. This undignified and depressing procedure occupied what turned out to be Benjamin's last sustained period of work, leaving him disillusioned and embittered. The piece of work in question was the essay 'Paris of the Second Empire in Baudelaire's Work' which, after exhaustive revisions, was finally allowed to appear in the *Zeitschrift* under the title 'On Certain Motifs in Baudelaire'.

The sequence of events with this essay was much the same as it had been in Benjamin's correspondence with Adorno over the Kafka article, the 'Reproduction' essay, and others. The difference now, though, was that Benjamin could not reply with discreet evasion, for Adorno was in the editor's chair. When Adorno's usual massive critique arrived in November 1938, after a year in which Benjamin had spent most of his time working on the essay, it no longer constituted friendly competition, but outright editorial rejection. Whatever Benjamin thought of Adorno's objections, he was unfortunately no longer in a position to ignore them. This regrettable situation was exacerbated by the fact that Horkheimer took it upon himself early the following year to warn Benjamin that he might have to lose his Institute allowance.[128]

Not surprisingly, Benjamin felt that the Institute was treating him inexcusably, and he wrote to Scholem to tell him so that spring.[129] But since Benjamin now had no income except from the Institute – Scholem's own approaches to possible sources in Palestine had also been fruitless[130] – he had no choice but to do what Adorno and the Institute were insisting. Accordingly he settled down, with understandable resentment,[131] to rewrite the Baudelaire article. This was finally finished, in a form now acceptable to Adorno, shortly before the outbreak of war. Benjamin's next move was into a French internment camp, an oppression which in itself lasted only two months, but signalled the beginning of a refugee existence which only ended with Benjamin's suicide in September 1940.

The strained relations between Benjamin and Adorno were expressed also on the personal level. It has been remarked that Benjamin could behave with 'Chinese politeness'.[132] This was undoubtedly true of Benjamin's relations with Adorno, but certainly did not characterise his associations generally. It is noticeable, merely with the ambit of Benjamin's Institute connections, that his letters and references to Adorno are far cooler than those, for example, to Horkheimer, which seem to be characterised for the most part by a genuine affection.[133] He never got beyond the formal '*Sie*' with either Horkheimer or Adorno, but this was not characteristic of Benjamin, who had many '*Du*' friendships. One of the most notable in this context was with Gretel Karplus, Adorno's later wife. Benjamin seems to have had a relatively close relationship with Gretel whom, at one point, he tried to persuade to come to Ibiza.[134] His letters to her, which are in the relaxed and intimate style Benjamin used so well to friends, bear no comparison to the stilted professions of collegial loyalty that predominate in the letters to Adorno. Benjamin also preferred Gretel as recipient of his work. The copy of 'Kafka' which Adorno eventually obtained (and blessed with one of his critiques) had in fact been sent to Gretel. Benjamin's last work, the theses on history, was first announced to her.[135] And, in an attempt once to avoid becoming involved with Adorno's professorial disputations, Benjamin answered a missive on the 'Arcades' synopsis by writing to Gretel instead.[136] In all this it is noticeable that Benjamin was not invited when Adorno and Gretel were married in Oxford in 1937.[137]

Benjamin's relationship with the Institute for Social Research is of crucial importance if we are to understand the context of his later work. A great deal of energy has been expended on arguing the character of this relationship. Members of the Institute, and particularly Adorno himself, were of course largely responsible for the Benjamin renaissance after 1945. Much of Adorno's writing, and that of his pupil Tiedemann, was devoted to assimilating

Benjamin's position to that of the Institute, and demonstrating the extent to which the two were compatible. The weakness of this approach lay in its continuation of the editorial policies originated by Adorno, filling the posthumous selections with politically sanitised texts – the revised Baudelaire essay rather than the first, for example, and the second 'Reproduction' essay rather than the first. The undeniably Bolshevik works like the 1933 essay on the politicisation of French writers, or 'The Author as Producer', were either suppressed altogether or offered with the caveat that they reflected Benjamin's unwholesome fascination with Brecht.[138] When directly hostile references to the Institute were unearthed by the editors of the complete Benjamin edition, they were put down to 'amoralism', the result of the regrettable persistence of a bourgeois mentality.[139]

The editorial problems raised by the first posthumous editions of Benjamin were undoubtedly worrying. But it is doubtful whether the high moral outrage voiced by Adorno and Tiedemann's many critics was entirely apposite.[140] Certainly the undeniable differences between Benjamin and the Institute cannot usefully be discussed on the level of morals. The relationship was that of a productive ideological organisation. The Institute supported Benjamin so that he could produce the sort of material they wanted. Benjamin believed that his obligations towards the Institute, although occasionally onerous,[141] were a reasonable exchange for the amount of intellectual freedom he retained. If he was occasionally resentful, that has to be seen in the light of a relationship that was in essence that of employer and employee. This is not a moral verdict; even co-operative labour inevitably involves a certain degree of alienation.

The fundamental problem is whether Benjamin's own original project suffered from his association with the Institute. This, ultimately, is the focus of all the disagreement over the interpretation of Benjamin's work. It was an old Bolshevik principle not to accept minority participation in a bourgeois government. Private or minority reservations are irrelevant in the functioning of an organisation; 'like it or leave it' is the only realistic principle. The fact that Benjamin did not leave the Institute may be an indication that he liked it. Alternatively, it may have been misjudgement, or a compromise forced on him by the exigencies of the time. The expectations raised by Benjamin's career *until* 1932 rather suggest it was the latter. If so, all we can ultimately hope to gain from his later work is a damaged torso, the remains of a theoretical corpus which had to submit itself to *force majeure*. That need be no less valuable than a carefully perfected and homogeneous structure. But, like an archeological fragment, it has to be excavated with enormous care from its surroundings.

3
The Intellectual Background

Benjamin's work drew on two very disparate theoretical traditions. On the one side lay German academic philosophy and the rich ideological milieu in which his own thought first developed. On the other was the Bolshevism which he first encountered in the years after the First World War. Some understanding of this context is necessary if we are to follow the path along which Benjamin's thinking developed. It is particularly important if we are to make sense of the unattributed citations which fill Benjamin's writings; failure to identify these citations, and to recognise the ideological background which for Benjamin himself gave them their political colouring, can lead to serious misunderstanding of his point of view.

A further point is that academic philosophy and the Bolshevism of the time were not really comparable in scope. German academic philosophy of the early twentieth century was a rich theology embracing a multitude of different areas from metaphysics to political and aesthetic theory. Bolshevism's theoretical nakedness was so far only covered by the most rudimentary garments. That is not to undervalue what Bolshevism did have; simple clothing is doubtless more practical than flowing ecclesiastical vestments. And indeed Engels, at least, had proclaimed the 'end of philosophy'. None the less, Benjamin's work sometimes shows an uneasy awareness of the gulf between its Bolshevik aims and the theoretical resources which only seemed available in the storerooms of the bourgeoisie. But his appropriation of those resources has to be identified as borrowing, not endorsement.

Traditionalism

Rise of the cultural sciences

The dictum that 'there's nothing new under the sun' is obviously false if applied to the organisational and technological development of human labour. It is, however, true of philosophy, or rather of systematic philosophies, the grand theologies of social self-consciousness. The relations of production create a second world which grows and changes; the theologies that accompany them run through a constant cycle, whose features depend more on the balance of class power than on the imagined innovations of the clerisy. This is clear to anyone who studies ideas not as an isolated intellectual struggle, but within their practical context. The progressions of twentieth-century thought, from critical realism to new ontology and back, are pre-figured in the battles of the medieval Christian Church; and Benjamin picked out the features of Kantian ethics against seventeenth-century Lutheran ideology. The resources of metaphysics are few; the task of the philosopher is to see that they disappear as lubricants into the social machine. To the extent that the social machine changes, so does the expertise of the philosopher. But nothing could be more reactionary and mystifying than the new corpuses of belief which periodically spring up; each one, nowadays, another modish metaphysics for a decaying capitalist world. Autonomous philosophy, like the systems that are naively abused as 'scholasticism', is a sign of nothing except ideological reaction. Its subtlety is the subtlety of the serpent.[1]

The academic philosophy within which Benjamin grew up was firmly rooted in the ideological campaigns of the time. Some of his thought, inevitably, had to make use of the resources of that philosophy. In other places his thought is a direct attack on it. The attacks are the most successful parts of his work; as we shall see in the final chapter, the ambiguities in his last writings are linked with his failure ever to carry out the intended full critique of traditional philosophy (especially as represented by Heidegger). One thing is quite sure: it is futile to cast across Benjamin's work with a few flies picked from modern French thought. No doubt fish will be landed. But the historical and ideological naivete of much French writing, especially in its Anglo-Saxon appropriation, will only ensure that the nature of this catch remains obscure.[2]

The task of a patriotic German philosopher had become complex by the end of the nineteenth century. Before the empire, the direct Prussian nationalism of a historian like Ranke had been sufficient ideological support for the state's expansionist ambitions. Ranke's 'realism' was, as Meinecke later confirmed, a good basis for the 'unconstrained political thinking' of Bismarck.[3] But this unsentimental and objective approach to the Machiavellian problems of foreign policy became less appropriate when, after 1871, the Second Reich had to contend with the more subtle internal problems of Catholic ultramontane resistance to Prussian hegemony, and the growth of Social Democracy among an organised industrial proletariat. This was clearly recognised by such academics as Wilhelm Dilthey, who, originally an enthusiastic supporter of Bismarck and a simple German nationalism,[4] realised towards the end of the century that the ideology of a large industrial state would have to be more complex. After the resignation of Bismarck, accordingly, Dilthey himself turned to the elaboration of more adequate theories of historiographic activity and the *'Geisteswissenschaften'*,[5] recognising that at least one of the attractions of Ultramontanism and Social Democracy was their great coherence as ideological systems.[6] The first of Dilthey's great writings on the theory of cultural history, *Introduction to the Geisteswissenschaften*, appeared in 1883, by which time Dilthey himself was already fifty years old.

The problem with Ranke's bluntly 'positivist' method was that it was altogether too indiscreet about political issues. In suggesting that Germany's struggles with her neighbours were part of a legitimate progress towards the sovereignty of the nation state, he had done little to isolate such 'legitimate' struggles from the 'illegitimate' struggles of particular social groups for emancipation. Objectivist history was altogether too close to the scientistic notions of progress ('Darwinism') endorsed by political revolutionaries and Social Democrats. A clear view of what had happened and what was still going on was liable to lead to the conclusion that human struggle *did* improve the lot of the human race, just as scientific discovery broadened its mastery of nature, and that the present state of affairs could not be regarded as the best of all possible worlds. This kind of attitude, flattered by the industrial upsurge of the later nineteenth century, was obviously likely to be threatening to the stability of established social interest groups.

Establishment philosophy had a number of answers to this. The outstanding one was to stigmatise belief in continued progress, and in any kind of materialist view of knowledge, as 'old-fashioned'. As Rickert put it rather quaintly in an essay on 'Values of Life and Values of Culture', 'These days nobody who wishes to be modern wants to know about materialism.'[7] Much of the historiography of the mid-nineteenth century (which included notorious liberals like Gervinus) would have been abandoned.[8] One way of looking at it was to regard it as a 'new Enlightenment' – another epoch of the same Gallic rationalism which, as was well known, had been vanquished by the better insights of German Romanticism.[9] The celebration of German Romanticism from Herder to Schlegel became, in fact, one of the central interests of cultural historiography, emphasising the 'modernity' of its abandonment of rationalistic norms, belief in progress and the like.[10]

As Rickert loftily declared, 'Truth is not subject to the domination of development or change.'[11] And certainly as far as culture was concerned, 'the concept of historical development . . . is to be explicitly distinguished from that of progress'.[12] For Simmel, relatively empirical sciences such as political economy could only stand philosophical scrutiny if given foundations in the metaphysics of 'value'. So, while conceding some positive aspects to Marx's work, he declared his own intention in *The Philosophy of Money* (1900) of 'building an additional storey beneath historical materialism, so that . . . economic structures themselves are seen as the result of deeper values and currents and of psychological and indeed metaphysical preconditions'.[13]

Dilthey was perhaps the most radical in the assertion of a transhistorical realm of permanent values which cut across any progress. For Dilthey, human history was not so much a chain of material causality as a tissue of 'significance' (*Bedeutung*) and 'sense' (*Sinn*). Causality, Dilthey declared in a Schopenhauerian vein, was itself merely an abstraction from a world of experience whose motor lay elsewhere, in the 'life of our will'.[14] Reality, for him, lay in 'inner experience';[15] images of nature were merely a shadow of this concrete inwardness. Will was the realisation of values, and also the peculiarly human facility, asserted over the tediously mechanical necessity of external nature.[16] And so the 'sense' which the historian had to construct from the manifold display of events was that which emerged from the interplay of values.[17]

For Dilthey this task was best approached through literature, whose 'permanently fixed expressions of life'[18] were the pre-eminent organon of all history. The literary work offered two major advantages. In the first place, engagement with the literary involved valuation; consequently, literary criticism reached to the deepest levels of the will and the constitutive powers in it.[19] Second, language, and especially literary language, was the most 'complete, exhaustive and objectively understandable expression of human inwardness'.[20] Language was the most adequate vehicle of what, in the neo-Kantian systematisation of this position, could most appropriately be called objectivity: the articulations of a consciousness immune from the ebb and flow of the material world. This process of the transfer of 'sense' from one 'inwardness' to another, across the hostile chasm of material change and degeneration, was best achieved by the language of literature. And the reception of this inward sense by other readers and critics was what Dilthey called *verstehen,* the mysterious hermeneutic act which joined humanity in the celebration of its own proper history.[21] Here, in Dilthey's argument, was a permanence and objectivity infinitely superior to the contingent phenomena of natural history.

From this vantage point, and particularly from his vision of the magical continuities of a literature that could rise above 'causal relations' to the 'inner unity and power of a second World of the fantasy',[22] Dilthey attacked those who believed in 'the autonomy of reason, the solidarity of society, and its progress towards the best possible world by means of control over nature, the regulation of state and law, and the overcoming of all ecclesiastical and political resistance'.[23] Dilthey did not believe in the autonomy of reason because its dictates were clear for the mystique of a reactionary *Weltanschauung;* and once this autonomy had been destroyed by the construction of a will-dominated 'second world', the crushing of all remaining political enlightenment was a simple matter.

Dilthey capped his comparison of human and natural history with a Nietzschean motif, the theory of eternal recurrence. In this interpretation only human history had the freedom actually to develop. Human actions, proceeding from the spontaneous valuative roots of the will, set their own conditions and established their own objectivity. Natural events, however, were always part of a chain of causal determination, a mechanical sequence which at any moment contained the elements of what was to follow. Only the human individual could go beyond this 'empty and barren repetition of the course of nature'. And yet, as Dilthey remarked bitterly, for the 'idolators of intellectual development' this very course of nature supplied 'the ideal of historical progress'.[24]

Neo-Kantian logic

Dilthey's political commitments are relatively easy to document.[25] This is less the case with other contemporary philosophers of patriotic persuasion. But with all of them a persistent attack on alternative world views such as Catholicism and 'international Democracy'[26] is discernible. The purely philosophical attack on what was believed to be the Social Democrat position was the most sophisticated and productive part of this movement. Its banner was the condemnation of 'materialism', 'naturalism', 'Darwinism' and 'positivism'.[27]

This involved the appropriation of neo-Kantianism. Neo-Kantianism was not in the first instance a particularly 'establishment' or 'reactionary' philosophy, having in one of its streams received much encouragement from the liberal author of a *History of Materialism*, F. A. Lange. Lange, and his successor at Marburg, Hermann Cohen, were both strongly attracted by the advances of natural science, and used the epistemological disciplines as a basis for the systematisation and encouragement of those advances. Cohen's interest in the Calculus is symptomatic of this. This was the kind of Kantianism that the empire's later philosophers declared 'one-sided'.[28] But the Kantian model still had useful instruments to offer those in the 'South-Western' school at the universities of Heidelberg and Freiburg, people like Rickert and Lask who were more interested in the cultural and ideological potential of philosophical speculations.

Rickert's philosophy was based on a 'logic of judgement'. It has also been termed 'logic of validity' (*Geltungslogik*);[29] but the term 'logic of judgement' (*Urteilslogik*) was used by Heidegger[30] and specifies more precisely the point at which he and others (including Benjamin)[31] concentrated their revision of South-Western neo-Kantianism.

'Logic of judgement' involved four stages. In the first place it abandoned the Kantian thing in itself, or any notion of a substance that transcended its knowable appearance.[32] Equally, correspondence theories of truth, or any reflection theory of knowledge, were rejected.[33]

Second, the dichotomy of form and matter, or, as Rickert also put it, of thought and experience, was to be abandoned.[34] In orthodox Kantian thought knowledge was only given by the coincidence of the 'aesthetic' (that is, time and place) with the 'logical' (that is, judgement). By means of 'synthesis' it was possible to generate a number of abstract instruments of understanding, such as mathematics[35] and the 'table of categories'.[36] But as Kant repeatedly emphasised, these instruments only had a legitimacy in so far as they were used on the 'objects of experience', that is to say, things that appeared in time and space.[37]

Kant's opposition between the two formal conditions of objective knowledge, aesthetic and logic, was effectively replaced in Rickert's work by a dichotomy of representation (*Vorstellung*) and knowledge (*Erkenntnis*). The purpose of this was to disengage objective truth from the obligations of the empirical. If for Kant truth had been a compound of the logical and the aesthetic, and if the aesthetic was only operative under the impact of real sensory input, then sense experience and its co-ordinates, time and space, were all inseparable from objectivity. In Rickert's scheme, the formal co-ordinates of time and space were, so to speak, all bundled together into the logical realm, which was then left face to face with an evacuated and meaningless realm of representation. This meant that the logical no longer had to obtain clearance from the aesthetic; the aesthetic forms were now only one of a variety of categories which might or might not appear in theoretical knowledge. The purpose of all this was to weaken the force of Kant's original scientism, and to confer the dignity of objectivity upon what under the original programme might have seemed sheer metaphysical speculation, namely the 'cultural sciences' as understood by Dilthey and his followers.

Accordingly, the third stage of Rickert's argument is to identify the character of the logical. Having determined that representation itself has 'no theoretical significance', and does not embrace the sphere of truth,[38] Rickert turns to knowledge itself. Knowledge, he proposes, coincides with judgement; an act of knowledge is necessarily also an act of judgement (*Urteil* – in the sense of forming a logical proposition).[39] Judgement, he next states, is 'practical';[40] every element of consciousness that is not mere representation, and that involves judgement's attitude of affirmation or negation, is part of the sphere of 'wanting' (*Wollen*).[41] And just as practice, from a traditional Kantian perspective, is essentially free from causal constraint, so also Rickert's 'judgement' is not causally constrained by the empirical.[42] You do not reach logical certainty because matters of fact compel you to; you do it because of what Rickert calls 'judgement necessity' (*Urteilsnotwendigkeit*), which he also characterises as a 'feeling'[43] and an 'imperative'.[44] Equally, the practical judgement that underlies all objective knowledge is guided not by the empirical 'must' but by the ethical 'should'.[45]

Judgement needs to be able to appeal to a criterion.[46] But since the empirical, or world of mere representation, no longer has the stature to supply criteria (which it would have done in terms of correspondence), Rickert has to look elsewhere. He finds his criterion in what he characterises as 'value' (*Wert*).[47] Values, which guide judgemental necessity, are 'never real'.[48] They are not identical with empirical or immanent phenomena such as the sensations of pleasure. So they are only articulated in the logical judgement itself. And every time such a judgement happens it 'announces' (*Kunde geben*)[49] or 'acknowledges' (*anerkennen*) value.[50]

The final stage in Rickert's argument was his identification of what he termed the 'realm of values'.[51] This he characterised as 'a "power" to which we submit, from which we take our direction, or which we recognise as binding for us'.[52] Values alone guaranteed objectivity, at least in the only sense that Rickert admitted. 'They form a realm in themselves which lies beyond subject and object.'[53] The conventional distinctions of epistemology were thus subordinated to a kind of higher truth, a truth which, as Rickert repeatedly emphasised, lay beyond the individual circumstances of time and place.[54]

It would be instructive, if we had the space, to uncover the thinly concealed theology in this viewpoint. Here we can only note that Rickert's 'realm of values' was clearly in the first instance designed for the philosophical legitimation of cultural study. Rickert's examples, typically, were artistic even in his more strictly metaphysical writings;[55] and one of his principal works was an attempt specifically to underpin the cultural sciences.[56] The importance of Rickert's work, however, is mainly transitional. Its conspicuous feature, an ahistorical hypostatisation of practice, was carried over into the next stage of Heidegger and 'new ontology'. Its weakness lay in its failure to determine the status of the 'object' which, while not fully ruled out, appeared to have no position in knowing except as a shadowy 'representation'. In particular, the rather abrupt differentiation between the grandiose timelessness of 'values' and the temporality of the subject-object encounter meant that the natural sciences still retained their grasp over time and space, however shadowy those factors might now appear. This reached its expression in the rather unsatisfactory 'two-world' paradigm of Emil Lask's early work,[57] where cultural study with its values got all the glory, but the natural sciences were still the ones that made the world turn over. The natural sciences' grip on the objective world had not yet been shaken, and neither therefore had the unpleasant presence of positivistic socialists with their economics and their institutional analysis. The scientists had to be pursued to their inner stronghold – real being and real time.

New ontology

Dilthey's position, even with support from the neo-Kantians, was not felt to be sufficiently secure. As Husserl remarked, 'It is easy to see that any fully thought out historicism [that is, Dilthey's standpoint] must turn into an extreme sceptical subjectivism.'[58] The 'second world' of this theory of culture was an arbitrary substantialisation of purely subjective facts; and Dilthey's suggestion that the truth of these entities could be established by learned debate[59] was held by Husserl to be philosophically absurd.[60]

Dilthey in fact died in 1911, and Husserl's attack on Dilthey in the prestigious new journal *Logos* in 1910 marked the beginning of a swing towards a radical new 'ontology' replacing some of the more simplistic aspects of neo-Kantianism. One thinker whose work reflected this move was Emil Lask; but the most important was Martin Heidegger, who was in those years a young man writing his Habilitation at Freiburg. Heidegger has since emerged as perhaps the most influential non-materialist philosopher of this century.

The 'modern ontologists', as Rickert dismissed them,[61] worked to develop a more substantial theoretical infrastructure to replace the blithe spirituality of thinkers such as Dilthey. None the less, they took over the basic orientation of his work. Husserl, for example, confirmed that the object of philosophy was the identification of ideal unities which stood above space and time, and which had their location in 'consciousness' rather than in 'nature'.[62] Furthermore, these ideal unities were articulated in 'absolute, timeless values'.[63] The spiritual roots of reality were also emphasised by Heidegger,[64] who made a point of reiterating the secondary status of 'natural-scientific knowledge'.[65]

The goal of the ontologists was a more adequate theory of categories. The steps in their argument are not easy to follow, but since they have a direct relevance to Benjamin's early metaphysics we shall have to make some mention of them. Basically, they involved a more radical theory of individuation. The South-Western neo-Kantians had depended on a notion of individuation – Rickert, for example, had based his theory of the *Geisteswissenschaften* on the contention that they were 'idiographic' or concerned with individual events, as opposed to the generalising aims of the 'nomothetic' natural sciences[66] – but the inadequacies of the two-world theory had made it difficult to ground this epistemologically. This was precisely the difficulty that led to Husserl's reproach of 'subjectivism': the choice seemed to lie between the natural sciences, which did have a claim to generality, and the poetical intuitions of 'history', which confounded their own claims to generality by also claiming to be unique and individual.

The ontologists attempted to resolve this by resorting to a more radical principle of individuation. This involved, in the first place, a reinstatement of material perception. Whereas Lask's 1910 *Philosophical Logic* had attempted to set out a doctrine of categories relating to the non-sensory 'world' systematically opposed to those of the sensory world, his *Doctrine of Propositions* in the following year carried a quite different emphasis. There, 'formal logic', or the activity of the intellect alone, was relegated to serving the central purpose of logic, now seen as 'exploration of the structure of the object' and 'penetrating to the primary phenomenon [*Urphänomen*]'.[67] Heidegger, in 1915, made a similar point when he declared that: 'Knowledge is only knowledge when it is knowledge of an object. No object without a subject and vice versa.'[68] It is important to note that neither Lask nor Heidegger is actually reinstating the principle of sensory apprehension of matter. 'No object without a subject' says nothing about the ontological status of matter. But it does transfer attention from the weak abstractions of a purely spiritual 'doctrine of categories'.

This new objectivity, manifest in Husserl's slogan of 'to the things themselves' (*zu den Sachen selbst*)[69] required a new approach to individuality. The neo-Kantians had fallen foul of the logic of singular knowledge by claiming that the 'second world' carried the understanding of individual human activities, but leaving it unclear how this individuality was constituted. Within a Kantian scheme, individuality is dependent on some material ('aesthetic') component, since the realm of transcendental logic is entirely concerned with general concepts. But if individuality was dependent on the material, how could it or its 'values' claim to be timeless and absolute?

The solution adopted was to propose that individuality was part of the formal realm rather than merely of the material realm. This meant that apprehension of the individual object was not merely an 'aesthetic' event instantaneously consumed by the generalisations of subjective categories. Rather, the individual object itself contained some active principle which made it accessible to the intellect directly and without mediation by general categories. In this way an object could be both individual and intellectual at the same time, the main advantage of this being that it was liberated from any general material forms such as time and space, and thus also from causality in the scientific sense. Individual objectivity was possible, in other words, without relapsing either into the world of natural necessity – governed by sensory forms – or into a world of subjectivist abstractions which lacked any element of concrete singularity. Much of this rather abstruse opposition between the 'ontologists' and the neo-Kantians was in fact a recapitulation of the revision of Thomism by Duns Scotus – something of which the 'ontologists' were well aware even if they were not always explicit about it.[70] It is clear in both Husserl[71] and Heidegger[72] that individual disclosure of essence is epistemologically fundamental in the system's operation.

The principle of individuation was clearer in its consequences than in its theoretical roots. In the first place it was reflected in a strong playing-down of the role of propositional logic – precisely the 'judgement' emphasised by Rickert. The centrality of the proposition or judgement was firmly resisted by 'ontological' thinkers. Lask, for example, claimed 'transcendental logic' for his newly *material* conception of categories, and asserted that the fundamental task of a new treatment of the proposition would be to isolate its concepts and conclusions from this 'transcendental logic'.[73] Heidegger pointed out in his Habilitation thesis that, at least in Scotist terms, the sense of a proposition could not be compared with a 'real object';[74] and later strongly criticised the assumption that language was essentially propositional.[75] Husserl claimed that the discipline of 'grasping the essence' (*Wesenserfassung*) – in other words, an understanding on the basis of individual apperception rather than universalising propositions – was more profitable to philosophy than 'all indirectly symbolic and mathematical methods', or the 'apparatus of conclusions and proofs'.[76]

So the object was held sufficient for understanding in itself, with no need for the 'subjectivist' instruments of universals and propositional logic. This is important first because, as we have said, of its overcoming of the material principle of individuation still implicit in the old 'two-world' theory. Second, it necessarily throws upon the object an active spiritual force of its own; or, to put it another way, the object becomes endowed with something that makes it intelligible without the intercession either of the senses or of conceptual algebra. The study of 'objective categories' announced by Lask in the *Doctrine of Propositions* becomes one step in the move to investigate the nature of this primary intelligibility.

This was the sense of the term 'ontology'. Ontology is the science of Being; and in this particular context it meant the science of individual beings and their manner of being together in a world. The question that arises is, if the 'scientific' co-ordinates of reality, such as time, space, and propositional logic, have all been relegated to second place as inadequate for the purposes of defining 'Being', then what is to take their place? The answer must be the 'objective categories', or something on a similar plane.

Heidegger on language

Fortunately, a set of what might be regarded as objective categories already exists, namely natural language. In one regard, language may be seen as a repository of universals linked in propositional statements. But in another way, it may be seen as more typically 'naming', that is to say, more properly constituted in singular objects than in a tissue of transferable signs. If it is taken in that sense, then the investigation of language can be not merely a revelation of the grammar of combinations, but of the ontology of Being as well. This is a view allowed in Husserl's comment on scholastic ontology;[77] and then pursued more and more systematically in Heidegger's work.

In his Habilitation dissertation Heidegger says that reality, the empirical world, has a categorical structure: 'that means it is formed, determined, ordered'.[78] This raises the question of how that order is articulated. Heidegger's answer (in terms of his exposition of Scotus) is *analogy*. Analogy, in scholastic logic, is opposed to univocation. Univocation is the application of a term to different objects with the same signification; analogy is the application of a term to different objects but with a different signification. 'Woman' is used univocally of two female persons; it would be used analogically when applied to an adult female and a little girl.[79] As Heidegger presents the Scotist standpoint, analogical gradation characterises the scale of truth and falsehood in reality. The highest principle, the divine, is 'absolute reality', of which anything may be properly predicated;[80] below this there are gradations of reality where the attribute becomes steadily more 'analogical' as the distance from the highest point increases. This, Heidegger claims, avoids all the difficulties both of 'dualism' (that is, the two-world theory, which can never allow absolutely true objective knowledge) and of 'monism' (in which knowledge is merely a reflex of material causation).[81]

The second relevant part of Heidegger's construction of 'Being' as a structure following linguistic and grammatical rules comes in his major work, *Being and Time*. This appeared in 1927 and became a text to which both Benjamin and Brecht were devotedly opposed. It does, none the less, elucidate some of the problems of ontology and language in a way that casts light on earlier parts of Benjamin's work. Heidegger's principal discussion of the relation of word and Being occurs in paragraph 7B 'The Concept of Logos'. This makes a series of points. The fundamental one is that the individual object is primary. 'Objectivity' is not, as in Kantian metaphysics, constituted in the application of transcendentals. 'Truth' is therefore not in the first instance a quality of knowledge involving transcendentals or formal operations; it is a quality generated in *aesthesis*, 'the simple, sensory perception of something'. And the something that is truly perceived is *idia* – the irreducible but intelligible individuality of the object.[82]

Intelligible individuality has a number of consequences. In the first place the object is, so to speak, active. In Heidegger's terminology, it 'shows itself' (*sich zeigen*).[83] It does not depend on subjectivity to process it in some sense before it can be 'objective'. It does not, for example, need to be identified *as* something by a categorising intellect.[84] It is exhaustively intelligible in its phenomenal form.

Second, the object is immediately present in speech. This does not mean, and Heidegger does not say, that the object's intelligibility is the same as its appearance in speech. But it does mean that 'allowing something to show itself' (*Zeigenlassen*) is a primary function of speech. Heidegger develops this around an exploration of Aristotle's *apophainesthai* (ἀποφαίνεσθαι), a term that means 'declaration' or 'statement', but is compounded of the root 'to be manifestly so' together with a prefix indicating agency. The 'apophantic' function of language – declaration – is one in which the object becomes manifest, as it were, by its own agency; language 'allows' it to do so. 'Speech [*die Rede*] "allows to be seen" ἀπὸ . . . by the agency of that [*von dem selbst her*] which it concerns.'[85]

In practice, Heidegger notes briefly, speech (*das Reden*) has the character of talking, that is, giving phonetic expression. In other words, there is a continuum between the appearance of the object in speech and the phonetic. None of these stages can be seen as primary or secondary. Just as speech 'makes way' for the appearance of the object, so too the phonetic is an integral part of the process of objectification.[86]

In Kant, the 'base unit' of knowledge is the propositional judgement completed after the aesthetic and the logical have been combined. In Heidegger, the base unit is given by the immediate entry of the object into speech itself. Synthesis, says Heidegger taking direct issue with Kant,[87] is not a 'busy concern' (*Hantieren*) for the combination of psychic events; it is the simple 'being together' (*Beisammensein*) of something with something. Heidegger does not specify what these somethings are; but presumably they are the traditional poles of subject and object, except that even to go that far in a purely formal distinction distorts the simplicity of the basic 'allowing to be seen' of language.[88]

The basic point emerges as follows. The object and the subject of speech (*Rede*) are functionally indistinguishable. On the 'subjective' side that means that, as Lask had written, the propositional functions of language are subordinate to its 'material' function. Language *can* be symbolic or representational, but this should not obscure its radical materiality.[89] Also, the role of language as an instrument of social influence is secondary; this again is possible, but it does not have the same character of direct revelation.[90] The object rises up in the medium of speech; the conceptual and phatic instrumentalisation of speech introduces an element alien to its primary *apophansis*.[91] Finally, the radical inseparability of subject and object in speech means that speech is itself a direct means of access to Being. It can, as Husserl had suggested, lead to ontology.[92]

A few brief remarks may help to identify the importance of this 'ontological' theory, and particularly its elaboration by Heidegger. It represents a sophisticated consolidation of a position whose foundations had already been laid by Dilthey and the neo-Kantian cultural philosphers. As Husserl had protested, the tackling of the age's 'need for a world view' (*Weltanschauungsnot*) had been rather excessively obvious in simple theories of *Verstehen*.[93] 'Ontology' could be just as useful for generating ideologies, and it did so with a more coherent theory and a more powerful set of claims.

The neo-Kantians' antiscientism (and thus their antimaterialism) was fully preserved in the new ontology. Heidegger's phenomenological theory of the relation between word and object firmly consigned any instrumental uses of language to a level of ontological inferiority. The 'real' ontology of objects, which was by definition more fundamental than scientistic formalisations such as causality, supplied a very much more impressive arena for philosophy than the abstractions of the 'second world'. The '*Existenzialontologie*' of *Sein und Zeit* is very much more powerful than Lask's earlier attempt at a non-sensory 'doctrine of categories'; and Heidegger's rejection of the primacy of propositional logic seems far more disciplined than Dilthey's rather petulant objections to the 'autonomy of reason'. Above all, of course, Heidegger's theory had a convincing appearance of materialism, and could thus, rather like Simmel's 'additional storey' underneath

Marxist economics, be said to be outdoing the socialists at their own game.

Beyond the metaphysical area, Heidegger's thought also served to confirm what had gone before. Dilthey, without any very solid theoretical foundation, had held up literary study as the backbone of historiography. Heidegger more than confirmed this; so much so that one of his later followers (H. -G. Gadamer), working with the principle that 'Being which can be understood is language', converted the whole of history into a 'universal hermeneutics', a cosmic textual critique.[94] The overthrow of 'positivist history' could hardly be more decisive.

Benjamin's work was considerably influenced by Rickert, who was one of his professors at Freiburg. Furthermore, his attack on 'judgement' as lying at the root of language's degradation after the Fall is obviously a close parallel to the work of Lask and Heidegger. The problem for us is that after 1924 Benjamin more or less abandoned the technical reaches of philosophy, while at the same time embracing a political vision largely incompatible with his previous speculations. As we shall see, he was aware of the incompatibility of his later work with that of, say, Heidegger; but he never carried out the critical project which would have been necessary to make these differences clear and systematic. What is even more confusing for the reader is Benjamin's reversion in his last writings to a position that seems to owe much more to Heidegger than is consistent with any of his intermediate statements. But the crucial purpose of this section has been to clarify what parts of Benjamin's thought may be regarded as innovation, and what parts are preparatory and derivative. Theories that seem unfamiliar now were not necessarily unfamiliar to the trained philosopher in 1915. In particular, it must not be thought that the naming theory of language, either as it appears in Benjamin, or as it appears (as 'material categories') in the new ontology, has anything to do with materialism.

Interventionism

Philosophical socialism after 1918

In Germany, the ideological impact of the First World War was as

great as its social consequences were. The political right were just
as disenchanted by the conduct of the war as the left, and with
both groups the most popularly compelling focus of this disen-
chantment was the disparity between the *Fronterlebnis* of the
front-line soldier and the hypocritical patriotism of ministers and
generals at the rear. But this rudimentary socialism could develop
in any direction. For Heidegger and other academic ideologists it
went towards nationalism (Heidegger became a member of Hitler's party on 1 May 1933). And while the effete pronouncements
of Wilhelmine neo-Kantianism were converted into the militant
ideology of *Volk*, military strategists ensured that in future the
demoralising gulf between front line and general staff would be
bridged by 'total war'. For others, socialism could only mean
Bolshevism, international class struggle. This is the position I
would term 'interventionism', in every respect the opponent of a
sceptical traditionalism. Its most prominent representative at this
time was Lenin; and it is towards Lenin that the major theories of
Benjamin's mature period move.

Two of the earliest left-socialist conversions to result from the
war experience were those of Bloch and Lukács, both of whom
exercised a considerable influence over Benjamin. Their earlier
works, the first edition of Bloch's *Spirit of Utopia* (1918) and
Lukács's *History and Class Consciousness* (1924), are rather problematic as statements of the interventionism that Benjamin
eventually embraced. None the less, both reflect the initial impetus towards socialism. Bloch's book passionately reproached those
responsible for the 'lies' that had concealed the nature of what was
actually a 'naked war of the entrepreneurs'.[95] The liars were the
academic ideologists; Bloch referred to Simmel, 'the patriot from
methodology',[96] and to Max Scheler and 'other heroes of
thought'.[97] But bombs had shattered their spiritual speculations
and 'supratechnological sensibilities'; amongst those who actually
had to fight, 'the artillery killed off the mysticism'.[98] As critical
intervention, this was effective; but as a programme of political
action, Bloch's book was weakly utopian, putting its faith for the
future in a 'spiritual state'[99] and notions of 'nationality'[100] and
even *Volkstum*.[101]

Lukács's book, like Bloch's, had not yet developed a fully
coherent alternative to the positions it was attacking; both were
products of idealistic indignation and had the character of what

Lukács later identified as 'messianic utopianism'.[102] A central problem of Lukács's book was its continuing close involvement with the philosophical procedures we have considered in the work of Lask and Heidegger. Lukács said, in his 1967 self-criticism, that he had omitted the category of labour from his metaphysical position, and thus destroyed the 'ontological objectivity of nature'.[103] As a result, his theory of the commodity offered the same kind of speciously 'material' overcoming of neo-Kantian dualism as did Heideggerian ontology. Lukács conceded that the implications of this were far too close to what 'the philosophical, cultural criticism of the bourgeoisie' had in Heidegger.[104] But from the point of view of Benjamin's further development, Lukács's early Marxist metaphysics were less important than his expositions of Leninist political theory. Lenin, who only really came into the discussion in the final essay of *History and Class Consciousness*, and then became the subject of the monograph *Lenin* (1924), represented a turning point in Lukács's development, and thereby also supplied an impetus to Benjamin's thinking which he could never have acquired had he remained in purely speculative realms.

Leninism was a theory of political agency. It rested on the twin assumptions of effective autonomy of the mind, and of the identifiable and controllable nature of natural phenomena. As a political theory, it was concerned with the way in which rational intervention could best be effected – with ways in which what currently exists can most accurately be located in the causal chain; and with the ways in which rational force for change can best be mustered. 'The basis of the Marxist dialectic is that all limits in nature and in history are simultaneously determinate and mutable, and that there is not a single phenomenon which, under certain conditions, cannot be transformed into its opposite.'[105] Natural science investigates the determinants of natural phenomena, and devises ways in which they may be influenced and controlled for the benefit of human beings. Historical science, similarly, investigates the determinants of historical processes, and devises ways in which they can be brought under the control of human reason. Identificiation of determinacy and exploitation of mutability are the keys to rational human practice.

The key to the temper of Lenin's thought was his attack on the twin evils of 'economism' and 'spontaneism' in *What is to be Done?* (1905). 'Economism' meant the belief that political changes would eventually result from economic or trade-union struggles left to themselves. It was a kind of fatalism which contended that day-to-day natural processes had an 'objectivity' and 'spontaneity' which made it futile to try to intervene to change them. From such a perspective Marxism would be no more than the contemplative account of inevitable processes. Against this, Lenin argued that economic processes clearly did have immense self-sufficiency and in that sense 'objectivity'; but that they would never change from mere natural necessity, but only from the deliberate application of force upon the weakest point of the system – namely the political point. Planned tactics and 'The Party' were the intellectual and the organisational instruments needed to muster this application of force.

The reverse of economism was terrorism, but they had a common root, as Lenin pointed out, in 'the worship of spontaneity'.[106] While the 'economists' resigned themselves to the inevitability, or otherwise, of proletarian self-emancipation, the terrorists believed that only a radically transformative coup d'état could achieve change. 'The Economists bow to the spontaneity of the "pure" working-class movement, while the terrorists bow to the spontaneity of the passionate indignation of intellectuals.'[107] The 'spontaneism' of economists and terrorists shared a common scepticism about the possibility of controlled intervention in nature.[108] Economists submitted themselves to a process they thought they could not influence, while terrorists sought to destroy the entire process and to replace it with one created by themselves.

Both groups failed to understand the nature of practice. Economists did nothing because they despaired of the possibility of productive intervention; terrorists did *anything*, and for the same reason. Economists believed that trade unions and proletarian institutions generally were the sacrosanct 'subjects' of history, and should not be interfered with; terrorists believed that these institutions were condemned to futility, and should therefore be ignored or annihilated. Both positions were based on despair of ever integrating the theory of the revolutionists with the practice of proletarian institutions. But, as Lenin's theory indicated, such an integration was the only worthwhile result of the revolutionists' efforts; without it there could be no success. His theory of the party was built up on this demand. In Benjamin's work, the same position emerged in the critique of Stoicism, which was to form the basis of his political thought from 1925 onwards.[109]

Organisation theory

The need for a unity of theory and practice introduced the philosophical basis for other speculations. As Lukács commented, the 'basic Marxist category' was labour.[110] In so far as 'subject' and 'object' were identical in materialism, it was in labour that they became so. This was a dialectical identity, in that while subject and object were formally distinct, in the actual process of reality they were inseparable. Labour was the category in which their identity was established, the 'consummation' of the unity of theory and practice.[111] This could also be stated in more concrete terms in the theory of organisation. The last and most Leninist of Lukács's essays in *History and Class Consciousness* was entitled 'Towards a Methodology of the Problem of Organisation', and in it he stated that: 'Organisation is the form of mediation between theory and practice.'[112] Lenin's theory of the party, the theory of the unity between revolutionary intellectuals and the working class, could thus be generalised as a theory of organisations, the concrete historical form of the unity of theory and practice. Organisation was the historically observable phenomenon, the objectification of the abstract category labour.

These principles were taken furthest in Bogdanov's *General Theory of Organisations*. As far as Bogdanov was concerned, the category of organisation supplied an analytical model for all the sciences, and in that sense could eventually expect to make philosophy as such redundant.[113] The theory of organisations, which he called 'tektology', generated a dynamic logic which avoided the static formalism of disciplines like mathematics as well as the naivete of commonsense experience.[114] He suggested that all products of human labour, from objects to ideologies, should be thought of as 'organised', and warned that the commonsense world of expressions such as 'sewing a coat' or 'writing a book' obscured the complexity of the productive process, reducing it to one very small component of the whole.[115]

Bogdanov's concretisation of labour in the category 'organisation' had a number of consequences in the practical realm. It led to a strong endorsement of Lenin's view that a full development of communism should lead to a disappearance of the split between mental and physical labour.[116] This split reflected historic inhibitions; a more enlightened social order would see it disappear not so much for ethical reasons, as because it was restrictive and

inefficient.[117] Bogdanov interpreted the Marxian principle that the
conditions of socialist revolution arise within the womb of capitalism in terms of the increasing efficacy of labour. Whereas early
manufacturing industry had demanded the division of labour into
intellectual direction and physical implementation, the development of high technology meant that each worker concentrated the two aspects in his or her single person. The development
of 'automatically functioning machinery', said Bogdanov,
converted the worker's role from mere carrying out of tasks into
'lively control and conscious intervention'.[118] This must inevitably
have profound consequences for the social construction of labour
and the relations of production.

Obviously, however, technological development in the means of
capitalist production was not being followed by changes in the
relations of production. This was because those with a vested
interest in the present relations of production – the propertied
bourgeoisie – were deliberately retarding further rational development.[119] The capitalists were caught between the need to
achieve higher productivity through technological investment on
the one hand, and the greater power this gave their workers on the
other. So, they attempted to maintain an artificial distinction
between production and administration, because this devaluation
of the 'practical' aspect of work helped alienate the worker from
its 'theoretical' aspect, and thus from more general possibilities of
deliberate social control. The sentimental polemic against technology from the bourgeois intelligentsia was another aspect of the
capitalist recognition that mechanisation is a two-edged weapon.

Beyond the specific context of industrial labour, resistance to
reciprocal development of the means and the relations of production took on more general forms. The most important of these was
tradition, which in Bogdanov's view tended to be the usual substitute for rational pragmatism.[120] 'Traditional' organisation was
characterised by such things as the oral transmission of lore, sacred
scripts, and a general reliance on cult and image rather than on
control and reason.[121] This found a conspicuous development in
traditional academic philosophy and particularly in its view of
language. Language, suggested Bogdanov, arose as one of the
earliest instruments for organising labour.[122] But as such, it had to
be seen in the functional context of all instruments, and subject to
historical developments in that context. However decisive a role

language may once have played as part of the 'tektological' process, it was now a relatively subsidiary instrument.[123] The same applied to any formal and epistemological instruments: 'The methods of knowledge cannot be explained . . . without relation to the methods of living praxis. In trying to do so philosophy took the road of empty abstraction and became perverted into a new Scholasticism.'

It was important for the socialist intellectual to know how to break down the capitalist division of labour and its reflection in ideologies of tradition and the 'empty abstraction' of academic philosophy. This could be achieved through an understanding of the general conditions of social organisation and associated ideologies.

The general form of social organisations was class. Classes were political interest groupings formed to defend economic positions. Like commodity exchange,[124] classes were structures expressing organisational relations, and not general conditions of all behaviour or consciousness. Class relations that adequately expressed the material conditions of production were desirable and fruitful. The general division between mental and manual labour which characterised the capitalist class order was doubtless at one stage progressive, although now obsolete as the result of technical progress.[125] Administration and subordination were necessary even in a socialist society, at least to the extent that it still lacked the material conditions for overcoming the division of labour.[126]

But clearly class meant more than simply chance membership of a particular social group. There would always be a tendency for those on the bourgeois side of the division of labour to hypostatise the intellectual aspect of labour, and to build up their world view with ideologies which denied the indispensability of practice.[127] Equally, an industrial operative, because of his or her situation in the labour process, would at least *tend* to have an understanding of the world which was, in a materialist epistemology, more objectively accurate.[128]

On the other hand, it was apparent, as Lenin argued, that the tendencies of proletarian consciousness, however correct, were not in fact sufficient to break through of their own accord into scientific political action. There had to be an additional element brought into proletarian consciousness 'from outside'. And this 'outside', inevitably, was the bourgeois intelligentsia, for only they had sufficient access to the scientific resources necessary to achieve this advance. Lenin quoted Kautsky:

> Modern socialist consciousness can arise only on the basis of profound scientific knowledge. Indeed, modern economic science is as much a condition for socialist production as, say, modern technology, and the proletariat can create neither the one nor the other . . . The vehicle of science is not the proletariat, but the bourgeois intelligentsia.[129]

And so there arose the problem of the 'bourgeois specialist', a problem that was not merely speculative, but very real, both for post-revolutionary Russia and for would-be class-conscious Bolsheviks like Benjamin. As Lenin explained, the 'bourgeois experts' whose help was needed for the revolution were inevitably 'filled with thousands of bourgeois prejudices'.[130] From the point of view of a systematic materialist epistemology, it was doubtful whether a bourgeois was intellectually capable of the same practical consciousness as a proletarian. At the very least, the bourgeois specialist had to be a dying breed. As Bogdanov argued, specialisation was only one moment in the dialectical progress of means and relations of production; and although it had been progressive once, it was now only reactionary.[131]

The ideological and cultural realm, however, remained a powerful sphere of political organisation which was in no sense superseded by the progress of industrial technology. Bogdanov, as could be seen from his involvement in the *Proletkult* movement, was convinced of the real organisational contribution made by art.[132] This was distinctly 'left' of orthodox Party views in the later 1920s, which increasingly tended to see literature as an uncontentious way of entertaining the masses and of appearing respectable in the eyes of other cultured nations. For Bogdanov, however, there was no decisive break, such as between base and superstructure, between 'organisation' in the sense of industrial production and 'organisation' in the sense of ideologically directing general social attitudes.[133] It was not enough to suggest, said Bogdanov, that because ideological forces were dependent on the relations of production they were therefore also determined by them. Art was not merely a decorative ornament which happened to reflect the conditions of the base. Ideology had its own objective role in society. It obeyed the same laws as other organisations in that while being determined by existing material conditions its aim was productive intervention in them. This was the basis of the *Proletkult* view that specifically proletarian art was urgently needed not for philanthropic reasons but to establish progressive organisation in areas hitherto bereft.

Assuming they remember him at all, modern Marxists are liable to associate Bogdanov with the glib optimism and philosophical naivete of the Second International. But it would be a mistake to turn back too hastily to the mandarin scepticism of conventional philosophy. For as we shall see, Benjamin was able to convert this interventionism into a brilliant analytical instrument for dismantling even the most sophisticated parts of bourgeois cultural theory.

III

Benjamin's Work

1

From Ethics to Politics

Benjamin's early work culminated in his Habilitation thesis, *Ursprung des deutschen Trauerspiels*, which was completed in 1925. This text brought Benjamin to the full height of his philosophical powers. It was also a representation of the development he had undergone in the ten years or so during which he prepared it. The *Trauerspiel* book's central dialectic of symbol and allegory, with its resolution in practice, offered a philosophical generalisation of the positions Benjamin had confronted in his work since the outbreak of the First World War. Symbol was the standpoint of the George circle, a standpoint Benjamin himself had never fully adopted, but which was closely associated with the ideology of the youth movement and also with the most advanced positions of cultural theory. Allegory was the austerely ethical and religious viewpoint into which Benjamin retreated after the break-up of the youth movement. And the resolution of this conflict was the political Marxism Benjamin embraced on Capri in 1924 in the theory of Georg Lukács and in the person of Asja Lacis. It is perhaps unwise to try too hard to identify the protagonists of this *Bildungsroman* in Benjamin's biography; but one thing is certain – the final position, like the conclusion of all *Bildungsromane,* has to be seen as a *result*. The historical materialism which Benjamin reached at the end of his long apprenticeship cannot be fully understood without the sometimes rather arduous negotiation of what led up to it. Accordingly, this chapter is not, in the first instance, about politics. It is about the complex procedure that resulted in Benjamin eventually getting there.

Critique of symbolism

Symbolism and the George circle

Benjamin was centrally concerned in his early work with a reassessment of the nature of art. As we have seen, German theories of art and artistic interpretation during this period were dominated by an attempt to revise Dilthey. Dilthey's notion of the autonomous and exemplary status of the work of art was accepted, but not the neo-Kantian transcendentalism that seemed to remove art from the domain of immediate experience. In strictly epistemological terms, these questions only began to be answered by the work of Lask and particularly of Heidegger. But a very influential practice of art interpretation had already developed early in the first decade of the century around the George circle. The strategy of this group might be described, using a line from George's poem *Knights Templar,* as 'deifying the body and embodying the deity'[1] – integration of the sensory and the intellectual in art and in life.

As we have noted, Benjamin was strongly influenced by ideas of this sort during his years in the youth movement. The moral calamity of 1914 took away much of the basis for his early commitment, however, and thenceforth the work of the George circle played a role mainly as a foil for his attempts to establish an alternative ethical position. Indeed, the question was whether this work *could* generate any alternative position after its apparent failure to stem the betrayals of 1914.

One of the outstanding thinkers of the George circle was Ludwig Klages (1872-1956). Klages, while an indifferent epistemologist, was one of the most influential cultural theorists of the circle, and a member of the so-called 'Cosmics', a group that also included Karl Wolfskehl, Ludwig Derleth and Rudolf Pannwitz.[2] Klages is a rather ambiguous figure, since he was an anti-Semite, and his theories of myth and ancestor cult gave direct support to the fantasies of Nazi ideologists like Alfred Rosenberg. On the other hand, he cannot have been very pronouncedly anti-Semitic, since Wolfskehl was Jewish; and neither was he a nationalist, for he left Munich in protest at the 1914-18 war.

Benjamin, at all events, was considerably impressed by Klages, whom he met in Munich in 1914, and whom he seemingly persuaded to address the 'Free Students' in Berlin a month later.[3]

Benjamin's hopes of re-establishing contact with Klages when he went to Munich for the winter semester of 1915 were disappointed because of Klages's protesting absence in Switzerland.[4] In subsequent years Benjamin retained his esteem for Klages; as late as 1930 he wrote of Klages's newest book that it was 'without doubt a great philosophical work'.[5]

Klages is important in a consideration of Benjamin's work because he is a theoretical presence which helps resolve ambiguous polarities. Although Klages is mentioned only once in Benjamin's major texts, and that critically,[6] his thought supplies a coherent structure against which much of Benjamin's own commitment assumes shape. Named targets of Benjamin's criticism, such as Gundolf and Kommerell, were surrogates used to protect Klages's identity; and even central categories of Benjamin's work, such as the Klagesian term 'aura' were not credited to their progenitor. Klages's anonymity is puzzling, but is probably connected with Benjamin's 'mortificatory' criticism; the living cannot be mortified without arousing misunderstandings and the clamour of disagreement (as happened, for example, in the case of the Kraus essay). Benjamin preferred to take only the dead to pin out as trophies, or else to use the untalented, as he considered Gundolf, for minor encounters in a greater campaign.

In any event, the problem for the young Benjamin was how to reassemble a convincing ethics and a convincing soteriology – doctrine of religious salvation – from the ruins of a crude interpretation of the 'deified body'. Klages's thought provided the best instruments for such a reconstruction within the realm of Benjamin's particular competence, namely, cultural criticism. Klages's position was what may in broad terms be called symbolist. There is no doubt that Benjamin was already familiar with French Symbolists like Mallarmé at this stage; but it is also clear that the symbolism of Baudelaire's seminal *Correspondances,* for example, can be integrated with that of Klages. It seems more likely that Benjamin acquired his knowledge of symbolism from Klages in the first instance; but anyway it makes no difference for an understanding of his work, which is in fundamental respects a transformative *rejection* of symbolism.

Symbolism, in the work of Klages and generally, may be defined as the belief that objects are symbols. Symbol, which is an ancient theological concept, is distinguished from sign in that it is not referential. A symbol does not *refer* to anything; it *is* something. The Greek *symbolon* means a token or tessera – half a broken bone or pot which may be reunited with the other half in order to prove the identity of the bearer. Theologically, the Christian symbol was the Creed, the means of identifying and uniting the believer into the body of the faithful. In this respect it is wrong to talk of a symbol 'of' something. A symbol is something that is significant by virtue of what it itself is. The tessera is not a symbol 'of' a pot; it actually is the pot, or at least part of it.

In symbolist terms, the belief that objects are symbols is an attack on any kind of transcendentalism. The object, as symbol, is directly integrated into a world of meaning which dispenses with concepts, universals, and the paraphernalia of transcendentalism. 'Logos' and the intellect (*Geist*) are for Klages the arrogant destroyers of the primal integrity of 'soul', producers of a web of deluded conceptuality which entangles the semantic sufficiency of natural life.

The basic symbolist position has four main extensions. First, it postulates what might be termed a panaesthetic notion of meaning. This claims that if the natural object is sufficient symbol in itself, and the significance of the object lies in its material presence rather than in any analysis by concept, then sensory attributes must count for more than linguistic formulations. In Klages's theory, the 'picture' counts for more than the concept. And equally, access to the ontology of an object lies through the senses and not through the intellect. The manner of this access is characterised by what Klages calls *Schauung* (insight), which, as he says, relates to the 'appearance of the god (epiphany, parousie)'.[7] The result of this 'insight', the 'picture', is then an item of knowledge that dispenses with *conceptual* objectification; Klages contrasts the picture, which is 'unspeakable', with the thing, which is 'speakable' – already processed by the intellect, in other words.[8] The implication of this idea of sensory priority also affects the other senses apart from sight. Hearing, of course, is the vehicle of speech and intellect; but Klages makes a point of emphasising the access to meaning of touch[9] and the olfactory senses in addition.[10]

The second extension of symbolism is the epistemological spontaneity of the object. For Kantianism the 'external' world could not by itself mean anything; only the subject's transcendental functions endowed it with meaning. In symbolism, by contrast, the object is semiotically active. As Klages describes the process at one point, insight is 'born' of the communion of an active daemon – the object – with a receptive soul.[11] Klages adds in connection with this theory that a pure insight, conceived under the action of the object, is characterised by a 'nimbus' – 'the radiant trembling which surrounds it in the moment of becoming'. Elsewhere Klages instances the 'aura' as a special case of the nimbus when applied to persons.[12] In either event this phenomenon indicates the active contribution of the object to its own perception.

The third extension of symbolism is the principle of unity, or of metaphysical monism. Just as the significance of objects is immanent in them, in their capacity as symbols, so too the teleological significance of the world in general is immanent and not transcendent. Klages attacks Plato and other idealists for searching for truth outside the material universe, 'blaspheming against the wondrous image of a cosmos which bore them also'.[13]

And finally, symbolism seeks to determine the kind of non-intellectual intuition that will result in natural understanding. It is of necessity anti-rationalist, for rationalism can only clutter up the pathways that lead to intuition of the individual object. Klages's term for the appropriate frame of consciousness is 'ecstasy'. Freeing both soul and body from the 'yoke of concepts', declares Klages, 'is the secret purpose of all mystics and neurotics . . .; and this is fulfilled in ecstasy'.[14] Klages particularly mentions drugs and intoxication as one valuable means to this end, and dismisses any doubts on this score as 'the intellectual arrogance of a life-hating moralism'.[15]

Those are four fundamental characteristics of a symbolism that may also be recovered from, for example, Baudelaire's poem *Correspondances*. Klages's own views generate two additional aspects which accord with the more philosophic projects attempted by Benjamin, and with the intellectual landscape described earlier.

The first of these is Klages's treatment of the problem of time and space. In common with the ontologists who revised neo-Kantianism, Klages abandoned any attempt to identify a transcendent realm of spirituality outside time and space, and sought his fortune in transforming the notion of time and space from within (as did Heidegger, especially in *Being and Time*). Klages marked out his position by attacking 'Logos' and the intellect precisely on the grounds that they were 'outside time and space'.[16] Klages, while retaining a dichotomy of matter and concept, reversed the conventional evaluation of them. Salvation and the good things of life were now to be found within time and materiality, and not beyond it. But a non-logical time was necessarily a rather different entity from 'objective' time. Just as Klages wished to locate true knowledge in the intuitive, sensual, symbolic 'picture', so too he wished to see an understanding of time which disdained the abstract constructs of conceptuality. This had two elements. In the first place, non-conceptualised time was for Klages strictly only the 'moment'. Any kind of continuing, contemplated, abstracted time necessarily destroyed the 'pictures' which were its proper content. Or, to put it another way, 'pictures' only came in 'moments', instantaneous flashes; any other kind of 'picture' must be false because tangled in the time-continuum of analytical reasoning.[17]

The second element is Klages's theory of a single-axis time. Conventional time, he argued, envisaged two axes radiating from the extensionless point of the present, namely, past and future. The future was a fantasy (*Hirngespinst*), he declared: only the past was a valid axis. Everything that had been, and indeed *only* things that had been, had reality; but this could never be conceded to the speculative and conceptual quality of the future.[18] So, instead of being a continuing progress into the future, time could realistically be regarded only as a relation spanning past and present, the 'poles' of time.[19] This relation, Klages proposed, was one of 'pulsation'; as each moment slid away from the present into the past, another would be thrown up – out from eternity, or the past, the repository of 'real' time.[20] So, instead of being an open-ended sequence of transformations, as in 'conceptual time', it was a sequence of cyclical recurrences indexed by the distance between the present and particular segments of elapsed, or about-to-elapse, time. There was therefore no infinite progression into a vacant future, but only the one axis of distance relating the individual to any point within an ever-present cosmos. Time, said Klages, was the soul of space, and space the body of time.[21]

The second aspect of Klages's work which moves him towards current philosophic concerns, and also explains important aspects of Benjamin's work, gives rather more point to what is on its own a very abstruse theory of time. This is the theory of 'primal pictures'. Klages's hyper-materialism, his insistence that everything, including meaning, is in essence immediately physical, natural, and sensory, leads him to reject any notion of a transcendental logic. But in the end, this symbolism is a form of objective idealism, because it has to collapse inwards upon a form of ideal order in order to explain the coherence of the world.[22] In Klages's case, these are the 'primal pictures', a paganised version of Plato's 'ideas'. And they are open to the same means of access as the Platonic idea, namely anamnesis.[23] The intriguing twist given by Klages's version, however, is that the 'primal pictures' are of a material reality; memory of real things, things which may well pulsate again from the distant pole of the past to the near pole of the present. In this sense, Klages's doctrine of time and primal pictures gives him a direct magical access to a mystical realm which in Platonism is by definition always 'beyond'. And so, because of this, the real world lives in a pulsating, cyclical relation between the things that happen to be momentarily, and the things that were and may be again. And the whole procedure is determined not by conceptually accessible forms, such as homogeneous time or causation, but by natural magic and ecstatic anamnesis, the symbolic communication of a universe mystically corresponding through all the natural languages at its disposal. Furthermore, these languages extend much further than conventional ones; the universe is full of 'pictures' radiating their symbolic meaning for those who can understand. Astrology, palmistry, graphology; through such techniques mankind can read the languages of the earth. Klages spoke on graphology before Benjamin's group in Berlin. And Benjamin himself attempted to earn money by graphology. But we shall see how misleading it would be to take this at face value; for these were the languages of myth and fate, and in fundamental respects unacceptable to the deeply ethical Benjamin.

Doctrine

We have seen that the outbreak of war in 1914 was a traumatic experience for Benjamin, confirming his scepticism about the German universities and shaking his confidence in the predominant ideologies, particularly that of Wyneken and the Free Students. He reacted by withdrawing to a more or less religious level, from which he contemplated the nature of salvation from the horrors of this earth. The essay, 'Two poems by Friedrich Hölderlin', written in the winter of 1914-15 after the suicide of his poet friend Heinle, was perhaps the high point of this retreat, embracing a vision in which the poet, as the spiritual centre of the world, does not even have to fear death – 'he is a hero, because he lives at the mid point of all relations'.[24]

But this essay was a religious counterpart to the natural symbolism of the George school, not its overcoming. The world of spontaneous natural correspondences, of mythic connections, was not abolished, but merely transposed into the work of art, itself still 'not intelligible to any further extent'.[25] Benjamin made no attempt to extract an ethical position from this modified magical immanentism, and it is unlikely that he could have. Stoic submission was its character: 'Set in the middle of life, nothing remains to him [the poet] except unregulated existence, the total passivity which is the essence of courage – complete surrender to the relations of life.'[26]

Symbolism of the kind expounded by Klages, and dominant in the George school, could not generate an ethics because it had no basis for a theory of free decision. All choices had to be natural, in that they 'corresponded' with the order of the cosmos, or unnatural, in which case they were illusory or without significance. But an ethical decision, in the sense of a decision that intervened freely and from outside in natural processes, was not to be accommodated in this framework, even in the rarefied 'relations of life' of Benjamin's Hölderlin essay.[27]

In order to establish an 'outside' from which the ethical decision could transcend natural processes, Benjamin turned to what he termed 'doctrine' *(Lehre)*. Doctrine, at first sight a rather bizarre intrusion, is a central category in Benjamin's early period,[28] and remained a descriptive model even after changes in his metaphysics had removed its systematic role. 'Doctrine', it may be supposed,[29] corresponded closely to the Judaic 'Torah', which in Hebrew means doctrine and also law, and is commonly used to designate the Pentateuch. Certainly Benjamin's use of the term indicates that his 'doctrine' shares two pre-eminent qualities of the Torah, namely, transcendence and verbal codification. In certain Rabbinic traditions the Torah is held to have existed before the world was created; this is an indication of the sense in which God's 'doctrine' transcends all material existence. The Torah would be ethically categorical in the Kantian sense. Also, the Torah is a body of doctrine formulated in Hebrew, traditionally the divine language, and in that respect a 'Logos' which transcends any profane forms of language. Both of these qualities of the Torah are essential to Benjamin's use of the term.

Benjamin's appropriation of 'doctrine', with all its religious dimensions, was an attempt to make ethical sense of a world over which natural symbolism appeared to have no control. The combination of a transcendent ethics and an immanentist theory of meaning was to dominate his work for nearly a decade. It produced a set of difficult and at times almost impenetrable positions. But it is important to identify their main features if only to make sense of the transformation his thought underwent after 1924.

The basic problem for Benjamin was to account for the relation between God and the world. His ethical position insisted that God, the source of the ethical imperative and of doctrine, should be transcendent, providing a principle of moral choice which was genuinely free of natural determination. At the same time, Benjamin accepted the symbolist view of the world as in essence a tissue of meanings, correspondences and languages. Language was not simply a part of conceptuality, thrown upon the world at the whim of the subject. The world was itself language, in a myriad different forms and levels. But in that case, what was the order that underlay these languages? Wherein lay the structure that could transcend the disorder of natural processes? This question had to be answered in order to make sense of God's relation to the world as its ethical legislator.

Benjamin's answer was to construct a principle of the hierarchy of languages. If the world was a tissue of languages, then it was a tissue that could be resolved into an order, at the summit of which was divine language. Benjamin's theory of divine language and of its relation with human and natural languages was the basis for his account of the Fall – the gulf between what is immanent in the world and what transcends it.

This position had two slightly more accessible articulations in Benjamin's theory of intellectual activity. The first was the theory of monadology and the tractatus, and the second was the theory of translation. Both were reflections on what Benjamin saw as the purpose of his own work.

Human and divine language. In Benjamin's view an uncontrolled symbolism could only result in myth and intellectual chaos. Myth had no limits and no governing principle; it abandoned all attempts at critical analysis and collapsed into 'idolatry of nature'.[30] Benjamin suggested that Goethe's theory of 'primal phenomena' (*Urphänomene*) – and the same objection may be raised to Klages's 'primal pictures' – was nowhere subjected even to a simple conceptual ordering. The end result was nothing but a 'chaos of symbols',[31] a chaos distinguished principally by its inability to separate sense from reason, the natural from the ideal.

In opposition to this, Benjamin raised a hierarchical theory of linguistic orders. This theory accepted the symbolist position that 'everything speaks', but sets out a hierarchy of levels at which this took place. The logic of Benjamin's argument rested on a distinction between language and 'spiritual essence'. 'Spiritual essence' is what is communicated in language, and the two must to that extent be distinct from one another.[32] None the less, this is not a distinction between sign and referent, word and object. This is because the sign or word has no place outside the object; there is no subject present to supply such a place. Benjamin expressly rejects any dichotomy of subject and object.[33] The object does not appear because it has been objectified by a subject. It does so spontaneously, in the communicative reaches of 'spiritual essence'. Language is in that sense not an external instrument for the communication of an object, but is itself the object, or essence, being communicated. 'Every language communicates itself.'[34] So the distinction between language and 'spiritual essence' is not epistemological but metaphysical. Benjamin is not claiming that there is a barrier to understanding between world and cognition, for the world, being 'spiritual essence', is itself essentially linguistic. The point is rather that language in *use,* for communication or whatever, can never be the same as language in creation, which is the only point at which the 'essence' of the world is fully taken up into 'language'.

God created the world in His word.[35] All other languages are only an attenuation of this highest word, and obviously not themselves creative. None the less, there is a continuum between the divine and the profane languages, and that is in the character of 'naming'. God's 'naming' actually creates. As a reflection of this most potent form of language the first linguistic act carried out by mankind (in Genesis 2) is the naming of the world. The 'parallelism' between God's creative word and man's naming cognition (*Erkenntnis*) determines the relation between essence and Logos. God created things in the word, and in that sense things also have natural names – this is what makes them cognisable.[36] But it is mankind's peculiar heritage to be able also to name, even though such names are only communicative and not creative.[37]

The power of naming is what distinguishes man from nature. All creation, all 'essence', has a language, but only human language names. This privilege, a 'reflection' of God's absolutely creative activity,[38] endows mankind with a power to establish itself as 'lord of nature'.[39] Although it is the character of all things to communicate themselves, only human language, because of its access to names, has the power to allow this. So 'things' have to communicate in human language; human speech, we might say, is the only cognisable form of an otherwise incoherent display of symbols.

The relationship, as Benjamin saw it, between Logos and essence may also be described genetically. The highest form of Logos, divine language, is identical with the language that creatingly 'named' the world. In one sense, then, this highest language is 'revelation';[40] its naming is identical with what it names, and to know it would be to know in an absolute and unlimited sense. This is a rather academic project, but since creative and cognitive language are essentially linked,[41] it is a real possibility. The notion that, as it were, God created in Hebrew, and that the Hebrew language is in some sense a 'real' part of the world is a significant part of Kabbalism.

The problem is that because of the Fall, man's relation to language is no longer as direct as it was during the time of Adam's naming in paradise. The reason for this, in Benjamin's exposition, was that our ancestors ate the fruit of the tree of the knowledge of good and evil. This was disastrous because the distinction between good and evil was entirely unreal. God had already established, at the end of the sixth day, that everything he had created was 'very good';[42] thus, any suggestion that there could be such a thing as evil was pure fantasy, and an abuse of the powers of language.[43] According to Benjamin this myth established three specific points. First, the use of language for 'judgement' (as between good and evil) was an illegitimate extension of the primary use of language for simple knowing, as indicated in the ability to name. Second, the fact that language was no longer rooted in the direct materiality of naming reduced it to the level of a conventional sign system, thus paving the way for divergence from the divine language and the general degeneration of linguistic activity. And third, said Benjamin, the Fall represented the entry of abstraction as an illegitimate latecomer into the realm of language.[44]

So, because of the entry of 'judgement' into language, Benjamin argued, man had become alienated from the magical language of things.[45] On the day of naming, things were named in the same language within which they had been created. Mankind was then indeed part of the universe of symbolic correspondences. But when, at the Fall, language degenerated into being used as *signs,* things found that they no longer had their one divine name, but were being referred to by a whole variety of different names according to the different languages. Because of this, things became 'overnamed', sad and silent. According to Benjamin, being named is always a source of some sadness; but being overnamed is altogether unacceptable, and causes profound estrangement between nature and the speakers who so carelessly abuse their position of name-givers. Nature cannot be expected to speak freely under such conditions and so it 'falls silent'.[46]

Benjamin's approach to language, despite its mystical air, was in fact quite close to the work of other thinkers of this period, and it may be that many of them shared a similar impulse to integrate the influential cultural mythologies of the George school into a more controllable philosophic framework. Benjamin's account of language, for example, is comparable with what Heidegger produced some years later in *Sein und Zeit.* Benjamin's theory of naming may be classed as a theory of formal individuation similar to the Scotist variety that Heidegger used.[47] The theory of names indicates that cognition does not depend on universals, but that the form is given in the individual name. Direct and complete access to the material individual is made possible by the fact that its 'name' is not merely a sign – as in nominalism – but a form guaranteed by the creativity of divine language itself. The relation between knower and known is not the reflection of an 'object' by a 'subject', but a communion in which both poles are spontaneously active. Benjamin uses the formula that self-declaration and universal address coincide in the name;[48] 'naming' is not the imposition of a constructed meaning on an inert object, but a self-identification by the object to the totality of the listening world. Benjamin uses an image similar to one of Heidegger's: meaning is a 'togetherness' of language with an object (*magische Gemeinschaft* in Benjamin, [*das*] *Beisammen mit* in Heidegger)[49] in which the phonetic form of language, the sound itself, is the symbolic completion.[50] The object and its phonetic naming form an irreducible unity in the symbolic world. The task of philosophy is to order these unities.

Benjamin's argument represents the adoption of an 'ontological' rather than a 'propositional' basis for this ordering. We have already seen the attack on the 'proposition' in writers such as Lask and Heidegger, and indeed Klages's rejection of *Geist,* the intellect, is a similar project. Benjamin's interpretation of the tree of knowledge of good and evil is concerned with this question. Knowledge of good and evil, or so the implied argument runs, necessitates the ability to judge. But such judgement, as the Bible showed, was a sinful misapprehension of the true purpose of language. And logical judgement, the use of analytical propositions, was the same kind of activity. Both sorts of 'judgement' were therefore equally reprehensible.

Like Lask, Benjamin criticised the Kantian table of logical categories for being too restricted, claiming that it was based on an impoverished 'mechanical' view of experience, and should be enriched with principles for the whole extent of existence.[51] In fact, Benjamin went further than Lask by demanding that the categories should now be seen as a 'doctrine'. 'Art, jurisprudence and history – all these and other areas must orient themselves by the doctrine of categories with an intensity quite different from Kant's.' In part, the young Benjamin noted with approval, this project could draw on what the Marburg School (Rickert and Lask) had accomplished in 'removing the distinction between transcendental logic and aesthetic'. And the whole of the system envisaged in this scheme would be able to anchor Benjamin's demand for a transcendent ethics firmly to a corresponding ontology – the divine hierarchy of the world.

Monadology and tractatus. Benjamin's more esoteric speculations about language and creation were confined to his student years during the war. By the time of his first major writings in the early 1920s his philosophy had assumed a slightly more accessible form. One aspect of this was the theory of monadic ideas.

In essence, Benjamin's theory of ideas is a systematisation of his theory of language. The idea is language at the level of pure naming, language in the condition of immediate correspondence with God's creative word, language that is total revelation. Now it is clear from Benjamin's theory of the Fall that profane communicative language never reaches this point. In that sense the language of pure revelation is 'unspeakable', or at least not spoken at any time since the Fall. Because of that, the language of this level, now characterised by Benjamin as the level of ideas, is not directly accessible to human beings. Its force, and this would be a Platonist position, was to 'irradiate' the objects of perception, although not itself part of any intuition.[52] Ideas were 'represented' in the medium of the empirical.[53] And in being represented they drew the empirical phenomena up to their own exalted level of truth. The mediating role was played by 'concepts', which collected the phenomena and distributed them up among what Benjamin called the 'eternal constellations' of the ideas. Benjamin called this process the 'rescue' (*Rettung*) or 'salvage' (*Bergung*) of the phenomena, safely installing them in the ideas.

(It might be objected, incidentally, that 'concepts' deploy precisely the kind of logical judgement that Benjamin had condemned as incompatible with the true nature of language. But he had foreseen this objection: when concepts were used to rescue phenomena into the ideas, he affirmed, they were proof against the 'suspicion of destructive hair-splitting' which might attach to them in any other role.[54] Benjamin's choice of the term 'concept' may have been influenced by Hegel, for whom the concept was the dialectical transformation of analytical and synthetic judgement, and the last step before the 'absolute idea'. But Benjamin's theory of ideas bears little resemblance to Hegel in other respects.)[55]

It is clear from Benjamin's argument that the ideas are not so much logical or formal entities as words at a certain level of purity. 'The Idea releases itself as the word which once again claims its rights of naming.'[56] 'An idea' is more a way of using words than any particular word or concept, whether in a divine language or elsewhere. 'Ideas are given not so much in a primary language as in a primary understanding where words retain their nobility as names without having lost them to cognitive signification.'[57] So, while he identifies various specific literary-critical and seemingly analytic notions such as *Trauerspiel,* Baroque or Renaissance as

'ideas', it is clear that Benjamin's guiding purpose is to integrate
the project generally into his vision of a material logic founded in
the principle of naming. This is confirmed by his characterisation
of the kind of knowledge to which the ideas, as a method, give
access. It can be described as monadic and supra-historical; and its
most appropriate vehicle is the 'tractatus'.

Ideas are monads because they are finite in number and fixed in
character. Just as the 'name' is ultimately rooted in the language of
creation, the words in which God created the numbered components of the world, so also the 'idea' is fixed in the unchanging
order of the universe. The idea, Benjamin stated, was a 'pure
essentiality' (*reine Wesenheit*) analogous to the fixed and eternal
celestial spheres.[58] Philosophical 'contemplation' was a 'renewal'
of the principle of naming which underlay all language not conta-
minated by the demands of profane communication. As such it
dealt with the same recurring and limited set of words – 'the
ideas'. And equally, as part of this, philosophy had to avoid the
introduction of new terminologies while it was dealing with 'the
ultimate objects of investigation'. Benjamin argued that the Romantics had no respect for the sanctity of language as a set of
eternal names. As Benjamin pointed out in his doctoral dissertation on this topic, Schlegel had been a passionate inventor of new
terminologies as part of his attempts to embrace the world in
abrupt systems and sudden conceptual visions.[59] But this process,
for which Benjamin employed the Fichtean term 'Reflexion', did
violence to the word as eternal name. 'In their speculations truth
took on the character of reflexive consciousness instead of that of
language'.[60]

The monadic discontinuity of the ideas, also described as 'isolation' and 'complete independence'[61] was matched by something
that was in effect an echo of the universe of symbolic correspondences, although Benjamin formulated it in terms of Leibnizian
monadology. If, as he suggested, the discontinuous ideas could be
regarded as Leibnizian monads, then a further feature of these
monads – their unclear representation of the rest of the universe –
might be incorporated also. So, 'every idea contains the image of
the world'. And the philosophic representation of the idea, or
perhaps the representation of the empirical by the light of the idea,
should end up with the idea's image of the world in the perspecti-
val foreshortening through which the idea saw it.[62] In this sense it

was possible to achieve a 'totality' through idea-guided contemplation. The individual empirical phenomenon which remained isolated when shunted about by mere propositional analysis, was rescued into 'totality' as soon as it was seen in the light of the idea.[63]

Monadology also gave Benjamin access to what was in many ways the crucial religious component of his doctrine of ideas, namely, anamnesis. Anamnesis is a central component of the Platonic doctrine of ideas, and we have also considered its function in the theories of Klages. In either case it may be defined as the belief that 'truth' is already and eternally present in the world, and that in order to get at it we need only 'remember' it. The precise technique involved in this 'remembering' is a disputed issue. But at all events the belief itself almost inevitably entails deep scepticism about history as a record of changes – for if 'truth' is *already* there, the particular changes that history undergoes in its unending struggle will clearly not be very significant.

So Benjamin's monadic ideas emerge as a vehicle for generating anamnesis. The foreshortened image of the universe which each one supplies is not only foreshortened in space, but also in time. And the discipline involved in reconstructing this image is pre-eminently one of covering its *entire* extent, temporally and spatially. So, while the discipline he characterises (disparagingly) as 'literary-historical' seeks only to convert all divergences into an indifferent historical motion, Benjamin's favoured 'art philosophy' uses the extremes to construct the extensive unity of the idea.[64] The extremes are envisaged as the border posts of a tract of land; Benjamin uses the image of 'pacing out' the circle of an idea's possible extremes.[65] In fact, Benjamin suggests, these extremes do not occur at the same point in history, but as a succession; this is what leads to the illusion of development as portrayed by 'literary historians'. By contrast, the 'art philosopher' removes the dimension of time and leaves history only as the 'colourful border of a crystalline simultaneity'.[66]

Benjamin's notion of the monadic idea, it will be clear, has a distinctly religious flavour about it. To complement it, he suggests the 'tract' (or 'tractatus') as a suitably styled literary form for giving expression to it. Indeed the 'tractatus', he points out,[67] is essentially a theological mode. Its purpose is the dogmatic revelation of divine truths, not intellectual exercise. The philosophical discourse, which Benjamin understands his *Trauerspiel* book to be, should adhere to the principles of the tractatus. The philosophical tractatus, bathed in the eternal light of the ideas and aligned according to the purity of naming, does not concern itself in the first instance with the trivialities of communication and the abstraction of conceptual form. The tractatus, as Benjamin emphasises, is concerned with the representation of ideas as Being, not with the mind's own spontaneous exercise of its conceptual faculties.[68] Accordingly, it avoids such methods as the chain of deductive argument, or the polemical refutation of opponents, in favour of 'the fullness of concerted positivity'.[69] All of this has to be included in the 'philosophical style', the attitude of revelatory instruction, or authoritative citation, the pronouncement of the scholastic cathedra.[70]

Translation. There was, in addition to the tractatus, another literary mode that Benjamin thought could do justice to the transcendent focus of languages. There is no systematic link between the theory of the tractatus with its monadic ideas, and the theory of translation, which revolves more around Benjamin's hierarchical understanding of language. But in his eyes both could equally be seen as 'theological': and as late as 1927 he was declaring that his own translation work had brought him closer to Judaic belief.[71] The theory of translation was elaborated mainly in the preamble to his own renderings of Baudelaire ('The Task of the Translator' (1921)). The theory of translation was a useful clarification of the principle of 'doctrine', and of the connection between Benjamin's ethics and his revision of the symbolist theory of language.

In Klages's symbolism there was an indifference between the various types and levels of symbols. Human language, in such a perspective, was no more than one part of the general semantic activity of the universe. This is what Benjamin dismisses as 'chaotic'.[72] His reply was to devise a careful hierarchy of symbolism. Language, he allowed, was indeed symbolic. But it was *only* symbolic in relation to one of its functions, and that was the function of naming.[73] The naming function of language restored it to communion with the creative word of God. But at the same time, this naming function was opposed to the communicative function. Communication, because it depended on analytical judgements, was a debased form of language; but on the other hand, of course, it was its characteristic form in 'profane' use. In that sense, the symbolic potential of language was concerned precisely with the uncommunicable, the divinely unspeakable. The two potentials co-existed in human language: 'language is . . . not only communication of the communicable, but simultaneously symbol of the incommunicable'.[74]

This has two consequences. In the first place, although Benjamin asserted that 'things' also had a language, it could not be symbolic in the proper sense of human language. Symbolism, in the sense of direct communion with the divine, could only take place between divine language and its extension in the weakened form of human naming; the language of things did not name.

On the other hand, human beings, with their language, could act as mediators in the communication of the universe from its lowest levels upwards to God.[75] And the term Benjamin proposed for this was 'translation'. Human semantic activity was a 'translation' of lower languages into higher ones, with a final goal in the creative word of God. 'Every higher language is a translation of the lower ones, until in the final clarity the word of God unfolds itself, the unity of this movement of languages.'

This provided Benjamin with a scale of values for artistic products. Sculpture and painting, for example, were the translation of certain sorts of 'thing-language'. They were a raising of the level of that language to one 'infinitely higher',[76] although still, presumably, this language was infinitely lower than the naming language of words. Benjamin, whose lover Jula Cohn was a sculptress, did not say this; but it would fit in, among other things, with the Judaic interdict on the graven image.[77]

This hierarchy also applied within the literary arts. In 'The Task of the Translator', Benjamin suggested that every translation, even in the literal sense of translation from one tongue into another, was a raising of the spiritual level. This was because translation took the text further from its communicative origins, as a natural part of the author's language, into a realm where it was closer to 'pure' language.[78] Purgation of the profanely communicative resulted in an increased role for the 'unexpressed and creative word', the divine origin which underlay all human languages. This argument, in support of which Benjamin adduced Hölderlin's impenetrable translations of Sophocles,[79] seems to imply that the more incomprehensible the result, the better the translation. Fortunately, Benjamin did not adhere to his own principles.

But what is interesting in this position is its implication for the status of poetry. The poet's intentions, says Benjamin, are 'naive, initiating, intuitive', while those of his translator are 'derivative, final, and idea-like'.[80] So, poetry – or at least poetry such as Baudelaire's: presumably Hölderlin would not come in this category – is at a lower and more natural level than its translation. The translation is one step further up the ladder to 'truth, or doctrine [*Lehre*]';[81] indeed, says Benjamin, it actually stands 'between poetry and *Lehre*'.[82]

We may make two brief comments on this. First, 'translation' is clearly an answer to the Romantic notion of *Kritik,* on which Benjamin wrote his doctoral dissertation – indeed he compares the two in the Baudelaire preface.[83] The Romantic art philosophers had developed a principle of criticism which, by reflective absorption in the single work of art, was to 'raise the power' of that work. The goal of this intensive contemplation was the creation of a fresh and even fuller universe of meanings. The young Benjamin was very taken by this notion.[84] As we saw, he felt that Romantic 'reflexion' theory got lost in the infinities of its own conceptuality. But their *Kritik* was an attractive paradigm for intellectual activity outside the confines of the purely poetic.[85] This could be retained by converting its conceptuality into translation, which was rooted in the divine logic of name theory.

Second, and more seriously, this theory of translation is at the root of Benjamin's principles of 'mortification' and later of 'destruction'. In terms of natural symbolism, all symbolic activity was good, and in a sense the 'earthier' the better. But the whole tenor of Benjamin's argument moves in the opposite direction, away from luxuriating sensuality and towards the ascetic minima of reason and necessity. From such a perspective the poetry of sentiment – even Baudelaire and Kafka – had increasingly little to say, while the critic, not as complacent *belletriste* but as a warning Joshuah, had a more and more urgent task.

Ethics and myth

The heavily theistic orientation of Benjamin's philosophical speculations during his earlier work has to be approached with great caution. Benjamin's own belief in God, then or later, is not directly at issue. What is important is that the concrete tasks he set himself did not always allow him to reach the conclusions apparently anticipated in his introductions. Benjamin's theory of language was intended as a prolegomenon to a full-scale critique of existing philosophical positions. But the practical task that he confronted – making ethical sense of the 1914 war and later of the post war revolutionary era – reduced his seemingly decisive initial declarations to a mere transitional status. The most obvious example of this internal development is the great *Trauerspiel* book itself, whose introduction is not so much a methodological framework as the first moment in a continuing dialectical transformation. Benjamin's theory said one thing; but his actual practice, as polemicist and historian, said something rather different. And his personal standpoint, if that is an appropriate term for it, can only be seen in the summation that results at the conclusion of the whole process.

The final result at the end of the process was to be the Marxism Benjamin adopted after 1925. This will be discussed in the next chapter. Meanwhile, we have still to consider how Benjamin applied the theoretical positions we have just described, and how they changed during the application. The two steps in this development were the major texts written in the early 1920s, the article on Goethe's novel *Die Wahlverwandtschaften* in 1922 and the *Trauerspiel* book itself in 1925. The Goethe article is closest to Benjamin's original starting point – the ethical critique of the George circle's cultural theory.

Benjamin's development was precipitated, as we have argued, by his search for a coherent ethical alternative to the chaotic faith in physical nature implied by Klages and the George circle. This search reached its climax when Benjamin turned to direct confrontation with these thinkers. The first encounter in his 'attack on the ideology of the George school'[86] was the Goethe article in 1922. This was a more or less direct response to the pompous *Goethe* by Friedrich Gundolf, a Heidelberg professor popularly regarded as the 'chancellor' of George's spiritual empire.[87] In this article, which was sharply and explicitly critical of Gundolf, Benjamin defended Goethe against what he saw as an attempt by the George school to co-opt the poet into their mythic world view. Klages was not mentioned; but the impress of his thought was as clear in

Benjamin's arguments as it was in the Gundolf book itself.

Gundolf's position in his *Goethe* was essentially an appropriation of Klages's mythic view of the world for the purposes of
literary history, and the book reflected the need to establish a
substantial foundation for the ideological disciplines. The theoretical centre of the book was the symbolist principle of semantic
unity, the notion that the being of an object is identical with its
meaning. In this sense, lyric verse was for Gundolf the highest
form of literature. In lyric verse, form and content constituted an
inseparable unity of 'lived experience' (the Diltheyan *Erlebnis*);
experience and its representation were identical.[88] Gundolf used
the term 'symbolic' for a slightly different kind of literature,
namely, those productions in which lived experience reached its
representation in the medium of 'alien' materials: in other words,
in objects and events rather than, as with lyric verse, in pure
subjective sentiment.[89] But *Erlebnis* was the root of both modes.
In the third level of literature, the 'allegorical', this root was
lacking, or at least obscured. Instead, the product was characterised by concern with the *Bildungserlebnis*, a debased form of
Erlebnis generated by *Bildung*, or education.[90] This was the arrogant realm of intellect and the concept. In allegory, poets trifled
with wit and topicality, rather than immersing themselves in the
serious sensations of the *Urerlebnis*, the 'primal experience'.

These literary propositions demanded some metaphysical consolidation, which Gundolf supplied in terms based on Klages. The
essential being was 'dumbly formed life' (*stummgestaltes Leben*), a
world that had form but dispensed with human language. Indeed,
language was only an inessential offshoot of life's basic unity, 'for
the body itself is soul'.[91] The difficulty was that this unity was a
primal condition now torn apart by the progress of a conceptual
civilisation. The 'immediate forces of primal life' had lost much of
their power.[92]

None the less, there was a level of modern life at which this
wholeness could be recovered, and that was the level of art. In
particular, it was the life of the great artist, the genius, which still
incorporated the primal unity. For Gundolf the lives of artists, and
not merely their work, offered the much needed reintegration of
body and soul. The artist's life overcame the dichotomy of body
and soul, of outside and inside, of necessity and choice, thereby
transforming external constraint as in the 'original condition of

humanity'.[93] And the particular term for this incorporated necessity was fate, *Schicksal*. The fate of the artist was the material aspect of this character; it was his *daemon*. And so the artist stood in a tissue of material correspondences in which his own linguistic creativity was only one strand in a centred universe of symbols. Gundolf's intention was to present Goethe as that kind of artist, the heroic object of a neo-pagan cult of nature.

In the essay 'Goethes Wahlverwandtschaften' Benjamin's response to Gundolf and the George circle has a tone of high moral censoriousness about it, which accords strangely with the fact that it was dedicated to Jula Cohn, Benjamin's current mistress. It was the critic's task to 'assess morally' the events of a piece of imaginative writing, he declared.[94] And the essay is full of references to the divine dignity of ethical matters in comparison with the profanities of aesthetic ornamentation. But this primness was a reflection of Benjamin's uncertainty about his own position, and the fact that, as we shall see, it was a moment of transition in a continuing development. In any event Benjamin had chosen his target well, even if his missiles did not always seem entirely apt.

Gundolf's comments on the *Wahlverwandtschaften* were not in themselves of any very great consequence. Benjamin chose to concentrate on this novel in his attack on Gundolf because he saw in it a test case for the George school's 'heroising of the poet'.[95] As Benjamin argues in the essay, Goethe's novel is precisely *about* the kind of fateful correspondences that concerned Klages. (They concerned Gundolf very much less, to do him justice; but as we have argued, Benjamin was using Gundolf mainly as a surrogate target.) The novel concerns the fate that befalls a married couple who invite two friends to stay with them, fall in love with their guests, and are then destroyed by their passions. The whole narrative is accompanied by a stream of omens and portents – what Benjamin calls 'death symbolism'.[96] And the ethical problem of adultery, particularly as it affects the husband's 'innocent' beloved, supplies the principal tension in the book. So it clearly had the required ingredients for Benjamin's attempt to define the relation between the mythic and the ethical.

Benjamin's response to Gundolf had two aspects. In the first place, he offered a brilliant new interpretation of the novel, which must serve as a model for any criticism with aspirations beyond the disordered and *inconsequential*[97] modes of symbolism and its variants. In this respect, Benjamin's determinedly ethical and practical approach is entirely vindicated.

His view, in brief, was this. Goethe was a deeply superstitious person whose relation to fate and natural correspondences was not the sublime creativity attributed by Gundolf, but simply fear. Goethe's elaborate theorising about symbols,[98] his references to the daemonic and the astrological,[99] his insistence on finding everything 'significant, wonderful, *incalculabel'*,[100] were simply instances of the many grotesque variations of mythic fear.[101] The quintessence of this fear was his fear of responsibility,[102] the fear that seeks to evade decision by appealing to the oracular compulsions of natural correspondence.

But Goethe was aware of this in himself, and much of his work could be seen as a 'struggle to escape the embrace' of the mythic world.[103] An approach that, like Gundolf's, ignored this practical (in the Kantian sense) orientation of the work, and indeed actually tried to describe it as mythic, was guilty of the gravest misapprehension.[104]

Benjamin's interpretation rests on the assumption that the *Wahlverwandtschaften* were an attempt by Goethe to come to terms with his fear of the mythic. Benjamin's evidence for this was principally the 'death symbolism', which he presented very ably as the implied object of the narrative's criticism, and a short *Novelle* which is told in the middle of the novel by way of redemptive contrast. The contrast lies in the way the figures in the *Novelle* grasp their fate by firm decision, while those in the novel allow themselves to be sucked in by mere 'choice', the process of natural 'election' indicated in the title itself. (The title is usually translated as 'The Elective Affinities'.) So, while the characters in the main novel behave like chemicals in a natural process *(Wahlverwandtschaften* is a technical term for a kind of chemical reaction), those in the *Novelle* interlude are seen to grasp their practical autonomy.[105]

Benjamin's interpretation is ingenious, whether it is legitimate or not. What concerns us rather more, however, is the superstructure he adds in order to substantiate his own ethical position. This draws heavily on the doctrine theory of language. In his comments on Goethe's death symbolism Benjamin suggests that it is underpinned by a language motif. The doomed foursome of adulterers, those who are unable to take their fate in their own hands, are overshadowed by a strange unexpressed guilt. Benjamin characterises this as the order of the 'nameless law', a namelessness that is also reflected in the minimal naming even of the main characters in the book.[106] Furthermore, the decline and destruction of the husband and his beloved, in particular, are characterised by a 'falling silent', a 'speechless drive', the inability to confront practice in the clarity of articulate decision.[107] By contrast, the language of the interlude *Novelle* is described as being 'prose of a higher order'.[108]

The language motif is also brought out in Benjamin's attack on Gundolf's mythic appropriations. For Benjamin, Gundolf's unwillingness, like that of Goethe's doomed characters, to enter the clear light of decision and the articulated word, was reflected in the extravagant terminology of his book – 'a jungle where words swing like gibbering apes from bombast to bombast avoiding at all costs the ground which would reveal they cannot stand – for this is the Logos, where they should stand and give an account of themselves'.[109]

Benjamin's perhaps somewhat forced introduction of the theme of language enables him to continue with an underlying 'theological' project originally broached in one of the early essays on ethics. This is the critique of original sin. Benjamin had had an interest in the Catholic doctrine of original sin since his earliest student days.[110] This interest had no doubt deepened into hostility during his prolonged and intensive reading of the Lutheran theologian Harnack.[111] In 'Fate and Character', written in 1919, the doctrine of original sin had been roundly ascribed to 'Heathenism'.[112]

From this perspective it becomes clear that Benjamin had something relatively concrete and topical in mind in his criticism of the mythic consciousness. The Lutheran reproach of Catholicism, very crudely, was that Catholic concern with the earthly presence of the divine in such institutions as the Church led to a mystification of religion. Luther's attacks on justification by works were based on a rejection of the worldly structures and hierarchies by means of which ecclesiastics could exploit the credulity of their flock. The institutionalised Church's claim to be the sole earthly means towards redemption inspired Luther's attacks on this despotic exclusiveness, particularly his criticism of the Church's attitude towards the anointed priesthood and the sacraments, and his translation into the vernacular of the otherwise inaccessible Gospel.

It is important to remember that at the end of the nineteenth century these seemingly 'theological' issues were again, or still, matters of direct political topicality. The systematic attacks by Prussian thinkers on the priestly tradition[113] were not mere random theological speculation, but part of political struggles within the new German Empire. Hermann Cohen, the Jewish philosopher, and Adolf von Harnack, the Lutheran Church historian, were united in their support of the Wilhelmine state against the Catholic-backed resistance from newly annexed Bavaria. This support, it might be noted, continued until 1914, when Harnack drafted the Kaiser's declaration of war, and Cohen too emerged as a loyal advocate of the military effort. In one sense, the discrediting of the Prussian establishment and its ideologues by the disasters of 1914–18 was an indirect cause of the development we considered earlier – the defeat of the dualistic neo-Kantianism of Prussians like Cohen and Dilthey by the new ontology of the 'South-Western' school. The interweaving of the intellectual and the political in Germany is more profound than most Anglo-Saxon readers can imagine; and the threads of that interweaving, *at least* until 1945, were mainly religious.

Benjamin's letters reveal a profound interest in Harnack's massive *History of Dogma*. And it is also clear from his work that the often cited Hermann Cohen was an important influence. Scholem's attempts to portray Benjamin as antagonistic towards Cohen[114] are entirely a reflection of his own quite different position.[115] Cohen was not, of course, a Christian; but throughout his career he sought to demonstrate the compatibility between Judaism and Lutheranism,[116] and as an ideological–political enterprise his work is congruent with that of Harnack. In a few words this may be described as follows. God is entirely transcendent and not in any sense materially present in nature. Each individual's access to God is therefore exclusively spiritual, an access that may take place through the sacred texts or through reason.[117] These roads of access stand open equally to every person, regardless of their material situation in the world. Because of this, all ecclesiastical establishment and all ritual are at best secondary, and at worst an intrusion of cultic 'polytheism' (a favourite term of Cohen's).[118] All 'conventional religiosity'[119] is a barrier in the way of pure and direct access to God, whether it takes the form of an institutionalised priesthood,[120] a misconceived mysticism,[121] or idolatrous concern with the visible trappings of wordly cere-mony.[122] Catholicism, at least in the eyes of 'Reformers', both Lutheran and Rationalist–Judaic, was guilty of precisely these aberrations, and in doing so was creating a kind of cultic theocracy designed to interfere in affairs of state.

These questions had direct implications for ethics and aesthet-ics. In Catholic eyes the world was a blend of good and evil. To the extent that the world was good, God was present in it. This presence was principally in the Church and its sacraments, which were a kind of spiritual garrison in a world beset by the armies of the devil. The doctrine of original sin was designed to explain the soul's defection, as it were, from the side of the devil to the side of God. Born in sin, amongst the hordes of evil, the soul could rescue itself by seeking asylum in the Church. The institutions of the Church acted in order to purge the soul of its inherited evil, and to prepare it for its eventual ascent into heaven (possibly with a further spell of de-programming in purgatory). The doctrine of justification by works was devised to enable the soul to chart its progress by visible achievements.

When Luther rejected justification by works and substituted justification by faith he necessarily also abandoned the Catholic view of original sin. If, in Lutheran terms, there is no divine presence in the world, and thus no continuity between good and evil in this life or elsewhere, the calibration of different degrees of sinfulness is basically irrelevant. Either the soul is in communion with the transcendent God, or it is not. And this can only be established by the once-and-for-all decision of faith, not by the petty accumulations of 'good works'. One further aspect is that the claims of God and Caesar, as it were, are radically separated. Good works and ethical conduct are related only very tenuously to the expectations of a pure faith. The whole realm of earthly behaviour, and certainly politics, is to a large extent immune to the interventions of the divine. No credit may be expected for ad-herence to earthly norms. In conventional Lutheranism this leaves a free hand for the natural authority of the ruler. In Antinomia-nism, however, the opposite conclusion is drawn – namely, that the faithful are under no obligation to observe the edicts of this earth. This paradox is vital for the later development of Benja-min's thought.

Benjamin's initial understanding of guilt and moral commitment was antinomian. His strongest 'political' statement of this was the anarchistic 'Critique of Violence', written in 1921, in which he used the Pauline opposition of law, which is a human institution, and justice, which is divine,[123] to argue for the moral superiority of 'pure' action over any kind of established law. (Benjamin actually uses *Recht* instead of Luther's *Gesetz* for 'law'; but none the less this is a classic Protestant topos.)[124] In Benjamin's argument, 'law' is associated with mythic fear of nature. 'Law' is ambiguous and devoid of ethical content precisely because it strikes blindly and without respect for persons: the law forbids both rich and poor to sleep under bridges.[125] The roots of this kind of law are the unwritten and unknown ordinations of mythic fate, and the sufferings of the convicted can only be called expiation, never punishment.[126] The millenium will arrive when this cycle of 'mythic legal forms' has been broken,[127] whereupon 'pure divine power' will resume the forms that had been usurped by 'law'.[128] As Benjamin concedes, it is not at present possible to say how divine law will differ in its actual manifestations.

The essay on Goethe's *Wahlverwandtschaften* is on one level an attempt to concretise Benjamin's view of real ethics. In the light of the essay's theological background, the development of the Logos theory of ethics is a straightforward 'Protestant' answer to Benjamin's opposition to Catholicism as ritualistic and mythic. In Protestant theology,[129] and very strongly also in Cohen's rationalistic interpretation of Judaism, 'the word' is a central instrument of man's salvation. In Protestantism 'the word' is particularly the Gospel, but more generally also Christ. For Cohen, reason, the intellect, the spirit, were all primary means of man's access to God;[130] and in his later work he also, like Benjamin, came to use the term *Lehre* to indicate God's law, the Torah, which in Protestant terms is directly parallel to the Bible with its new and old 'laws'.[131] So, when Benjamin argues that any primacy of cult over *Lehre* is 'heathen', and that ethical truth is inseparable from the Logos,[132] he is standing in a well established tradition, however obscure this might be to the unsuspecting literary reader. It is in fact a hard-line exposition of the doctrine of justification by faith, with language standing in for the more conventional understanding of faith. (Benjamin in fact makes *Treue* – faith in the connubial sense – central to his ethical demand.)[133] The core of Benjamin's argument is precisely that the adulterous lovers are damned not by what they *do* ('good works', or their absence), but by what they *are* (in this instance secure in the linguistic faith, or not). The characters are 'deaf to God and dumb to the world. Justification fails them not because of their actions, but because of their being. They fall silent.'[134] And again, because the characters lose the 'supernatural life' (that is, language) in themselves, they fall victim to the encroachment of 'natural guilt', 'without their actions necessarily offending against morality'![135]

To resume Benjamin's very daring interpretation, he is arguing that Goethe's novel was an attack on his own mythic fears and heathen tendencies, an attack that was resolved precisely not by throwing himself into the welcoming arms of the institutionalised Church, with its established ethics, but into a radical act of faith towards an extreme Protestant vision of God. As literary criticism this is sensational, and all the more so because it takes an exceptional amount of perseverance to understand what Benjamin is saying. But the message is so bizarre that it is not really surprising he did not wish to make it too obvious.

This, however, is not the conclusion of our progress through this step in Benjamin's development. Nor is it the end of the essay, which has a third section following the two from which we have drawn most of our material so far. The last section is an attempt to re-establish some notion of the 'symbol' in the light of the extreme anti-representationalism implied in the theory of linguistic redemption. Benjamin does this with a metaphysics of art, and in a way that strongly suggests he had drawn much from Cohen's *Religion of Reason*, with which he had been concerned since 1920.[136]

The problem with a strongly transcendentist religion like Protestantism and, in Cohen's interpretation, Judaism, is that it virtually rules out the substantial bases of institutionalised religion, namely, ritual and mystery. This means on the one hand the established priesthood together with the visible trappings of the church, the ritual objects; and on the other hand it means any mystery of death, belief in immortality and the like. A strict religion of the transcendent spirit rules out the one as a mendacious distraction, and the other as tendentiously animalist speculation about what is necessarily inconceivable. Outside the immediate confines of religion, this also poses problems in aesthetics and ethics. Any of the arts, and particularly the visual arts, are liable to be reproached with producing cultic objects; and in ethics, as we have seen, antinomianism and a bleak Stoicism about the future are implications difficult to avoid.

The purely aesthetic question is difficult to resolve in this context, although Cohen does endorse music as 'the most ideal of the arts' and hence a legitimate ladder to God.[137] The real question centres on ritual, which to some degree is obviously indispensable to religion with any public presence at all, and with a need to express the expectations of its congregation. Cohen has an interesting answer to this. He says that the central motif of a transcendentist religion, as expressed by the Old Testament prophets, is hope. Cohen, more conventionally than Benjamin, directs this hope towards the future and the messianic age that it heralds. The sense of this hope is straining away from dismal continuing existence, 'the dominant universal power of reality'. And Cohen compares the manner of this hope with the idealism of philosophy; the attempt, as he describes it, to liberate being.[138] As far as ritual is concerned, he says, it is a symbol, 'the paradigm of all symbols'. But it is not symbolic in the sense of the mystic material correspondences of Klages and others. In fact it is quite the reverse. It is a liberation from the appearance (*Schein*) of mankind's dependence on these material evils, from the appearance of 'an indissoluble share in evil which, because of his finitude, he cannot escape, but which also he is not subject to'. And in these terms the most complete ritual, says Cohen, is the Jewish Day of Reconciliation, 'the symbol of temporality' – the symbol, in other words, that establishes at one moment mankind's access to the spiritual absolute and also its freedom from the bonds of time and matter.[139]

The highly obscure third section of 'Goethe's Wahlverwandtschaften' is an appropriation of this theory to Benjamin's aesthetics. What makes it more than usually baffling is that it also contains themes drawn from Klages and the George school, resulting in a strange mixture of the heathen and the fundamentalist. Basically, however, the position is this. Although Benjamin had declared his intention of examining Goethe's novel as a moral entity, it was clearly not very satisfactory to dismiss the attractive and moving heroine, Ottilie, as no more than a demonic presence abandoned by faith and Logos. And further, as we have noted, a simple fundamentalist iconoclasm made it difficult to account for beauty, whether as a category of art or generally.

So Ottlie's very moving death, the death of a beautiful person, is installed by Benjamin precisely as the kind of religious symbol Cohen envisaged, and thus also as a model for the direction art should take. The experience of beauty is an experience of the symbol of reconciliation. (It is noticeable that Benjamin speaks of 'reconciliation' – *Versöhnung* – throughout his analysis, rather than the *Erlösung*, redemption, which he usually uses in this context – a further confirmation of his reading of Cohen.) But just as reconciliation is only real when it is with God, so also beauty is not real; beauty and the reconciliation promised by beauty are both appearance (*Schein*).[140] But reconciliation with God is in any case only possible beyond materiality. It is necessary, in fact, to die to this world before being born again, or reconciled.[141] Because of their readiness to undergo this, the *Novelle's* central characters *are* saved, while those in the novel itself are not[142] (the *Novelle* characters throw themselves in a dangerous river). But this is also the key to the reconciliatory force of beauty. It is precisely the passing (*Vergehen*)[143] of beauty that points beyond it. Essential beauty, Benjamin indicates with a reference to Plato's *Symposium*, exists only in the realm of ideas; as a result, phenomenal beauty is always 'essentially' appearance.[144] In that respect, beauty is always 'transition' (*Übergang*) for the real poet.[145] This has to be understood in three senses. In the first place the passing of beauty, and the emotion this causes, are a symbolic gesture towards the purer realm.[146] Second, the conspicuous nature of appearance in beauty gestures strongly towards the 'inexpressible' which corresponds to it in the realm of ideas, but which only exists in relation to this *Schein* of phenomenal beauty.[147] And third, beauty in art is a transition to the true aim of the artist, which is the 'mystery of hope'.[148] 'That most paradoxical and fleeting hope finally surfaces from the *Schein* of reconciliation, just as, in the setting of the sun, there rises an evening star which will survive the night.'

And in that sentence we can also see how Benjamin has added the ingredient of Klages's mysteries to Cohen's doctrine of hope. The ingredient is immortality, which appears in two instances. In one, Benjamin mentions approvingly Ottlie's vision of going to her ancestors, an image Benjamin explicitly associates with Val–halla.[149] And in the other there is the star – an image that occurs in almost exactly the same situation in Klages,[150] and which gives Benjamin the opportunity for an extraordinarily ambivalent reconciliation of the mystery of hope with George's deification of the body in the last lines of the essay. A brilliant conclusion to the composition, this is also a signal of more to come.

Ethics and practice

Christian Stoicism

The problem with Benjamin's antinomian ethics was that their transcendentism gave very little guidance for practice in the material world. Just as 'pure' action (in 'Critique of Violence') was never identifiable according to concrete norms, so also artistic beauty (in the Goethe essay) seemed doomed to a self-immolation on the altar of 'hope'. The only specific ethical values offered by Benjamin were the remote existentialist notions of faith[151] and responsibility.[152] The ultimate site of the ethical decision was, as Benjamin repeatedly emphasised, the individual's lonely reckoning before God.[153] As a symbolic ritual in Cohen's sense even the work of art was devoted to extinguishing its practical reality. In Benjamin's terms, the 'mystery' of the dramatic – what we might call its symbolic integration – took place when the ladder of language reached the higher level, the level of the inexpressible.[154] So, ultimately, even Logos was consumed in what would seem to be truth of an entirely formal and abstract kind. And from this metaphysical perspective the world was reduced to no more than the opposition between an 'empty' heaven on one side, the infinite realms of an inexpressible and unrepresentable truth, and a necessarily evil materiality on the other, a material that could only redeem itself by explicitly flaunting the fact that it was *Schein*, appearance. The symbol of the star, pale remnant of the natural correspondences of the symbolists, seemed poor consolation for this, particularly as this star, a meteorite,[155] was only nature's expression of its own transience.

This is the condition Hegel described as 'Stoicism' in the section on unhappy consciousness in the *Phenomenology of Spirit*. Stoicism, defines Hegel, is a concept of freedom that embraces the 'pure generality of thought'.[156] This 'freedom of self-con-

sciousness' is 'indifferent towards natural existence'. Such a freedom has only 'pure thought as its truth, without the complement of
life'.[157] As part of its struggle to give this freedom some direct
significance the mind attempts to become one with the formal
generality it conceives of as Being. But each time it is confronted
with a real entity it is disappointed by the fact that this single
phenomenon cannot be the same as the universal Being. 'By the
nature of the *single existence* it happens that as soon as it assumes a
reality [*Wirklichkeit*] it disappears into time and space, [and reveals itself] to have been distant, and to be remaining distant.'[158]
So, unity with this formal absolute remains always without 'fulfil-
ment and present' (*Erfüllung und Gegenwart*), leaving nothing
except a perpetual hope.[159] Hegel gives a striking image of the
mind's fixation on 'the beyond', the other side of space and time.
'It is only the *grave* of its life that can assume a present reality for
consciousness.'[160] The stoical consciousness, despairing at the inaccessible presence of the absolute, finally turns to its one sure
present reality, the symbol of its material transience. And this,
says Hegel, is the form the world spirit assumes 'in a time of
general fear and enslavement'.[161]

   This is the root of *Urspung des deutschen Trauerspiels*, Benjamin's greatest theoretical text and the basis for his work during the
rest of his life. Hegel's identified presence in the *Trauerspiel* book
is minimal, despite the reference to 'Hegel's dialectic' as one of
three 'great philosophies'.[162] But we have already seen that failure
to cite precisely his most important authorities was a characteristic
mannerism of Benjamin's. In any event, 'Stoicism', which has not
previously appeared in his work, now becomes a central theme.[163]
So does the grave. And as we shall see, the dialectical resolution of
the 'antinomian' dilemma[164] is entirely Hegelian.

   On a more explicit level, Benjamin's Habilitation dissertation is
a continuation of his ethical search in terms of the nature of art.
Or, in Cohen's terms, it is a further attempt to define the legitimacy of art as symbol. This time Benjamin is prepared to warn
the reader that a theological understanding is necessary to penetrate the argument;[165] and the thematic structure of the book is
founded on explicit comparisons between pagan, Lutheran and
Counter-Reformation theologies. The fact that he is so explicit
should warn us, with our experience of Benjamin's reluctance to
reveal his most valued sources, that he is no longer fighting from a

Rationalist-Protestant-Judaic position. We shall see in due course where he has moved.

The centre of Benjamin's project is to identify the symbolic character of the literary forms tragedy and *Trauerspiel* ('drama of grief') and thus to consider the theological legitimation of works of art. Theology is by now, as will become clear, no longer a secret dwarf, Benjamin's unconceded inner commitment, but an instrument of what might be called ideological history. Theology is the means by which societies organise their most fundamental problems of identity. 'Ideology' is, one must admit, not a very good rendering for this, since nowadays it tends either to mean false consciousness or the universal science of semiotics, neither of which corresponds to theology. Theology might be described as applied philosophy. That, at least, is how it served Benjamin.

The principal distinction in Benjamin's analysis is between Greek tragedy and Protestant German *Trauerspiel*. The similarities and differences between these two forms (or 'ideas', in Benjamin's terminology) enable him to locate them as part of a dialectic of theological enlightenment, a dialectic that finds its resolution in his own critique of Stoicism. By way of contrast and comparison the Spanish *Trauerspiele* of Calderon are also discussed. These are legitimate parts of the 'idea' of *Trauerspiel*; but their Catholicism means that for Benjamin they have a ritualist taint which rules them out of serious consideration within his historical dialectic. (This does not indicate lack of esteem for Calderon; but only Lutherans were 'stoical' in this argument.) As a rough guide to the book overall, we may divide it into the theoretical prologue, which seems at first conspicuously remote from the historical subject-matter of the book; a first chapter mainly concerned with the unfamiliar genre of seventeenth-century *Trauerspiel*, distinguishing it from Greek tragedy, but also containing the crucial section on Protestant Stoicism; and a second chapter, roughly corresponding to part three of the Goethe article, which describes the 'mystery'[166] or divine function of *Trauerspiel's* allegory and finally integrates the themes introduced in the prologue.

In Benjamin's view, the artistic 'mystery' has to be carefully sited against a framework of concepts drawn from the philosophies of religion or history.[167] Benjamin sees Greek tragedy as a form sited in 'prehistory' (*Urzeit* or *Vorzeit*).[168, 169] The basis of the mystery is human sacrifice,[170] but raised to a level of contract by the intercession of Logos.[171] The dramatic representation of traditional heroic tales, stories of the destruction of individuals by nameless law and unknown fate, is a ritual sacrifice to the mythic world of unpredictable deities. But at the same time it is a mystery, a symbol in the theological sense, because it indicates the direction of hope. And that hope, for the theological situation of the community, was Logos. The hero may have been 'tragically silent' before his fate, which was itself a formless destiny, a dumb propitiation; but the fact that the poet gave it representation in Logos enabled the community to transcend the first level of nameless natural fear. 'Faced with the suffering hero the congregation learns . . . gratitude for the word, granted to them with his death. And this word shone out as a renewed gift with every new variation that the poet extracted from the legend.'[172] The contract that emerged was one that bound the gods as well,[173] beating back unfathomable doom with the piercing rays of the word.

It is important to note that Benjamin's analysis did not merely prepare the ground for his major argument; he was also continuing the attack on the symbolistic interpretations of the George school. By using the term *Urzeit* as a way of identifying the historical and philosophical standing of tragedy, Benjamin was assimilating it to Klages's conceptions of primal myth, but also relativising it historically. This is a clear 'Whig' perspective: Benjamin did not believe that the Greek condition was either a desirable or a recoverable idyll, but strictly a moment in an upward progression. This was emphasised further by his endorsement of Wilamowitz-Moellendorff's dismissal of 'cultic' interpretations of tragedy; despite the cherished beliefs of Nietzsche and the George associates, Greek tragedy was not an ecstatic celebration of Dionysian rites, but a sober and eminently theological mystery.[174]

Accordingly, Greek tragedy contained the dialectical seeds of its own supersession by a superior mystery. This took place in the Socratic dialogue, in which the word and its acutely rational control drove out the dumb tragic hero. But as the other side to this, a new mystery was set up by what Benjamin called the 'purely dramatic' element in the word – the mystery of transcendence.[175] And the decisive signal of this was the great dialogue on immortality, Plato's *Phaedo*, which, in Benjamin's view, represented a complete abandonment of the principle of sacrificial extinction which had dominated the tragic hero's position.[176] The new mystery of transcendence leads straight to the next, and radically different, form – the *Trauerspiel*.[177]

The pure drama of a transcendent Logos thus presented itself as the centre and 'idea' of *Trauerspiel*. While the tragedy was the first struggle of an inchoate community against mute mythic law,[178] the mystery of 'pure drama' became a celebration of transcendence through the immortal word. While tragedy was a first distanciation of the community from nature, the *Trauerspiel* was a systematic opposition between the transcendent realm of heavenly truth and the immanent realm of worldly evil. The nature of the mystery, its theological function, and the direction in which it points must necessarily be quite different in each case.

But these differences can only be identified by proceeding beyond the more abstract levels of the 'idea', whatever Benjamin's prologue might have suggested. The *Ursprung des deutschen Trauerspiels* was much more historical, in its adducing of empirical evidence, than might have been expected from the prologue or from the essay on Goethe. This seeming inconsistency is an indication of the dialectical movement even within the book itself.

Accordingly, Benjamin's differentiation between tragedy and *Trauerspiel* is founded on three strongly historical propositions as well as the more abstract deduction of 'pure drama'. The first is a 'pragmatic'[179] distinction. Greek tragedy is modelled on the form of the judicial proceeding, the confrontation in this instance between the claims of mythic law and the resistance of the hero. Therefore, the action takes place in circumstances of cosmic pomp, and the dramatic unities conform to the strict timetable of Greek judicial processes.[180] But in *Trauerspiel*, which is mainly concerned with emphasising the poor figure the world makes in the remorseless light of transcendence, the action usually takes place on a temporary and moveable stage, a contemptuous emphasis on the insubstantiality of all worldly events.[181]

The second distinction is thematic. While Greek tragedy adhered closely to the traditional myths, remaining piously within the areas that constituted the primitive identity of the community, *Trauerspiel* roams freely through history for its material. And while tragedy was profoundly respectful towards the litigation repeatedly represented on its stage, *Trauerspiel* is intimate and casual in its attitude towards the histories it chances to incorporate.[182] For tragedy, the litigious deities had to be taken very seriously; but in *Trauerspiel* the view from a transcendent immortality can only regard historical events with sad resignation.[183]

The third and most important distinction concerns the function of these mysteries. Both, as Benjamin remarks, are to be seen as 'keys to the life of a people';[184] they are, as we have suggested, the theological dimension of community functioning. But both imply very different community structures. Benjamin does not go into the question in relation to the Greeks, although it is clear that they were in a 'prehistory' not merely religious but also social. The *Trauerspiel* on the other hand shows very distinct connections with contemporary social organisation and politics. Benjamin shows this both in relation to the authors of these dramas and in relation to their general political character. The authors, as Benjamin says more than once, were civil servants in professional life who looked out on historical events from the established perspective of civic office.[185] They occupy, as Benjamin comments, an *'intérieur'* from which they observe the coming and going of the outside world.[186] The *'intérieur'* is their office in the heart of the establishment. The *Trauerspiel* is also by nature resolutely apathetic in relation to political change. It is its essence to be anti-revolutionary; however much it may deplore the events of the world, it will never consider the possibility of active intervention. People who do attempt intervention appear in the *Trauerspiel* in the character of the 'intriguer', Iago-like figures whose satanic cunning and devious means of control only serve to hasten the calamities awaiting all material struggle. This is the only view of history that the *Trauerspiel* can conceive, framed by fruitless intrigue and doomed calculation. Moral dignity accrues only to the sovereigns, upholders of the natural order; and even this is the 'unhistorical dignity of the Stoics'.[187]

So, despite its absence in the 'prologue', it is clear already that history plays a significant part on two levels. In the first place, a literary form, even if it is an 'idea', has a historical location from which it cannot be separated. And second, that literary form, even if considered as a 'mystery', operates within a specific context and has a specific function. Benjamin's 'theology' is evidently not without its materialist components.

The *Trauerspiel* has two main functional contexts: Catholicism and Protestantism. The Catholic *Trauerspiel* is slightly anomalous because of the incomplete transcendentism of the Counter-Reformation. The sense of the 'purely dramatic' mystery is that Logos, so to speak, catapults sensibility into hope for the beyond. Awareness of the next life is a precondition and goal for the Socratic, or 'purely dramatic', use of the word. The word is the ladder into transcendence which cannot be interrupted by immanent realities.

But Catholicism – or so this argument runs – sees the possibility of a 'secularised soteriology',[188] salvation on this earth through earthly institutions of God, such as Church and monarchy. These establishments form a material ladder by which man may already on earth start the ascent to heaven. This is a contributory scheme very different from the abrupt award granted to those who are secure in faith alone. Accordingly, the Catholics manifest no messianic or apocalyptic expectations, but instead envisage a peaceful earthly existence under the sure protection of the Church.[189] So the Catholic *Trauerspiel* was effectively an encouragement to mankind to join this scheme. Moreover, the Catholic dramatists enlisted original sin as a way of constructing the mythic fate, 'creaturely guilt', against which the Church existed to provide protection.[190] The doctrine of original sin served as a ground for the satanic destinies of the natural world; and the divine institutions were the means of escape from this. Accordingly, the pagan repertoire of fate and mythic correspondences was brought back as the ominous nexus against which the Catholic sovereign restored a redemptive order. 'Astral fate – sovereign majesty, those are the poles of Calderon's world.'[191]

But Lutheranism, which produced 'the great German Baroque dramatists',[192] set an entirely different context. While the Catholics had earthly institutions and the attendant clarity of ethical discipline, the Lutherans were antinomian. The rigid transcendentism of the Lutherans gave them no sure basis for an ethics in this world, nor any access to concrete representations of the next. 'The next world is emptied of anything which might have even the slightest breath of this world.'[193] In this world, it must be conceded, the Lutherans had a greater sense of 'responsibility' than their Catholic counterparts.[194] (This was *Verantwortung*, individual ethical accountability before God.) But the Lutherans' dour reluctance to concretise the good and the true had paradoxical consequences. They felt themselves in a desolate landscape of valueless and inauthentic actions. But life resists this notion: 'Deeply

it senses that it is not there simply to be devalued by faith.'[195]
So the Lutheran consciousness responded by creating a new world,
a robotic caricature of the real. And it did this in *Trauer*, sadness.
'*Trauer* is the disposition in which the feelings reinvest the evacuated world with a life of masks, and find a mysterious satisfac-
tion in contemplating it.'[196] Lutheran drama shared the Catholics'
condemnation of 'the satanic convolutions of history, in which the
Baroque could see only political intrigue'.[197] But this was intensified by a quite unexpected 'flight into unredeemed nature',[198] a
sudden concern with the patterns and significations of what had
been abandoned by departing transcendence. And so, with a
dialectical paradox, the Stoical transcendence of the Lutherans
leads them back precisely to the starting point of the whole process
– myth and symbolic correspondence. The literary form taken by
this is allegory, subject of the remarkable final section of *Ursprung
des deutschen Trauerspiels*.

Allegory and melancholy

When we turn to Benjamin's account of allegory the dialectical
progress has to start afresh once more; or, in terms of the tractatus
form, 'thought constantly starts from new, pedantically it returns
again to the substance of the matter'.[199] 'The substance of the
matter' (*die Sache selbst*) is, as we should know by now, Benjamin's search for an alternative to the symbolistic 'materialism' of
the George school, the thematic text to which Benjamin's tractatus
constantly returns.

As we have already seen in the confrontation between Catholic
and Protestant *Trauerspiel*, the extreme transcendentism of the
Protestant dramatists tended to produce a dialectical counter-im-
age, namely the flight from an 'empty heaven'[200] and an 'evacuated world',[201] both desolated by the retreat of truth into pure
formal transcendence. The response, particularly on the Protestant side, was a reversion to 'unredeemed nature',[202] a 'passionate contemplation'[203] of what now seemed only a ghostly charade
of senseless correspondences. As a result of the 'depersonalisa-
tion' of the world, 'every trivial object, because the natural and
creative relation to it has gone, appears as the sign of an inexplicable wisdom, and enters an incomparably rich set of connections'.[204]

When we come to the final discussion of allegory the polarity of Catholic and Protestant loses its centrality. The fundamental question now is the relation of the artistic mystery to the world of objects, and since all *Trauerspiele* reject materiality as essentially satanic,[205] the greater transcendentist tension of the Protestants is no longer decisive. And so Benjamin reformulates the argument in the terms that come closest to the core of his position. The final section is primarily an attack on the artistic criticism of his contemporaries, and particularly of the George school.

The polarity that structures the final section is that of symbol and allegory. If we recall the positions of Klages and Gundolf it will not surprise us to see that it is 'symbol', or rather its mistaken interpretation, that is associated with the positions Benjamin attacks. Modern art criticism, says Benjamin, is 'barren';[206] it has taken over the Romantics' 'flirtation with a spectacular but ultimately commitment-free (*unverbindlich*) knowledge of an absolute', and converted the notion of symbol into a 'philosophical euphemism for powerlessness'.[207] In other words, the symbol has been used as a pompous way of escaping the ethical dimensions of art – its status, one might say, as a mystery functioning within the theological levels of a community.

The target of Benjamin's criticism is in effect a generalisation of the position Gundolf had adopted in his *Goethe* – the suggestion, in a word, that 'heroes' create their own 'fate'. In specifically aesthetic terms this is identified as the belief that there is a continuum between symbolic form and the divine, between the beautiful and the ethical.[208] It is a disregard of the boundary that divides the creaturely realms of immanent beauty from the transcendence of Logos, a boundary that can only be crossed by the 'mystery' – of hope or whatever. Ultimately, beauty is a mystery of the ethical; but the neo-Romantic beliefs of literary criticism put both beauty and ethics on a par in the notion of the 'complete individual', the creative genius on its 'soteriological, indeed sanctified path'. In the Goethe essay Benjamin had described this grandiose and mythic view of art as 'emanationism', the doctrine that art somehow ordered the primal chaos of the world.[209] In the *Trauerspiel* book, as in the earlier discussion, Benjamin's concern was with the role of the unattained, the 'inexpressible', behind art's character as mystery.

Part of the aesthetic position of the view rejected by Benjamin is, as we have already seen in the case of Gundolf, a distinction between symbol and allegory. Conventionally, this distinction was one of semantic value, with symbol substantially integrated as both Being and sign, while allegory was sign alone. Allegory, as Benjamin said, was 'denounced as being no more than a means of reference (*Bezeichnung*)'.[210] Benjamin's response was that such a view attributed more to the symbol than it could legitimately provide. He conceded that the theological symbol, at least, did manifest a unity between 'sensory and supersensory object',[211] and that arbitrary signification was indeed a part of the allegory,[212] but argued that the presentation of the two as part of an aesthetic hierarchy was quite misleading.

Benjamin's critique of symbol was congruent with his analysis of beauty in the Goethe essay, except that he added an important element derived from Klages. Symbol, like beauty, was to be disentangled from any false attribution of transcendence. Beauty, as we saw, was essentially impermanent; and it was precisely its temporal transience that identified it as part of the realm of *Schein* – mere appearance. Similarly, now, symbol was hailed as the 'transfiguration of decline' in which 'the light of redemption fleetingly appears'.[213] This is the same as the mystery of beauty and hope described in 'Goethe'. There was no identity between the beautiful and the true, between symbol and redemption; merely a mystery in which fading *Schein* led on to hope. The power of beauty and symbol lay in their death, their spurning of the continuity of time. 'The measure of time governing symbolic experience is the mystical instant.'[214] And so, with an ironical confirmation of Klages's opposition of time and symbol, the anamnesis of a transfigured creation took place only outside the intellectualised coordinates of time and space. And the character of the symbol was fundamentally pictorial rather than conceptual or linguistic. It was the 'picture of an organic totality',[215] the flash of a lost sensory wholeness. But this only served to confirm its irredeemable isolation from transcendence.

Allegory was different on all counts. It was described as being 'beyond beauty'[216] and as a 'later formation, based on extensive cultural debate'.[217] At least in a historical sense, in other words, allegory was a modern component of what was by implication a more enlightened theological order. And what was decisively important was the 'dialectical' nature of the allegory, both in its application by Baroque drama,[218] and in the internal tensions of the form itself.[219] In its application it was dialectical in the sense of being social, devoid of the 'unpolarised inwardliness' of symbolist individualism;[220] and in its internal tensions it revealed itself to be a continuation of the motion already identified in the progress from tragedy to *Trauerspiel*. In both cases it was historically active, while the symbol, even in the correct sense, was a kind of inert extreme.

Now if symbol is the momentary pictorial flash, allegory is the slow profundity of contemplation. Unlike the time-free symbol, allegory contains 'the decisive category of time'.[221] And, while symbol transfigures the process of natural decline, allegory converts history into a 'petrified primal landscape'. The manner of the flattening or petrification (*Erstarren*) is 'script'. Allegorical 'script' is the opposite of the symbolic 'picture'. While the picture generates a beautiful totality, 'script' produces fragments in which the beauty has been exorcised by learning, particularly theological learning.[222] The direct sensual picture of the symbol is replaced by the 'picture' of the 'script' (*Schriftbild*, which actually means typography); Benjamin saw in Baroque typography the hieroglyphics of immoveable divine wisdom.[223] Beyond this, the 'script' of the allegory is an antidote to the pictures conjured by the symbol. The picture's 'symbolical beauty evanesces when it is struck by the light of theological learning. The false appearance of totality is extinguished.'[224]

In the allegory, devoid of symbolic illusion, transience is not transfigured but remorselessly framed into an inescapable *memento mori* of decay. History can only be irreversible decline;[225] and in the allegory its decay becomes permanently accessible to contemplation. This is the essence of the 'ruin' motif in Baroque literature, where it serves as the perfect encapsulation of natural decline, the fully adequate image of history.[226] It also serves, superseding the earlier theory of hope, as a new mystical basis for art. Hope is here replaced by the notion of 'mortification', which becomes the goal of artistic experience. Just as allegory disperses an illusory symbolic beauty, so mortification examines the beautiful under the auspices of knowledge. Here Benjamin reverts to a discussion originally broached in the first paragraphs of the Goethe essay, namely the goal of criticism and its claim to 'truth'. He uses the same terminology of 'truth content' and 'material content'; material content is what might be described as the immediate contemporary dimension of the work in its first appearance, while truth content is the underlying significance which only becomes clear with the fading of these 'earlier charms'.[227] The significant difference is that whereas in the first essay Benjamin had seemed to suggest that the two components of the work were basically discontinuous, here, with the technique of 'mortification', it becomes part of criticism to transform the 'material' into the 'true'.

In Benjamin's view of 'mortification' – and this passage, though brief, is crucial for his critical theory – beauty is necessarily bound to the side of materiality rather than truth. This does not have to mean that beauty is ephemeral, although probably attempts at 'naive enjoyment' of older works are simply 'dreaming'.[228] Enjoyment of such works has to be the fruit of a degree of technical understanding. A non-contemporary work is no longer materially alive, and so it cannot generate the same symbolic mystery, the passing of beautiful appearance, as a contemporary work. The beauty that it has is of a different order in that, once discerned, it is a lasting beauty (and in that sense, as Benjamin concedes, it may be wrong to call it beauty at all). But at all events, intuitive or empathic assaults on the historic work produce only sentimentality or the dreaming misrepresentations of nostalgia. Mortification extracts beauty from the object recognised as materially dead, and it does it by means of technical knowledge; 'so not Romantically, by arousing consciousness in live works, but by colonising them, as dead ones, with knowledge'.[229] And the remarkable feature of the Baroque 'ruin' is that it starts its own embalming, so to speak.[230] The refusal of the Baroque to rely on appearance,[231] even in its own contemporary material context, means that it stands ready as a 'ruin' when the later critic comes to it to begin mortification. It offers a technical account of its historicity even in its origins, and thus minimises the amount of appearance that has to be converted by the critic. The importance this allegorical form had for Benjamin is reflected in the last lines of the book, in which he again opposed symbolic and allegorical beauty: 'When others beam as gloriously as on the first day, this form [allegory] will hold fast to the picture of beauty even on the Last Day.'[232]

But whatever the power and dignity of the allegory, this does not conclude the argument for Benjamin. Religious allegory may supersede pagan symbol, but as it does so it is immediately embroiled in a dialectic of its own. The 'antinomy' of allegory[233] derives principally from its insistence on script, and from the attitude to language that this involves. The paradox of language, as we have already seen, centred for the earlier Benjamin around its incorporation of two distinct functions, naming and communicating.

As Benjamin presented the paradox in the *Trauerspiel* book, it was not in the first instance between naming and communication, but between script and sound. These two, the writing on the page and the sound of the voice, stood in 'high tension polarity' towards one another.[234] This was because – or so Benjamin interpreted the Baroque attitude – they had a different status in the divine hierarchy. The spoken word, and indeed natural sounds in general, were from the realm of matter. They were part of the 'free, original expression of creation', and, in the Baroque view, they were firmly linked with the processes of the natural world by such bonds as onomatopoeia.[235] But because of this, the spoken word was a kind of unthinking exaltation; Benjamin also describes it, using the term from Klages's theory of natural symbols, as an 'ecstasy'.[236]

Script, on the other hand, was entirely opposed to the material world. It encompassed the power and dignity of pure intellect.[237] In particular, it was the vehicle of significance (*Bedeutung*),[238] the divine order from which the natural realm was inevitably excluded. This, according to Benjamin, was why the Baroque paid so much attention to the imposing typography of its books, and so little to the natural rhythms of style and composition. The indigestible *Schwulst* of Baroque writing was a deliberate part of this programme.[239] Together with typography it was intended to press home the irresistible 'authority' of theological majesty.[240]

But more than either of these, allegory itself was at the heart of the Baroque's struggle for authority. The power of allegory, the play of sense, lay in its ability to convert objects into signs. The natural world lay at its feet as an inexhaustible store of signs which could be endlessly combined and related at the whim of the allegorist. 'Every person, every thing, every relation can signify any other.'[241] Objects could not retain their own identity; they were in perpetual danger of being summoned to appear in allegorical reference to something else. And it was this disrespect for objects that caused grief, Benjamin now declared, modifying his earlier view that it was *naming* that brought sadness into the natural world; 'Here we encounter significance (*Bedeutung*) . . . as the reason for sadness.'[242]

But the real treachery of allegory comes not with its high-handed disregard for the dignity of objects, but with its assault on the spoken word itself. The spoken word, as far as Baroque was concerned, was 'purely sensory';[243] and because of that it was itself part of the natural realm of objects, and fair game for 'allegorical exploitation'.[244] And so, allegory falls upon the sound, demolishing the organic homogeneity of speech and converting its fragments into new structures of allegorical reference. The communicative force of speech is shattered,[245] and its elements are given a substitute dignity in 'anagrams, onomatopoeic conceits and other linguistic tricks'.[246] The material presence of the spoken word, in Benjamin's image, is constantly overtaken by a 'sickness'[247] – the sickness of transcendence.

The height of this, Benjamin declared, would be to combine sound and significance in such a way that they did *not* come together in the organic unity of communicative speech. This ultimate piece of allegorical trickery was to be found in irony, the weapon of the intriguer. It was the force of the intriguer's irony to convert the intended or natural sense of words into something different, thus bringing about the final destruction of organic language.[248]

There was a resolution to this polarity, as Benjamin understood it. 'For there is no contradiction in conceiving of a lively, free use of revealed speech in which it would lose none of its dignity.'[249] But this resolution could not come about in the Baroque, for the Baroque was not consciously aware of the antinomy within its attitude to word and script.[250] As far as Benjamin was concerned, a dialectical account of the coeval status of word and script only emerged in work such as that of the Romantic, Johann Wilhelm Ritter.[251] Word and script were one aspect of the tension between ideas and empirical phenomena which Benjamin had introduced in the prologue. But an account of the Baroque could not yield a resolution of this tension on the level of language theory alone. To achieve that, Benjamin had to go back to another aspect of the Baroque, and that was the melancholy at the centre of its ethical transcendence. Melancholy will lead us straight to practice, the concluding moment in this remarkable book.

Melancholy, the sadness that overcomes the spirit faced with an evacuated world, and that responds by 'passionate contemplation' of it, has certain positive results. For example, as Benjamin had pointed out in 'Fate and Character',[252] it generates anthropological and physiognomic insights which may be regarded as adequate forms of scientific knowledge.[253] In general, the desolated contemplations of the melancholic may come up with a range of empirically based scientific theories and even 'the sublimest researches'.[254]

But the dialectical antithesis to this is the futility of such knowledge, and its irrelevance to any theologically legitimate practice. The paradigm of the melancholic is the prince, says Benjamin.[255] Despite the fact that he is a representative of God on earth, he is as much subject to the frailty of nature as anyone else. And the only purpose that can underlie his actions is the maintenance of an order awaiting its inevitable doom. So the dialectic of melancholy is that of penetrating intelligence and profoundest gloom, genius and madness.[256] And the final extreme of melancholy is the deadly sin of acedy, or torpor, set by Dante in the lower ice of Hell.[257]

The prince does not intervene in the run of the world because it is not proper for him to do so. Legate of an inscrutable transcendence, his only function is stoically to watch over the pointless processes of the natural world. Meanwhile, his dialectical opposite, the courtier, devotes himself recklessly to the manipulation of people and politics. The courtier is just as melancholic as his prince, and with no illusions about the futility of his deceitful intrigues.[258] And indeed the courtier's faithlessness and the prince's torpor are fixed as two poles in the same antinomy. It is the lack of middle ground for the practical exercise of human faith. 'For all essential decisions in relation to human beings can offend against faith; they are governed by higher laws.'[259] In terms of the Baroque image of transcendence, faith is a creaturely sentiment which has application only in the realm of things, a realm with no access to the 'higher law'. So, while the melancholic prince abandons human practice entirely, the courtier plunges to the lowest of all practices, the manipulation of natural necessities. The contemplative torpor of the melancholic and the mendacious politicking of the intriguer are the two lost poles of a practice exiled from the truth of human faith. Just as the Goethe article was a recovery of responsibility from the chaos of myth, so the *Trauerspiel* book is a recovery of human practice from the desert of religious transcendentism.

Practice

And so we come finally to the resolution. The symbolic world of material correspondences leads to chaos, and can offer no ethical guideline. Benjamin's theory of language and doctrine seemed to yield a principle of hope. But the formal emptiness of this principle, when set in a rigorous transcendentism, evacuated the practical content of ethics and left the world a petrified mask where only passive objects could demand faith. Meanwhile, the studies of the melancholic had accumulated an encyclopaedic but pointless store of material knowledge, and the Logos obsession of the allegorists had produced a complex of ritual hieroglyphics impervious to the practical application of the word. Enlightenment seemed confined to the despondent contemplations of the melancholic over his own grave.

But – 'The true being of a man is his *deed;* for in it individuality is *real';* and against the infinite transferability of the allegorical sign the deed '*is* this, and its being is *not* merely a sign, but the thing itself'.[260] Hegel's resolutions of the antinomies of unhappy consciousness are those that Benjamin uses against the melancholic allegorist. And he also uses them against himself, for the long self-citation from the 1916 language essay, which makes up most of the last paragraph of the *Trauerspiel* book, is modified by one crucial addition, namely the theory of practice. In the early essay the central distinction was between adamitic naming, given by God as the true basis of language, and judgement between good and evil, which formed the basis of conceptual language and brought about the Fall.[261] This dichotomy, we will recall, was integrated in Benjamin's account of tradition as 'doctrine', the formalisation of God's primal creative utterance. So, on one side we had the substantial reality of 'naming' and language which walked in the light of God's Word; while on the other stood the hubristic subjectivity of judgement, abstraction, and the debasement of language in mere human communication. And this position, although without the dimension of 'doctrine', was again resumed at the beginning of the *Trauerspiel* book.[262]

But, as we finally discover at the very end of the book, this was done not as a definitive philosophical statement, but as the beginning of a dialectical process which the rest of the book sought to complete. The epistemological prologue emerges as the abstract pole of an understanding which cannot dispense with the concrete historical development of the rest of the book. And the name theory of language is a text to which the rest of the book supplies commentary.

This is finally clarified in the last paragraph of the book, which in effect constitutes a commentary and interpretation on Benjamin's earlier language theories. In its alternation of sentences from the 'language' essay with new passages it is almost literally an 'inter-linear' commentary,[263] and as such, a textbook demonstration of dialectical ascent from the abstract to the concrete. The problem with Benjamin's earlier position had been its empty formalism. It was all very well to rule out the whole dimension of human communication, but this realm could not practically be separated from the 'material' realm of names. Insistence on naming and the sacred is as abstract as judgement and communicative chitchat were held to be. In the work of the Baroque allegorists, this dogmatic position had led precisely to the opposite of what had been desired; for in their emphasis on the sacred and the scriptural they drove out the free, lively use of revealed language,[264] and devalued the sound of speech, guarantor of the integrity of language and meaning.[265]

So, the question was, if a rigidly formal use of language tends to devalue the world of things and lively processes, then where are we to look for a language in which 'names' achieve their objects, and establish a material communion between the named and the namer? The simple postulation of an attitude of 'naming' in opposition to an attitude of 'judging' is obviously too abstract. The answer appears in Benjamin's interlinear commentary. 'Knowledge of evil has no object. Its object is not in the world. It is only posited by lust for knowledge, or rather for judgement, in mankind itself.'[266] Thus far Benjamin repeats his earlier position. Knowledge of evil is insubstantial, because God's creation is 'very good'. But what about knowledge of good? In the naming theory of language, which Benjamin's earlier text expounded at this point, knowledge of good did not seem to have any object either; or at least access to it seemed blocked by the general interdict on concept and communication, the free and lively use of language.

So now, in this later text, Benjamin gives an account of knowledge of the good. 'Knowledge of the good, as knowledge, is secondary.' Secondary to what? 'It follows from practice.' So the theory of the inferior or secondary status of conceptual judgement is here radically altered. It is no longer the assertion that 'naming' has a kind of self-evident presence in language, and that we need only turn to it to be saved. Rather, it is the assertion that 'naming', in its real and practical form, is practice itself. The ground of naming upon which 'real' language, the language of names if you like, is built up is the ground of practice. 'The deed . . . is not merely a sign, but the thing itself', in Hegel's words.

From this perspective the antinomies of both melancholy and allegory find their resolution. The torpor of the tyrant and the nihilism of the intriguer are revealed in their sinfulness by the principle that 'Knowledge, not action, is the authentic existence of evil'; and the object of their contemplations is shown to be 'the Fata Morgana of a realm of absolute, that is godless, spirituality'.[267] The 'three satanic promises' that have seduced them are the illusions of freedom, autonomy and infinity,[268] precisely the idealist magic Benjamin had discussed in the thesis on Romantic criticism. And the ultimate entity of idealist speculation, consciousness, is seen for what it is – a trickster's parody of the only true synthesis, namely life.

Allegory itself now reaches its dialectical resolution, the settling of the infinity of meanings within which its superabundance of signification threatens to disappear. Precisely in the allegory of the grave, the 'vision of ecstatic annihilation', it reveals its own limits. 'Here decay is not so much signified, represented allegorically, as itself significant, offered as allegory – the allegory of resurrection.'[269] And so the whole nihilistic technique of destructive contemplation at the last moment turns in on itself. Allegory is allegorised by reality. What had seemed the only sure foothold in a cosmos of desolated illusion, the 'inexplicable wisdom', is now brightly illuminated by the light of life itself. Like Faust on hearing the bells of Easter, the allegorist's thoughts of death are suddenly turned to life and resurrection. 'The allegorist awakes in God's world.' And everything he thought he had, including the chimera of 'hope', is suddenly lost: 'the secret, privileged knowledge, the arbitrary sovereignty in a realm of dead things, the imagined infinity of an empty hope'. But in exchange he receives what he did not have before, the sober reality of his own practice: 'All those things disappear with this one transformation, in which allegorical absorption has to abandon the last phantasmagoria of objectivity and, completely left to itself, finds itself no longer trifling with an earth-like world of things but sober under heaven.'[270]

Dialectical insights taken in static isolation are liable to seem rather trite. This is why Benjamin's *Trauerspiel* book, like Hegel's *Phenomenology*, does not schematise its position as a geometrical pattern. It is only possible genuinely to make sense of such a work if it is read as a totality, as an experiential world which cannot be reduced to formulae and sets of propositions. The search for an adequate understanding of such works has inevitably to be long and rather painful. Like the prizes in an Easter-egg hunt, the concealed revelations derive much of their value from the effort of looking for them. Because of that, a commentary such as the one we have just attempted risks trivialising the book and reducing it to what it cannot be reduced to. We have tried to avoid this by presenting Benjamin's thought as a process, rather than a fixed schema. But it must be remembered that much has been omitted by our dry and rather hurried rendering.

   Given these reservations, it is still possible to offer a summary of the practical implications of the *Trauerspiel* book, a work that was Benjamin's longest complete project and that supplies the foundations for what comes later. We have already pointed to the polemical impulses that informed much of what went into the *Trauerspiel* book, and the explorations that preceded it. The final result, however, goes some way beyond being a mere answer to hostile positions. In essence it is a description of the position of the intellectual in an ethical universe. And here the most important element, new in Benjamin's development and fundamental to what follows, is history. The 'heaven' under which the allegorist finally awakens is history, as is made clear when this motif is repeated in the 1940 Theses.[271] And the character of the melancholia that precedes this awakening is lack of awareness of history. The Stoic conception of history endorsed by the Baroque is unhistorical.[272] The only conception of history open to the Baroque is the mere politicking caricatured in the figure of the intriguer.[273] The real being of nature, which is inseparable from its historical development, is exploited and devalued by the Baroque as no more than inert material for its significant games.[274] And however many histories may be used as material for the Baroque drama, they are always subjected to the careless manipulations of the dramatist: 'total freedom of plot is appropriate to the *Trauerspiel*'.[275] The result is that history is ultimately reduced to lifeless caricature; all we are shown is its '*facies hippocratica*', its death mask in the 'petrified primal landscape'.[276]

And yet history is the medium in which reality lives, and although the 'ideas' may in some sense be transhistorical, the phenomena which they illuminate only exist in history. The historian may indeed rescue phenomena into the 'crystalline simultaneity' of the idea, as Benjamin's prologue affirmed. But in real existence, those crystals are dissolved in the stream of time. The dialectical opposition between the historian's melancholic contemplations and the unceasing flux of becoming is only resolved at the flashpoint of 'now', the present moment in which the intellectual project itself becomes a deed.

History is the arena of the present, the dialectical moment in which the living deed can burst the chains of seemingly valueless knowledge. It is not the past of the grave; it is the now of the resurrection. Historical insight is the practice that springs from the decay of preceding contemplations, not as the realisation of intention, but as affirmation of a reality for which all 'allegorical' absorption must only be a servant. And this is the purpose of Benjamin's book. For the critical mortification of the Baroque in the end leaves the critic with something real, namely the 'truth content' which is left after the dissolution of beauty. And the truth content recovered by Benjamin's project is that the Baroque *Trauerspiel* was a theological enterprise, an exercise in political ideology carried out by persons with a concrete interest in what they were doing – those authors who 'now and again gave gratefully rewarded service to the affairs of state'.[277] Against this, the modern period of German literature – Benjamin instances Expressionism and the George school[278] – although in important respects resembling the Baroque era, had failed to establish any political direction. But, says Benjamin in a sentiment that opens up the entire future course of his work, it did represent a decay which is 'preparatory and fruitful'.[279] For the rest of Benjamin's work we have to look to his mortification of the decaying and preparatory, and the release of the political fruits that lie within. From 1925 onwards the arena of historical practice is the arena of politics.

2

Historical Materialism

Benjamin's 'turn to politics'[1] with the completion of the *Trauerspiel* book is well documented in his letters. By the summer of 1925 he was able to declare that the 'academic intentions' of the book had been no more than an external occasion, and one that he viewed 'ironically'.[2] To Scholem he wrote that he now expected nothing from his plans for a lecturing career except a 'belated and bright red cactus bloom'[3] – this in recognition of the prickly nature of his new work with Marxism. From his own point of view, he now found himself no longer able to take a 'full interest' in the subject of his book;[4] it had to be 'a conclusion – not a beginning at any price'.[5] In later years Benjamin still regarded the tragedy book as the completion of his 'German literature cycle';[6] and from then on he saw his literary work as essentially a matter of making this field 'unpalatable' for the bourgeois critics.[7]

Despite these remarks it is important not to lay too much emphasis on Benjamin's sudden conversion. In the first place, his own assessment was perhaps influenced by anger at his treatment by Frankfurt University, and by the experience of an emotional link with Bolshevism in the person of Asja Lacis. In the second place, the more extreme expressions of a rejection of the *Trauerspiel* book are counterbalanced by later affirmations of a continuity in his work, and by citation of the earlier texts in several mature pieces. Over-emphasis of this 'break' by commentators probably results largely from the influence of Scholem and Adorno, both of whom had some interest in preserving the notion of a 'mystical' Benjamin still largely intact despite the supposedly unrelated political diversion.

As we have shown in the previous section, 'political' implications were already strongly present in the *Trauerspiel* book. Benjamin later characterised it as 'dialectical' but not 'materialist',[8] and this does indicate the direction in which Benjamin's further thinking moved. Not that the distance between the dialectic and the position he subsequently occupied as 'materialism' was in fact all that great.

The dialectic of practice

As we saw, Benjamin's *Trauerspiel* book reached a notion of practice from two more or less distinct starting points – one metaphysical and one historical. On the metaphysical side, the book resolved Benjamin's theory of naming into a theory of practice. Benjamin's original rather religious counterposition of language as naming, the state of paradisal creativity, and language as system, for conceptuality and communication, was transformed into a dialectical relation. In the Baroque era an analogous opposition had become locked into a variety of antinomies between transcendence and immanence, allegorical signification and material signifier, stoical contemplation and satanic intrigue. But these antinomies were all abstractions. The true character of language as naming did not appear in such things as allegorical signification; it appeared in practice. And in practice, in the primal simplicity of the deed, the world was restored to unhappy consciousness. Stoic apatheia was dissolved, and language, as names, again entered the divine realm of the idea.

Seen in this Hegelian light it would seem that Benjamin's metaphysics in the *Trauerspiel* book remained essentially idealist. This was perhaps inevitable, given his religious starting point. After all, Benjamin described as 'theological' the resolution that, in the final section, released the tensions carefully built up in the rest of the book. But this was theology of a very powerful order, and one that if anything expedited his critique of ideological structure and function. As history, the *Trauerspiel* book was in the first instance a reflection on the political nature of cultural practice, an exploration of the sense in which Baroque drama was a *political* theology (in Carl Schmitt's phrase). The antinomies of allegory were not merely a localised problem of poetic form; they were tensions inherent in the condition of the intelligentsia under absolutism.

The inability of the Silesians, as Lutherans, to round off their dramas in the same way that Calderon could in the Catholic south was not simply an aesthetic disability; it was an aspect of more complex political conditions in the advanced bourgeois nations of the north. The philosophical antinomies of language could be resolved with a theory of practice. But the corresponding antinomy in Baroque 'theology', the immobilised opposition of transcendence and immanence, could only be resolved in historical process – and that, in the real world, was an issue of practical politics.

The whole force of Benjamin's argument issues in this chain of practical implications. The *Trauerspiel* book appears at first sight, and has usually been read, as a standard academic work in which an introduction devoted to general theoretical or methodological points is followed by their application to a particular set of historical data. And it is imagined that Benjamin's own various commitments peep out at points along the road – in the doctrine of ideas, in the theories of melancholy and natural decline, and the like. But this is quite wrong. All that Benjamin actually embraces as his own, like Engels *vis-à-vis* Hegel,[9] is the dialectical method itself, especially as it emerges in the procedure of mortification. *All* the rest, *including* the elegant constructions of the 'epistemological prologue', are the abstract elements from which Benjamin reassembles the concrete historical whole. The theory of naming, which appears in the prologue as part of the doctrine of ideas, is just as abstract a moment as the theological opposition of transcendence and immanence. The abstract moment of language metaphysics may be resolved in a theory of practice; but although this completes the logical structure, that in turn demands a theory of nature and of history. And equally the historical moment, the exploration of Baroque theology, *also* demands a resolution in terms of the further processes of historical development. And those processes, the 'idea' into which history itself is seen finally to enter, is the present moment of political practice.

This is the sense in which the *Trauerspiel* book, perhaps more strikingly than any of Benjamin's work, exemplifies the principle of representing our time in historical time.[10] It is a scrupulously scholarly work, and absolutely disdains any attempt to draw parallels with the modern era; and yet it is not possible to follow its dialectical flow without seeing that it points beyond itself, towards the future in which we now are. It 'implies' us, as Benjamin later characterised this kind of link.[11] We can only follow what the book is about if we recognise that implication, the vacuum of the present into which the abstractions of the past rush at the moment of understanding.

So, on the one hand, the book is a dialectical resolution of Benjamin's own previous transcendentist approach to ethics and metaphysics. The ideas are taken out of the hands of God, and ethics is no longer a matter of the individual's confrontation with the transcendent absolute. The theory of practice releases the individual into the concrete world of the deed – a significant step for Benjamin's subjective development, if not necessarily for readers generally. But this reservation does not apply to the real historical dialectic of Baroque theology. The critique of contemplative absorption cannot itself remain suspended in melancholic inertia. The frozen immobility of transcendence and immanence has to find an issue. It does this either in the Catholic doctrine of the continuity of Kingship with the divine, or – and this is the more interesting response – in the destabilisation of the intellectual project itself. The Protestant melancholic goes too far in his insistence on the absolute inaccessibility of transcendence, because this destroys human trust, and with it the essential fabric of earthly society. So, ultimately, the rejection of politics as satanic intrigue must collapse in upon itself; the fragments of civil life must be picked up by the individuals themselves. The Silesian dramatists' stoic attempts to protect the status quo backfired by revealing their project as itself a part of ideological production.

The methodology of the *Trauerspiel* book, prologue notwithstanding, is based on a conception of 'theology' as the integration of intellectual enterprise with practical application. But this had to be extended if it was to be of value in the exploration of modern intellectual practice, the area 'implied' by the *Trauerspiel* book. Benjamin's mature work – from 1925 or so onwards – accordingly was concerned with the development of a general methodological scheme for the analysis of intellectual practice. This was mainly associated with the theory of *Technik*, which may be seen as a materialist adaptation of the principle of 'theology'. The theory of *Technik*, which is probably best understood in the light of other contemporary projects, such as Bogdanov's theory of organisation ('Tektology'), covered the conditions of intellectual practice set by technology on the one hand and social organisation on the other.

The purpose of the theory of *Technik*, furthermore, was to establish a basis for the critique of false consciousness. Just as 'theology' could trace the emancipation of seventeenth-century bourgeois intellectuals imprisoned in the opposition of transcendence and immanence, so *Technik* could determine the correct dialectical resolution of the tensions in modern intellectual practice. With the aid of it Benjamin was able to mount an extensive analysis of the modern ideological battlefield, fought over by the myth-builders of Fascist cultural history and the interventionists of Bolshevism. Behind them lay the various failed projects of the recent past, figures like Baudelaire, Kraus and Kafka, with their halting struggles to penetrate the mysteries of their own political circumstances.

Technik and intellectual practice

Technik, in German, means both 'technology' and 'technique'. As Benjamin uses it, it covers both areas. The term is stretched in the same way, and with the same intentions, as Bogdanov's 'organisation'. Just as Bogdanov uses 'organise' of things, in the sense of producing them, as well as of people in the conventional sense, so also Benjamin uses *Technik* to cover both the human and material relations of production. A piece of machinery is *Technik*, and so are the methods and organisations used to exploit it.

The reason for this apparent ambivalence is both writers' desire to emphasise the realm of practical material intervention as the integration of theory and practice. For Bogdanov, 'organisation' was the fundamental category of reality, the only sure path to an understanding of the dialectical universe. In Benjamin's work, similarly, *Technik* is the medium in which the antinomies of Stoicism and undialectical thinking are resolved.

In taking up this position, Benjamin is expressly *not* being 'technocratic'[12] or 'positivist'.[13] The technocratic, positivistic attitude to *Technik* believes that 'the world' is an inert object of the scientist's contemplations. But the dialectic of theory and practice insists there is no objectivity independent of the material act. A positivistic obsession with eternal laws of nature is almost as misguided as an obsession with the movements of the eternal spirit. Ontological speculations may only serve the demands of practice. And the epistemological 'deed', in the arena of *Technik*, concentrates the expertise of both the natural and the human sciences.

None the less Benjamin's choice of the term *Technik*, however dialectical his understanding of it, is also guided by a polemical rejection of petty-bourgeois hostility to technology.[14] Holding technology responsible for the evils of the age was then, as it is now, a central component in reactionary ideologies.[15] When Benjamin says *Technik*, he means 'technology' at least as much as he means 'technique'. And this 'technology' is precisely not futuristic aestheticisation of machines;[16] it is a hard-headed concern with their real scope and function. Esoteric celebration of machinery as a work of art or a semiotical construct is just as reactionary as the attempt to flee into the abstractions of the 'purely human'. Benjamin cites the Russian poet Mayakovsky: 'The era of the machine does not demand hymns in its praise; it demands to be mastered in the interests of humanity. The steel of skyscrapers does not demand contemplative absorption, but decisive exploitation in the building of housing.'[17] The ignorant apercus and opinions of bourgeois essayists have to be abandoned in favour of an appropriate expertise. In this the machine is the same as the social apparatus. 'Opinions are for the giant apparatus of social life what oil is for machines; one does not go up to a turbine and douse it with oil. One squirts a little into hidden rivets and joints which one has to know about.'[18]

As Benjamin understands the term, then, *Technik* means both the human relations of production ('technique') and the means of production ('technology'). This dichotomy corresponds in a general sense to other Marxist polarities, such as variable and fixed capital, superstructure and base, or even consciousness and matter. The term *Technik*'s deliberate ambivalence captures, perhaps rather better than Bogdanov's 'organisation', the dialectical unity which all these opposing elements enter in any concrete instance. The stress on this dialectical unity is perhaps especially important for Benjamin's project, the critique of intellectual practice. That is because traditional approaches and indeed previous 'philosophy' as an enterprise had tended to fracture this critique, either by abandoning the unity (positivism and analytical philosophy generally) or by subverting the dialectic (objective idealism). In the former case, philosophers had isolated conceptuality from the real world as two supposedly autonomous realms; and in the latter, the dialectic of reality and consciousness was ultimately crippled by the undialectical victory of the one over the other, as in Hegel's theory of spirit. In either case, 'philosophy' was sealed off from its real context, and in particular from politics. But intellectual practice is mediated by political organisation. In order to become a historical, practical phenomenon, 'thought' submits to conditions of organisation; and the conditions of organisation are what integrate the abstraction 'thought' into the concrete realm of politics. *Technik* is a concrete unity; but at the same time it must be understood through the twin dialectical moments, consciousness and matter, technique and technology.

Benjamin's analysis of intellectual practice revolves around the consideration of these two moments and the relation between them. There are four distinct elements in his discussion: political conflict and revolution; the general character of intellectual practice; intellectuals and class; and the principles of progressive intellectual practice.

Conflict and revolution

In Benjamin's conception, political advance and, if necessary, revolution, are the adaptation of human organisation (or 'techniques') to what is demanded by alterations in the technological base. In Marxist terminology, this could be described as taking control of the means of production, and indeed Benjamin specifies socialisation of productive processes as being the principal consequence of revolutionary action.[19] The need for revolution arises when there is a mismatch between directive control and technological capacity, the component parts of *Technik*. 'The development of the forces of production, which include the proletariat and technology, has produced the crisis which is forcing a socialisation of the means of production.'[20] The failure of the established capitalist classes to allow full development of *Technik* as organisation as well as *Technik* as technology brings about the crisis of an uncontrollable technology. The strength of the 'new body' of technology has, as it were, outgrown the directive capacity of a mind befogged by the archaic relations of capitalist organisation.[21]

The immediate urgency of this task – the revolutionacy adaptation of social *Technik* to productive *Technik* – shows in the crude and destructive applications of uncontrolled technology. Modern war, says Benjamin, is a 'slaves' revolt' of *Technik*,[22] the outburst of a power that can no longer be kept in check by outmoded organisational techniques and the capitalist distribution of social power. In fact, war is in the capitalists' interest, because it is the only way in which the advance of modern *Technik* can be contained without actually endangering property relations.[23] War produces a vast acceleration in the development of technologies and organisations. And yet the only beneficiaries of this are the capitalists, whose refusal to allow the reform of property relations brought about the social instability in the first place. War is a grotesque self-immolation of *Technik*, a gladiatorial combat orchestrated by those who can profit from senseless destruction, although not from the rational progress of organisation and technology. Benjamin comments that the only rational war in the modern era is civil war – war to drive out those who cause the unnatural convulsions of repressed technical progress.[24] Meanwhile, the entire history of the last century, the century of imperialism, is one of 'the failed assimilation of *Technik*'.[25]

As we saw in the last section, Benjamin's early ethical position was strongly associated with a theory of language. This does not change with the introduction of *Technik,* and indeed the notion of the 'word' is converted to become part of the ethical legitimation of the new category. Benjamin stresses the moral dimension of *Technik:* disorder in the material arrangements of the means of production is reflected also in its moral arrangements. Benjamin speaks of the 'solidarity of moral disorder with economic purposelessness' in the bourgeoisie.[26] Equally, the political 'disorganisation' of intellectuals in the bourgeois world was a root cause of their moral contamination.[27] And, of course, the vicious and goalless nature of imperialist war was intimately connected with 'disorganisation' as well.[28]

This moral disorganisation, the loss of the ethical dimension, came about because capitalism prevented the integration of the spiritual with the technological – of theory with practice, in Marxist terms. Its irrational perpetuation of the division of labour made it impossible to assume the control that modern technology offered and demanded, and it plunged *Technik* into the dark of a spiritless and amoral practice. Ethical practice in the advanced technological age could only be achieved by organising humanity in the way demanded by *Technik* – that being, as Benjamin maintained in agreement with Bogdanov, according to the principles of codetermination.[29] Such an injection of practice into the paralysed body of technology would immediately sweep away the discrepancy between 'the gigantic resources of *Technik* and its minimal moral illumination', and thus avoid the cataclysmic war that must otherwise overtake humanity.

So it was *Technik,* uniquely, which could restore the ethical 'word' to the universe. For reactionary thinkers, technology was nothing but a 'fetish of the eclipse',[30] one symbol among many for the coming disaster, one more way of explaining man's alienation from nature. In a metaphor taken from the *Trauerspiel* book, Benjamin spoke of the hippocratic death mask being all that the reactionaries were able to extract from their view of existing nature.[31] But it was *Technik,* the arena of historic action, which could break the silence (*Verstummen*) of nature and restore it to an eloquent communion with mankind.[32]

Given favourable circumstances, labour and the word could combine with unprecedented clarity in modern *Technik.* In the newspaper, as appropriated by the post-revolutionary society of the Soviet Union, 'work itself is given the word' (*Die Arbeit selbst kommt zu Wort*).[33] The epoch-making achievement of the revolution had been reflected in the near abolition of illiteracy;[34] as part of this, the newspaper, which used to be the platform for self-regarding bourgeois reporters, had now become the means of expression for a whole class, a whole nation of producers. Benjamin anticipated the 'literary transformation of all relations of life',[35] a transformation characterised more than anything perhaps by the ability of the liberated labourer to 'give an account of' his or her labours.[36] *Rechenschaft geben* – this was an echo of Benjamin's early transcendentist ethics, the lonely account rendered before God. But here, with universal literacy and the self-determination offered by modern *Technik,* this proud ethical responsibility was to be possible for everyone, now, in this world.

It is interesting to note, in this context, how Benjamin's theory of *Technik* gave 'materialist' specification to a theory of language that had previously relied heavily on the problematic regions of creation myth. Bogdanov, as we saw, ascribed the genesis of language to the first primitive organisational communication during labour.[37] A divine origin of language was, from Benjamin's new perspective, obviously not very suitable. So he developed his own 'materialist' view in the shape of an onomatopoeic theory, described in the two essays, 'The Doctrine of the Similar' and 'On the Mimetic Ability', both written in the early 1930s. 'On the Mimetic Ability', in particular, is an intriguing re-statement of earlier symbolistic preconceptions in terms of a language theory which regards 'liquidation of magic' as characteristic of a modern highly developed language.[38]

Intellectual practice

Benjamin felt strongly that Marxist theory did not yet have an adequate model for the description of intellectual practice.[39] The self-definition of traditional intellectuals, as we have already noted, in effect ruled out the notion of a distinct practice. The intellectual project, as it appeared in traditional cultural history and in the work of philosophers such as Heidegger, saw its purpose in the recovery of a kind of inner truth already present in the world. Their work involved the expression of an existing authenticity, not intervention in a continuing process of change. So they concentrated on elaborating the timeless qualities of the truly human (or the authentically racial), and saw their role in promoting self-contemplation rather than purposive understanding.

Some Marxists had opposed this with an aggressive duality of base and superstructure. This did not necessarily involve the notorious 'determination' of superstructure by base; but from a theoretical point of view it did little to break free from the helplessly positivist (Benjamin, less misleadingly, called it pragmatic) historiography of the nineteenth century. Franz Mehring was an example of this.[40] The activities of the base were stressed as being obviously primary, which relegated superstructural matters to the dismal wastes of the pure cultural heritage. But this left intellectuals, at least in the higher reaches of production, doing little more than stocking shelves in the museum of eternity.

The need was for a methodology which, like dialectical cultural history, saw intellectual activity as united with all other levels of activity, but without engulfing the whole process in metaphysics of spirit. The young Marx had argued against viewing intellectual activities as if they took place on their own level of history. 'There is no history of politics, law, or science . . . of art or religion', he argued in a passage quoted by Benjamin.[41] This was stated more fully in the *German Ideology* itself:

> For materialism ideologies and their corresponding forms of consciousness . . . no longer retain the appearance of autonomy. They have no history, they have no development; it is only that human beings developing their material production and their material organisation [*Verkehr*] also change their thinking and the products of their thinking along with this reality.[42]

So, intellectual history, the site of intellectual practice, had to be identified in the reciprocal dependence of purpose and material impact – 'thinking and the products of their thinking'. Purely natural events are not 'history' because they are not the product of any thinking; pure thinking is not 'history' because it has no product. This principle had to be applied in the understanding of intellectual practice, part of the general dialectical unity of *Technik*.

So, in direct opposition to the traditional view, Benjamin adopted the technological criterion of innovation as the touchstone of intellectual practice. Whereas traditionalism demanded originality and 'novelty', the fresh view of an old truth,[43] Benjamin demanded real innovation as a means of real change. The question that confronted intellectual practice was the same as that confronting any other *Technik*: did it respond successfully to the circumstances of the day? Modern organisation, Bogdanov had argued, was distinguished by the fact that it did not rely on tradition and established custom. The break from habit into critical innovation was the leap into modern *Technik,* a leap that was demanded of ideological *Technik* as much as any other. 'There may be timeless pictures,' wrote Benjamin in a review of a George circle product, 'but there are certainly no timeless theories. Tradition does not decide about them, but only originality. A genuine picture may be old, but a genuine thought is new. It must be of today.'[44] But this innovation is precisely not the random modishness that characterises most intellectual 'advances'; it is innovation that embraces *Technik,* that improves the material apparatus of intervention. 'We are not suggesting spiritual renewal, as proclaimed by the Fascists, but technical innovation.'[45] The Fascists' 'renewal' – 'Germany awake!' – was the extreme low point of an ideology of the autonomous spirit.

Equally, superficial political committedness was entirely irrelevant to effective political intervention. In opposition to Lukács's demand for 'tendentious' left-wing writing, Benjamin declared that such a view missed the basis of serious intervention. Successful 'tendency' could derive only from the 'progress or regress of literary *Technik*'.[46] The productive author had to see that technical progress was the precondition of political progress, and the essence of technical progress was organisational adaptation to the changing means of production.[47] To establish what he meant by this in the area of artistic production we must look first at Benjamin's theory of class, the wider context of all political action.

Intellectuals and class

The technological pole of *Technik,* for Benjamin, implied specific organisational forms at the 'human' pole. The modern industrial proletariat was a function of changing productive technology. The 'progressiveness' or otherwise of a group of people was decided by the degree to which it had adapted to the demands of technical organisation, and in that sense the proletariat was the only progressive class, because it was the only one that, willy nilly, had adapted. Capitalists, who had merely succeeded in clinging to an organisational framework favourable to them were really only a 'class' by virtue of their opposition to the proletariat. So in what sense were intellectuals, and in particular intellectuals who regarded themselves as 'left-wing' or 'progressive', members of a class? Many intellectuals would disclaim any such membership; Karl Mannheim's theory of the 'free-floating intelligentsia' spoke for the attitude of many. But from the point of view of *Technik* such an attitude was obviously unacceptable.

The particular targets of Benjamin's attack were those intellectuals who, '*déclassé*'[48] by changing systems of patronage and intellectual function,[49] sought to make a virtue of this by claiming independence of class relations. This could involve the 'logocracy' of those who believed in 'the rule of intellectuals',[50] or the 'mimicry of proletarian existence'[51] by bourgeois who believed that this kind of ostentatious self-abasement automatically rid them of their background. Both positions involved a repudiation of the bourgeoisie, but combined with a reluctance to establish any adequate link with the proletariat. It was the anarchism of a bourgeois *décadence*. But its only consequence was to expel the intellectual into a classless and history-less limbo, an irrelevant 'private exist-ence'[52] between the great fronts of bourgeoisie and proletariat. 'For there is no more chimeric existence than existence between the class fronts at the moment when they are preparing to clash together.'[53] At best this was a futile reverie; at worst it was the prelude to treachery,[54] such as the treachery of those bourgeois intellectuals in 'one of the most important episodes of the October revolution, namely the sabotage of the new regime by broad masses of the intelligentsia'.[55]

As far as Benjamin was concerned, it was not in the last resort possible for a bourgeois intellectual to repudiate his or her class roots. This was not merely an empirical assertion; it followed from the fact that the very notion of 'an intellectual' reflected organisa-tional principles – the division of theory and practice – which only obtained in the bourgeoisie, the class organisation of capitalism. Intellectuals were at best an 'estate' (*Stand*),[56] said Benjamin, ironically echoing the terminology Fascism introduced to combat the theory of class struggle,[57] a group still integrated in the organ-isation of bourgeois society.

Thus, any attempt by intellectuals to free themselves from the bourgeois apparatus was futile as long as it was based on no more than 'sentiment' (*Gesinnung*).[58] There were, however, two ways in which the bourgeois intellectual could play a revolutionary role. The first was simple destruction. He could be a 'traitor to his class' and work from within for the collapse of the bourgeois appara-tus.[59] In essence this was the character of much of Benjamin's own work, as we have already seen in his notion of the 'destructive character'; and it was his own understanding of the work of many writers he admired highly, such as Siegfried Kracauer, whom he called a 'spoilsport',[60] and Baudelaire, whom he regarded as a 'secret agent against his own class'.[61] But the result of this was liable to be a chimeric existence worth little more than that of the sentimental leftists, an existence whose main result was 'loneli-ness',[62] leitmotif of Benjamin's later years.

There was a more constructive role, and that was as a 'special-ist'. 'Specialists' were not merely an analytical category, but a very real issue in the early years of the Soviet republic; they were those intellectuals who in large numbers sabotaged the regime, but whose help was none the less often indispensable. Lenin's writings of this period repeatedly turned to discussion of the problem.[63] Apart from their political unreliability, bourgeois specialists were from a theoretical point of view obviously undesirable, because they reflected the bourgeois division of labour. As Benjamin emphasised, the aim of future socialist education should be 'polytechnic' education rather than specialisation.[64] None the less, the specialist could be a 'starting point'[65] for what would eventually be the total re-education of the working population. And this was the point at which the bourgeois intellectual could claim a worthwhile and revolutionary function. The advantage of the specialist was that unlike the self-regarding 'free' intellectual, he acknowledged that his work was part of a 'great plan',[66] a wider functional totality. Vain intellectual creativity had no part to play in that perspective; the specialist was no more than an 'engineer' adapting a part of the productive apparatus to the purpose of the proletariat.[67]

Specialisation was dialectically self-consuming. The progress achieved by specialisation in the whole field of *Technik* would, if carried through properly, eventually lead to a 'polytechnic' condition in which everyone was his or her own 'specialist'. It was in Soviet journalism that Benjamin saw this happening most clearly. Specialist bourgeois journalists, once responsible for the 'unrestrained degradation of the word', had handed over their productive apparatus to the polytechnic literacy of reader contributions.[68] The role of the intellectual as specialist was to make himself or herself redundant.

> They can only work with the aim of placing power in the hands of those who will make this peculiar species of human being – which is only a stigma on the despiritualised body of the common weal – disappear as quickly as possible. In other words it is a matter of giving society that unreserved reasonableness, and with it that purpose in each of its innumerable functions, which will liquidate the pathological blockages whose symptom is the existence of intellectuals.[69]

In all this the sad realisation is inevitable that the condition of an intellectual is almost inescapably reactionary. 'For the intellectual's road to radical critique of the social order is the longest, just as the proletariat's is the shortest.'[70] The communist party's hostility towards intellectuals was in the end only too understandable.[71]

Principles of intellectual practice

Despite this rather pessimistic view, Benjamin obviously felt there was a sense in which intellectuals could be fruitfully active, as specialists if not indeed as members of a socialist productive team. But this depended, in his view, on the recognition of certain principles.

In the first place intellectual activity had to have consequences. Bourgeois writers prided themselves on their 'freedom'; but this freedom was only a reflection of their failure to establish any context of active intervention.[72] In the Soviet Union, by contrast, the spread of literacy and the 'literarisation of the relations of life' had meant that 'whatever is thought has consequences', a fact that was reflected in party control of thought.[73] This might not be possible in the West: but political writers had to realise that the task even of lyric verse should be the awakening of 'deliberation and action'.[74] And intellectual production should abandon the privacy of bourgeois speculations; what counted was the 'art of thinking into other people's heads', in Brecht's phrase.[75] Another of Brecht's notions appropriated by Benjamin was that of 'crude thinking' (*plumpes Denken*), a crudity that consisted in the thought's insistent gesture towards practice rather than in its actual content.[76]

Second, progressive intellectual production must organise, in the human sense.[77] Bourgeois thinking was characterised by the fact that it formed cliques (one thinks of the George circle); progressive thought organised political groupings and parties.[78] A piece of writing's 'power to change' could be judged by whether it brought about any 'regrouping'.[79] A writer's principal concern would obviously be to organise those within the same productive area, colleagues within the same *Technik*. Intervention would be directed through them in the first instance. 'An author who does not teach writers anything teaches nobody.'[80] Equally, 'For the critic his colleagues are the highest court of appeal. Not the public. And certainly not posterity.'[81]

In the third place the writers had to abandon the notion of 'the public', and realise that they were writing to organise a class. 'The public' was a degraded and disorganised form of the human collective, the passive consumer of products generated by an individual 'creator'. The masses on the other hand were the raw material of a responsive and collaborative proletariat.[82] Reactionary intellectual organisation counterposed the 'star', or the 'creator' or whoever, to the 'public' as a way of preserving the basic division of theory and practice, active and passive, creator and consumer. The 'public', in that sense, was 'a corrupt condition of the mass', a state that reaction promoted in order to displace the proletariat's proper class consciousness.[83] It was failure to penetrate the mysteries of the mass, the fact that it was a not-yet-organised class, that characterised the extremely defensive attitude of bourgeois writers like Hugo and Baudelaire. Baudelaire separated himself off from the masses as a 'hero'.[84] Hugo understood the masses as a 'public',[85] a group of 'clients'[86] from the *essentially* disorganised and random world of market exchange.[87] Failure to establish the continuity of intellectual *Technik*, the collectivity of production embracing both 'writers' and 'readers', resulted in the degenerate opposition of hero and public.

The final principle observed by the progressive writer was didacticism. 'Is there any genuinely revolutionary writing which does not have a didactic character?' asks Benjamin.[88] Written intervention depended centrally on the didactic character, the most direct way of 'thinking into other people's heads'. More than anywhere, this applied to the specifically academic enterprise. The division of labour had gone so far that even within the theoretical enterprise there was a distinction between the more 'practical' and the more 'theoretical' elements. With the abstract speculations of pure research, subjects such as literary history had lost the instructive purpose which, at their origins in more enlightened times, they still had. 'The crisis of education is closely connected with the fact that literary history has quite lost sight of its most important task – the one it had when it entered life as "science of beauty" – namely the didactic one.'[89] Academic study had to lose its quality of contemplation in museums. The basis of its revival should not be research; on the contrary, research should become the assistant of its revival through the processes of instruction.[90] And in all this, education should see itself as 'revolutionary education for labour' in the first instance, working towards a 'universal readiness for action' which could supersede old bourgeois specialism and the gulf between theory and practice.[91]

Benjamin's principles of revolutionary writing were shared with, perhaps to some extent even derived from, his friend Brecht. But there is no doubt that his general commitment to a 'materialist' intellectual practice, and his critique of the position of the modern intellectual, grew directly from his own experience and development. These resources gave his polemic the extraordinary elegance and vigour which it showed particularly in the work of 1926-32. This may be made clear by the conclusion of his review of Erich Kästner, one 'melancholic leftist' who had the misfortune to fall into Benjamin's net:

> His is the fatalism of those who stand furthest away from the processes of production, and whose dull efforts to identify economic trends [*Konjunkturen,* a pun on astral conjunctions] are comparable with the attitude of a man who submits himself completely to the inscrutable fortunes of his own digestion. Undoubtedly the rumbling in these verses has more to do with wind than with overthrow. Constipation and melancholy have always gone together. But since the juices have been coagulating in the body of society, stuffiness has greeted our every step. Kästner's poems do not improve the air[92].

False consciousness

Benjamin's theory of *Technik* is rooted in a materialist onotology, and this is crucial to his approach to the problem of false consciousness.[93] His position may be followed through in two aspects of his work; his historiography and his theory of social relations. Both of these must be examined briefly in order to disentangle his work from some of the misinterpretations to which it has been subjected. (The specific problem of history in Benjamin's last work will be considered in detail in the final chapter.)

Benjamin's historiography was highly empirical. His opposition to the positivist school and to Prussian historians such as Ranke was not epistemological, but moral and methodological – how could imperialist historians be expected to give an honest account of the world? When Benjamin spoke of history he *was* thinking of 'what actually happened', *not* of the movements of spirit or the reflexive constructions of our contemporary consciousness. He objected to the George school precisely because it was an 'exorcism of history',[94] a failure to establish the disciplined and philological understanding that alone could legitimate concern with the past. Attempts to 'mediate' between the events of the past and the sensibilities of the present were entirely misguided: 'the mediator who starts off with the idea of applying the criteria of the modern reading public (instead of the insights of modern science) is building fragile bridges'.[95] The climax of this tendency in academic historiography was the installation of 'cultural history' as the methodological foundation for 'pragmatic history' (by which here Benjamin meant political and economic history).[96] This trivialisation of the empirical, which Benjamin identified in 1931, has had its modern formulation in the 'universal hermeneutics' of H. -G. Gadamer. But in Benjamin's work cultural events could never be autonomous; they could only be enacted on stages set for them by the material, the economic, the political. This was clear even in the *Trauerspiel* book; and it became more and more prominent with his emphasis on the contextual approach to literary history. 'The existence [of the work of art] in time and its being understood are only two aspects of the same thing.'[97] The relation between the work of art and its historical context constituted its historicity, its significance, and our ability to understand it. Attempts to hijack the work into a safe haven of spiritual values and processes were futile. The obstacles to our understanding of the past were not epistemological, but political. A ruling elite which treated the cultural activities of the past as 'booty'[98] for its present enjoyment could not be expected to understand the dialectic of past or of present. That too was why the only true subject of historical understanding was the 'fighting, oppressed class',[99] the proletariat, which alone acceded to the dialectical demands of the modern age.

The proletariat's (potential) understanding of history was parallel to its position in the world of *Technik*. Private ownership of the means of production had distorted the co-operative patterns of control implied by modern technology. In order to retain this ownership, capitalism had resorted to a number of strategems of which the most important was the division of the world into thinkers and doers, directors and directed, controllers and controlled. And this in turn had been distilled into the reactionary methodologies of idealism. The proletariat was the subject of historical knowledge because every other class had destroyed the world before it set out to understand it. The mandarins of 'cultural history' obliterated the scientific facts of past events under the mists of spirit, and deliberately obscured the precise indicators of organisation and social control given by the hard material world of technology.

If the chains of archaic control systems, and of an ideology subservient to their interests, were broken, then clearly something historically fruitful would have taken place. Benjamin did not always choose the term 'progress' for this. He spoke of the 'awakening',[100] the advent of the Messiah who would only change things very slightly, but in doing so would redeem the entire world.[101] This would be the 'leap under the open sky of history',[102] a leap rather than a progressive step, but a forward move none the less. The procedure by which this happened would, as we have seen, be a matter of destruction rather than refinement. The proletariat was already awake, forced into wakefulness by a system that still withheld the rewards of this condition. It only remained to awaken the remaining classes, and particularly the redundant mass of the petty bourgeoisie, principal scource of a prostituted intelligentsia. And this had to be done by liquidating their false consciousness, their failure, or refusal, to understand the demands of *Technik* and their own historical superfluity. In Benjamin's account, false consciousness was something that did not in the first instance afflict the proletariat, or even the cynical capitalist, the 'real powers', but pre-eminently the petty bourgeoisie.[103] They were the people who were 'whiling away their time' until the day arrived that would plunge them into the labour market with the proletariat.[104] Their historic awakening, once achieved, really would lead to the collapse of capitalism. So it was to them that the revolutionary intellectuals had to turn, like the Talmudic angels who 'sing their hymn . . . and then disappear for ever'.[105] The explanation of the false consciousness that still enveloped the petty bourgeoisie was therefore an 'urgent necessity' for Marxism.[106] It became the focus of Benjamin's later work.

Benjamin's distinction between true and false consciousness, then, was not based on metaphysical considerations but on the political openness of the knower. False consciousness was objectively wrong, and could be dispelled scientifically. Also, the appearance of false consciousness was related to class. Class not only determined the general laws of political and economic behaviour, but also the reliability of consciousness. In that sense, class was crucial to the analysis of intellectual products, and also to the organising of intellectual practice. And finally, productive intervention was a real possibility. Benjamin declined (in the last essays, at least) to call this 'progress', but even there it still constituted real historic advance.[107]

The materialism of Benjamin's notion of false consciousness, and its appeal to 'scientifically' verifiable conditions, has to be stressed, for this is an area of some confusion among commentators. In particular, there was an unfortunate conflict here between Benjamin's ideas and those of Theodor Adorno, his influential literary executor. Adorno's position has been well described elsewhere.[108] Here we need only note that it was professedly 'melancholic' in precisely the sense criticised by Benjamin. Adorno was extremely sceptical about the value of organised political intervention, certainly as institutionalised in the Communist Party. He was also very sceptical about the value of philosophy as systematic practical guidance. The purpose of his theory of 'negative dialectics' was to provide a permanent self-undermining of philosophy, the remorseless recognition that the concept is always inadequate to the object. On both these counts Adorno's melancholia would seem open to objections from Benjamin's work. Adorno's rejection of politics is the Baroque suspicion of the 'intriguer'; and his negative dialectics conflicts with the Brechtian 'crude thinking', interpreted by Benjamin as the thought that indicates the deed. And the whole tenor of Adorno's cultural criticism, luxuriating in symbols and allegories, generates exactly the 'petrified landscape' that Benjamin rejected in the melancholic leftists. It also exhibits the kind of 'logocratic' retreat into the fastnesses of a purely culturalist avant-garde which Benjamin condemned.

Benjamin's theory of false consciousness itself could hardly be attractive to Adorno. Adorno's epistemology could not easily bear a correspondence theory of truth in any form. On the principle of 'mediation' (*Vermittlung*) every phenomenon had to be set in relation to the 'totality', without specification of its particular functional status.[109] Like the early Lukács, Adorno believed that the phantasmagoria of commodity fetishism were not misunderstandings but objective historical categories.[110] Consequently, it was dangerous to distinguish too confidently between the scientifically observable economic law and its false social appropriation. His demand that Benjamin should insert 'more theory'[111] into the Baudelaire essay was essentially a demand for the same scepticism towards the economic which characterised his own work. In the Baudelaire project, in fact, Benjamin did obediently retreat from the extremely empirical approach of the first version and into an 'epistemological' level.[112] This should not mislead us about the continuing sharp historical focus of the essay.

The role of class in Benjamin's theory of false consciousness was inevitably troubling to Adorno. As part of its general diffidence in the area of practical political intervention, the Frankfurt school always felt its 'insight into the historical obsolescence of the theory of the proletariat's revolutionary potential' to be a central plank in its own platform.[113] But as far as Benjamin was concerned, the theory of class formation and the role of the intellectual in it was a crucial theme in the Baudelaire essay and elsewhere.[114] Accordingly, it remained in a subdued form in the second version of the Baudelaire essay. None the less, Adorno did seemingly expunge this disagreeable theme elsewhere, namely in the Reproduction essay. The second version of this, which appeared in all the selections under Adorno's control and subsequently, lacks two crucial passages on the theory of class.[115] According to the editors of the collected works, the second version was produced to impress Brecht, and to 'outdo him in radicalism'.[116] If so, it is strange that Adorno and his successors should always have chosen that version to reprint, rather than the first version or that which appeared in the *Zeitschrift*. But in fact the second version is 'radical' mainly in its obscurity, an obscurity brought about precisely by its omission of passages which Adorno, *not* Brecht, would have found distasteful.

Finally there is the problem of progress. Adorno's rejection of any faith in technological progress was made clear in the *Dialectics of Enlightenment* (1947); doubtless Benjamin was already aware many years earlier of Adorno's suspicions towards any progress except the etherial ones of the musical avant-garde. In the first version of the Baudelaire essay there is no hint of the ambiguous comments about progress that appear in the paralipomena to version two (that is, *Zentralpark)*, and develop into full-scale attack in the 'Theses on History'. Possibly Benjamin thought this apparent change of tack, at least in the Baudelaire project, would placate Adorno while preserving (if obscurely) his own argument.

At all events it is worth noting that he announces the critique of 'progress' in the same early 1939 letter to Horkheimer in which he also announced the move to 'epistemology'.[117]

As far as Adorno was concerned, Benjamin was best restrained in areas of arcane abstruseness. 'You may trust us to . . . make the most extreme endeavours of your theory our own',[118] he invited, trying to point Benjamin away from hardheaded commentary on intellectuals and the class struggle. But Benjamin knew where his concerns lay, and was not put off by Adorno's somewhat condescending insinuations about his understanding of Marxism.[119] As Benjamin replied, with dignity and firmness, he had no interest in 'putting on the wax wings of esotery', and as far as his dialectical materialism was concerned it had nothing to do with tactics or the Institute, but was based on very real political experiences during the previous fifteen years.[120] The fact that Benjamin was not blown off course is revealed in his last review (none of which the *Zeitschrift* published), which continued to assert his rejection of culturalist avant-gardes,[121] and his insistence on real social change[122] guided by a naturalistic understanding of technology.[123]

Myth and tradition

Benjamin's model for the analysis of false consciousness drew heavily on Freud, most obviously perhaps on *Beyond the Pleasure Principle*. As with all of Benjamin's major influences, his debt to Freud tended to be very understated; those occasions, such as the second Baudelaire essay, where he offered explicit commentary on Freud, were very rare. It should be emphasised that Benjamin used Freud strictly as an analyst of pathology. Recent semiotic critics have tended to elevate *Beyond the Pleasure Principle,* in particular, to a transcendental account of consciousness or language formation.[124] Benjamin's position was entirely different. The analysis of dreams, and the child's games in *Beyond the Pleasure Principle* were for him means of access to pathological conditions. In the practical world, human beings wake from sleep, and they grow up to be adults; there was *no* sense in which sleep or childhood could healthily determine that world. Dreams were things to be understood and then forgotten; the child's compulsive repetition had to be dissolved.[125]

Benjamin's use of Freud demanded two things: identification of the patient, and a model for the analysis of pathological indicators. The patient was the social class that had lost its historical role, and therefore no longer had a 'day' it could wake up to.[126] Its ultimate fate had to be proletarianisation; but until this rude awakening it whiled away its time in dreams of an imagined past. It was this 'prehistory', and especially the loving descriptions of it by intellectuals, that supplied the object of Benjamin's 'Freudian' analysis.

The model for Benjamin's analysis was one we have already encountered, namely the mythic anthropology of Klages. This was the framework Benjamin meant when he said that the second Baudelaire essay would concentrate on 'epistemology'.[127] But of course this is not epistemology; it is the pathology of dreams and delusions. Although Benjamin's signposts are clear enough, many commentators have been misled by his loving 'mortification' into thinking that his descriptions of 'tradition', 'memory', 'experience' and the like, and essays such as the one on Lesskov or the second on Baudelaire, were laments for a lost culture. This is mistaken; Benjamin must be read with care and caution.

In Benjamin's view the class that had lost its role was the petty bourgeoisie. The petty bourgeoisie was the class that sustained the division of labour necessary for the maintenance of capitalist property relations. It was a class condemned to the chimeric and transitory role of experts, people who directed what increasingly had no need of direction. The insecurity engendered by their superseded organisational role made them cling convulsively to what they did still have – the pathetic authority of the white collar and the rich fabric of a culture of dreams. But just as their authority was only mimicry of the real authority of property ownership, so also their culture was worn out and second-hand. Like much popular art, it was 'only the debased cultural heritage of a ruling class'.[128] But still it was tended carefully by intellectuals unable to see the uselessness of such cast-offs. Educationalists and the academic world were worst in this respect. They had 'their fetishistic pleasure at the instrument itself, without recognising how unserviceable it is becoming. The real powers that be are however aware of this and hand over the worn out tools without resentment. Of all people, the academic elite should be most able to see through this.'[129]

But Benjamin's polemic against the academic world, although persistent, was incidental to his main theme. This was the identification of the dialectic of consciousness which led eventually to practice in the full sense, i.e. political practice. Benjamin was only interested in those few academics who represented a significant moment in the dialectic; Max Kommerell, the George disciple, was one of those. Benjamin found his best specimens elsewhere. In a three-stage dialectic, the first stage was occupied by writers such as Lesskov, Hebel, Kraus and Kafka, the second by Baudelaire and early Surrealism, and the last by late Surrealism, Bertolt Brecht, and Soviet writers.

The first moment in Benjamin's dialectic of modern intellectual consciousness, as in his earlier work on tragedy and *Trauerspiel,* is mythic, cultic, and religious. Again, Catholicism recurs as a signpost, now augmented by more generalised and explicit attack on 'spiritism', 'occultism' and modern religious esotery.[130] But in this mature project Benjamin's understanding of the first moment revolves around a Freudian theory of anamnesis, now termed remembrance (*Erinnerung*). Remembrance is the non-deliberate relation to the past which we have already met in connection with Klages. It is involuntary recall, the fruit of association and circumstance rather than of purposeful organisation. It operates on an individual and on a social level. On the individual level its medium is 'experience' (*Erfahrung*). 'Experience' is what is constituted not by the deliberate purposeful activity of an individual, but by repetition and habit. It is the medium within which the child's terrible 'primary experiences' are absorbed; and it is the medium through which unconscious and long-sedimented habits form character.[131] It is the content of the Proustian *'mémoire involontaire',* recall activated by arbitrary and unpredictable associations of smell and sound which lead the mind back to forgotten and functionless roots of experience.[132] In Freudian terms, experience is located in the conserving repository of the unintentional memory, the dull determinants of a character not yet integrated into full self-conscious clarity. For intentional memory, the instrument of conscious practice, is destructive, and obliterates the inertly conserved traces of 'experience'.[133]

For Benjamin this was important as a model for archaic ideological activity whose paradigm, he argued, was 'story-telling' (*Erzählen*). Story-telling had a number of characteristics. At a fundamental level it was historically specific and, in the modern world, a fading art.[134] Story-telling depended upon certain kinds of socio-economic formation, such as the craft system,[135] which supplied the right functional setting for this exchange of experience. Technological changes which affected this base, such as the invention of printing[136] and the development of industry,[137] also eroded the social structures necessary for 'story-telling'.

In addition to this, 'story-telling' implied a particular relation between the public and the ideological producer. This was a relation of 'authority'; the story-teller was an 'authority' in the community. Benjamin's account of this drew on suggestions, prominent in Klages and of course Jung, that non-functional anamnesis by individuals would approach elements of experience common to the whole human collective.[138] The most individualistic absorption generated the most general 'experiences'. Three points must be added about this principle. First, the individual mouthpiece of these collective experiences would play the role of an authoritative guru, immune to practical controls such as validation.[139] The authority of such persons rested not on their actions, but on their being.[140] It was an authority that reached out through the depths of the personality, never through rationally controlled criteria of accuracy and consistency.[141] The personality was the organ of pure collectivity, in these terms, and its manifestation was authority.

Second, because the charismatic individual articulated a moment of collective anamnesis, the procedure had an important element of ritual and cult about it. On the level of individual psychology the anamnesis of 'experience' was realised in habituated games and mannerisms.[142] But when this anamnesis was directed towards the anamnesis of collective experience, it generated the social form of remembrance, *Eingedenken*.[143] *Eingedenken* was remembrance on ritual days, the celebration of the general rhythms of a collective past, whose most obvious formalisation was in the calendar of ecclesiastical feasts.[144]

The third point is that Benjamin's evaluation of these phenomena, whether individual or collective, was that of Freud and not that of Klages or Jung. For Klages, as we have seen, anamnesis and involuntary recall were the means of access to higher truths of human existence, a means of overcoming the depradations of the modern intellect. Benjamin, however, reversed this account. Freud's *Beyond the Pleasure Principle* had drawn on studies of shell-shocked soldiers who, it seemed to Freud, were attempting to master their traumatic experiences by obsessively repeating them to themselves. From this he offered two conclusions. First, that a trauma consciously confronted, or 'remembered', was a trauma mastered. And second, that the instinct of repetition was more fundamental even than the principle of pleasure-seeking. An organism, in other words, was more interested in returning to its primal experiences, whether inherited or acquired, than it was in 'progressing' towards maximisation of its own pleasure. The organism, in fact, was innately conservative, and spent (according to Freud) its greatest energies in making sure only that it followed its own course in its own pre-established way. So the shell-shocked patient's compulsive repetition was a pathological variant of the organism's general instinct – to continue towards its own death in its own time and its own way. The instincts operative here were only apparently innovatory; they made 'an illusory impression of forces striving for progress and change, despite only trying to reach an old goal by old or new paths'.[145] But, as Freud made clear, this was 'purely instinctual, as opposed to intelligent, behaviour'.[146] The individual's compulsive protection of its own experiences, its own fate, turned the forces that appeared to be constructive and progressive into no more than the 'escorts of death', as Freud puts it in a memorable phrase.[147]

Repetition, for Benjamin, is the agent of a blind organic existence. In the individual, it is part of the habit-formation which develops in the play of children, and which precedes the deliberate practice of the adult. In the social collective, it is part of the elementary constitution of social forms, the first emergence of ritual from the darkness of mythic fear. But in either case, it is a form of consciousness which must necessarily be overcome. The *Trauerspiel* book gave one instance of this dialectical overcoming. The later work, supported by Freudian and Marxist analysis, gives another.

As Benjamin presented it, the epistemology of primitive anamnesis found in 'story-telling' and other archaic or mythic cultural forms corresponded to rules formulated by Klages. These, as we will recall, relied primarily on the principle of distance, both spatial and temporal. Benjamin's theory of 'aura' was taken directly from Klages. His definition of aura as 'the unique appearance of a distance'[148] is a rendition of Klages's view of anamnesis as non-deliberate and momentary understanding. And, as with

Klages, auratic distance extended along two axes, space and time.

The axis of mythic time was related to the 'primal', which could be either primal experience (in the individual)[149] or primal history (*Urgeschichte*[150] or *Vorgeschichte*[151]). In common with Klages, Benjamin emphasised that the distance of time reached not through the continuum of past and future, but into a 'beyond' situated in death. 'Death is the sanction of all things the story-teller may report. He has borrowed his authority from death.'[152] The 'other side' of death came and went with the cyclical generations of life; the living observed the distant past through an aura of remote authority. To some extent this was literally true: Benjamin pointed, perhaps a little facetiously, to the 'aura' surrounding the sitter on old portrait photographs.[153] (The dialectical twist, of course, is that this appeared for technological reasons.) Also, the 'original' and 'authentic' work of art had an aura,[154] presumably carried with it from the past. But the real site of temporal aura was tradition. Tradition was the bedrock of collective experience which supported the community, and which was articulated in the work of the community's most inwardly individuals. Death was a sanction of authority because it guaranteed the re-entry of the individual into the arms of ancestry, the living tradition which pulsated into the consciousness of the particular momentary now. Respect for tradition was a continuation and reaffirmation of the community's primal emancipation from darkness; it was the repetition which guaranteed the intact individuality of its fate. Collective remembrance was the substance of this tradition. 'Remembrance establishes the chain of tradition which leads on the past from generation to generation.'[155] And charismatic individuals such as the story-teller were the mouthpiece of this remembrance.

The second auratic distance was space. This was really only a synchronic restatement of what was already given in tradition, except that it referred to the orders of present nature rather than of deceased ancestors. These orders appeared in the principles of 'hierarchy'[156] and 'natural history' (*Naturgeschichte*),[157] the view that all created beings have a natural place foreseen for them in the divine arrangement of the universe.[158] This applied to human beings as much as to inanimate objects; in the mythic cosmos they were all distributed along the great ladder of creation stretching from the heights of spirituality to the depths of thingness. Safely fixed to this ladder, collective experience had an identity immune to the shocks caused by death or decline of any part of itself.[159] And with the aid of this scale, the primitive community was able to integrate its repetitious ritual into a world credited with the same fixity. Social relations were as 'natural' as the supposedly preordained relations of things and animals. Benjamin characterised this attitude as 'tact', the ability to treat 'not only the king as though he were born with a crown on his head, but also to encounter the lackey as a liveried Adam'.[160] Meanwhile, the inanimate extremes of this ladder were as interestingly auratic as its spiritual pinnacle, and the world of stones and minerals was as prophetic and as rich in significant correspondences as any other level.[161]

It will not have escaped the attentive reader that Benjamin's account of the mythic world view, particularly his association of the aura with the twin categories of tradition and natural hierarchy, comes close to a somewhat caricatured account of Catholicism and pre-Lutheran Christianity generally. Benjamin had good reason for drawing attention to the Catholicism of Kraus,[162] and for linking Lesskov (the modern 'story-teller') with 'Greek Catholicism'.[163] Lesskov's art, and his world view, were beautiful; but in accordance with Benjamin's theory of beauty, they were beautiful precisely because their historical redundancy was making them fade away.[164] Kraus of course was more contemporary, and in any case not a story-teller. But he still had the same ritualised, preindustrial view of the world, which allowed him to pin his faith on the 'natural' human being,[165] secure in a world in which all creation was a church 'where no more than an occasional breath of incense carried in the mists reminds you of ritual'.[166]

Kafka also belonged in this category for Benjamin, even though there was obviously no connection with Catholicism. None the less, Benjamin saw Kafka as an essentially religious writer, although from a perspective diametrically opposed to that of his more orthodox friend Scholem.[167] While Scholem saw Judaic doctrine as the substantial presence in Kafka's work,[168] for Benjamin it constituted only a painful absence. Kafka's characters persistently alluded to and gestured towards God's ordering law, but they never laid their hands upon it. 'Do we possess the doctrine which is accompanied by Kafka's similes and explained in the gestures of K. and the mimicry of his animals? It is not there; at most we can say that this and that alludes to it.'[169] In a similar way Kafka's attitude towards the primal world, which was implied by his religiosity, was in fact dominated by a kind of vacuum. The orders of the primal world were transposed from the past of tradition into a future of guilt and indictment.[170] So, the elements of this religious view were present in Kafka, but inverted into a desolated modernity, a soteriology of despair. As far as Benjamin was concerned, Kafka's importance was his demonstration, whether deliberate or not, of the bankruptcy of the religious approach as a means of ideological intervention. But it is not surprising that he felt unable to make this explicit to Scholem, who could only protest at the 'flagrant liberties' he saw in Benjamin's account, particularly over the handling of terms such as 'doctrine' and 'the primal world'.[171]

The allegorisation of Technik

Benjamin was mainly interested in the second moment of the dialectic – what he described in connection with the development of Surrealism as 'the overcoming of religious illumination'.[172] This is the moment of the 'threshold',[173] the moment which believes itself to be facing up to a modern secular world, but which is in fact still entangled in the modalities of ritual. The main subject of this historical threshold, as we have seen, is the petty bourgeoisie, the victim of industrial progress. The particular targets of Benjamin's analysis are their ideological producers, the modern urban intellectuals and their productive organisations, especially journalism and universities. Elements of the preceding dialectical moment are retained at the petty-bourgeois stage, and are revived in response to the need for reactionary resistance. Benjamin emphasises that the work of men like Klages, part of reawakening 'ritual and cultic traditions', cannot be dismissed as merely atavistic.[174]

The presence of 'cultic' elements in modern culture has two aspects. According to Benjamin, they usually appeared, as we shall see, cemented into reactionary ideology. But the cultic ecstasy could still be seen as a legitimate form of knowledge, an access to the original dynamics of cultural formations. Klages had recommended the use of drugs as a means of access to primal truths; Benjamin also found this in his studies of Baudelaire[175] and the Surrealists,[176] extended in the latter case by a general interest in the dream world. Benjamin himself experimented with hashish.

The importance of the dream was its blending of the empirical with the non-empirical. This was even more characteristic of the state of ecstasy or intoxication; as Benjamin argued, 'intoxicated persons are "still" aware of real circumstances'.[177] Intoxication had a 'dialectic' which exposed the twin poles of the movement of truth.[178] The opposition of 'reality' and 'ecstasy' might operate one way from one perspective, but reverse its polarity from another. 'Perhaps every ecstasy in one world is disconcerting sobriety in the complementary world?' This was the 'profane illumination' which drugs could help bring about, although, Benjamin remarked, the discipline of religious insight might be more reliable.[179] But both, religion or drugs, were only a propaedeutic (*Vorschule*). Benjamin evidently found such propaedeutic possibilities in Klages's occultism, and in palmistry and Kabbalism. But it is important to bear in mind how he envisaged the function of these disciplines, which was to release the 'revolutionary energies'[180] locked up in ideological formations. 'Profane illumination' revealed the dialectic of the social world, not merely as an anthropology of modern myth, but as a liberation into deliberate practice.

The polarities of this dialectic were *Technik* and 'primal history', and these were combined by false consciousness into ambiguous and indefinite images. The function of critical analysis, as it had been with myth (for example, in the *Wahlverwandtschaften* essay), was to pin down the ambiguity of the images offered,[181] and ultimately to force them to a historical and political release of the energies trapped in their ambiguity. Benjamin's term for this ambiguous stasis was the 'dialectical picture'. In myth, the site of ambiguity was the chaos of the natural symbol. In modern ideology, it was the blend of *Technik* and *Vorgeschichte*, the pre-conscious natural habits of the community. The ambiguity of myth had to be resolved because it blocks ethical responsibility. And the ambiguity of modern false consciousness had to be resolved in order to free the revolutionary energies of political practice. The dialectical picture was the moment of this modern ambiguity, the point at which consciousness crystallised into a rigidified blend of old and new. It was, in a term repeatedly used by Benjamin, the 'threshold' of a new historical era, the desperate hesitation of a community unable to take the step necessary to save its own existence. The task of the analyst was to shatter this hesitation, to break the inhibitions restraining the last step into conscious adulthood. Only in this way could the self-consuming energies of false consciousness be liberated into fruitful progress.

The step into adulthood was the step into *Technik*. The success or failure of a community's assimilation of *Technik* determined its ideological health, and its ability to take control over the conditions of its existence. The subject that was worst at assimilating *Technik* was the petty bourgeoisie because, in terms of Benjamin's understanding of the division of labour and its supersession, *Technik* must eventually destroy the class's functional identity. The ideological consciousness of the petty bourgeoisie showed an exaggerated pathology of the 'threshold', and was most properly the site of the dialectical pictures.

Benjamin incorporated the transition to technical social organisation into his account of anamnesis. The content of 'cultic' anamnesis, and of literary forms like story-telling, was, as we saw, 'experience' (*Erfahrung*). This was obviously not appropriate to technical demands for conscious self-control. In contrast to it Benjamin developed the concept of *Erlebnis*. This also means 'experience', but whereas *Erfahrung* was taken to mean the subliminal experience which the organism absorbs only half consciously and conserves as part of its structures of repetition, *Erlebnis* is immediate and pragmatic response to environmental stimulus. If *Erfahrung* is involuntary and subconscious, *Erlebnis* is deliberate and conscious. And each form of experience, in Benjamin's account, was matched by a corresponding form of memory, that of *Erfahrung* being involuntary, and that of *Erlebnis* being consciously instrumental.[182]

The importance of this distinction, and of the unique form of technical and instrumental memory, was that it corresponded to a change in the technical base. As Benjamin argued, '*Technik* has submitted the human sensorium to a complex training.'[183] And the predominant character of this 'training', as imposed by machinery, was the 'shock'. Modern industrial existence was a never-ending series of shocks to the individual's consciousness, whether from the buffeting of production technology, modern modes of information, or simply the crowds on the city street.[184] Under such conditions the 'shock experience' (*Chockerlebnis*) had become the norm.

This is where the implications of Freud's account of trauma became important. Becoming conscious of experiences which are otherwise conserved subliminally was, in Freud's terms, a means of defence, or of psychic hygiene. For the instinctual consciousness it provided a means of ensuring the continuation of the individual organism along the route prescribed by its primal experiences. But under pathological conditions, as with shell-shocked soldiers, the subliminally conserved trauma was obviously so intrusive that the stability of the whole system was threatened. The traumatic shock of modern warfare had exceeded the powers of this defensive system to preserve an equilibrium. Or, in more general terms, the comfortable mechanisms of habit and ritual repetition had become overloaded.

Now the 'shocks' of modern urban existence, in Benjamin's view, are similar to the shocks of warfare. They may not be traumatic to the same degree; but they do require the same persistent and intent conscious manipulation. The *Erfahrung* of instinctual conciousness deals only with the mild cycle of events in a craft-based society. Habit and ritual are quite enough to direct responses in that sort of setting. but the shocks and transformations induced by industrial technology throw the subject into a position where only constant alertness can parry the thrusts of the environment. The modalities of *Erfahrung* are not longer adequate; the environment of the city must be instantaneously processed through the defensive deliberations of *Erlebnis*. And all the dreaming poetic delights of the older form have to fall victim to this changeover. 'For the shock to be caught like this, parried by consciousness, the incident which sets it off has to acquire the character of an *Erlebnis* ... This means it would sterilise the incident for poetic *Erfahrung,* incorporating it directly into the registers of conscious memory.'[185]

Despite the fact that it 'shocks', there should be no reason why the modern technological environment should not be assimilable by social consciousness. The *Erfahrung* of an earlier age was rooted in social structure; it should be equally possible for the 'training' of contemporary *Technik* to estatlish the appropriate form of *Erlebnis*. But this does not happen The most common response to *Technik,* at least among the most ideologically productive classes, was interpreted by Benjamin as repression *(Verdrängung)*. In Benjamin's view this Freudian category supplied the best model for the understanding of false consciousness. And no class was more alienated from the realities of its existence, and more rich in repression of all kinds, than the office worker, archetype of the modern petty bourgeoisie. In his response to *Technik* and urban life could be seen the dismal extent of modern social repression. Benjamin assembled descriptions and pictures of the urban petty bourgeoisie in the nineteenth century and noted how, on the street, they were seen to give the impression of exaggerated uniformity, while at the same time their dissociated motions made an impression of 'half-drunk, wretched individuals'. In their abrupt gestures they imitated 'both the machinery as it batters the raw material and economy as it batters the commodity'.[186] That was the full extent of their assimilation of technology.

Meanwhile, this class sought to make ideological sense of its position, straddling the threshold of a new historical age. It did this with the aid of various sorts of dreamlike 'double exposure' (*Überblenden*)[187] in which the bitter realities of modern life were embedded among the elements of a pre-history of *Erfahrung*. The most obvious example of this was in utopian writing. Such writing mixes 'nature' with *Technik* without considering the ways in which nature has to be dependent on *Technik*. Like Kraus's moralism, it is rooted in a naive faith in the 'natural' order. As a result, popular utopias such as Micky Mouse and Jules Verne flee into a realm of unlimited technological possibility, in which everything is juggled around except for the social consciousness at the 'natural' centre. In Verne's novels, for example, 'it is still only little French or English rentiers who are whizzing around space in the craziest vehicles'. And the world of Disney cartoons, Benjamin commented, was 'full of wonders which not only exceed those of technology, but which make fun of them'. Only Paul Scheerbart, a science fiction writer much admired by Benjamin, was capable of imagining a human world whose radical difference matched that of its technology.[188]

The same thing could be found at a more theoretical level in the utopianism of Fourier and the Saint-Simonistes. Although these utopias were socialist, they were blind to the organisational implications of their technicist fantasies. So, in their dreams the future appeared 'wedded to elements of primal history, that is to say the classless society'.[189] Despite his interest in machinery, Fourier was able to produce no more than the 'colourful idyll of Biedermeyer' when it came to social organisation. And the Saint-Simonistes glorified the processes of commodity exchange, but without understanding the organisational and class structure on which it was founded. 'Alongside their share in the industrial and commercial enterprise of the mid-century stands their helplessness in questions affecting the proletariat.'[190]

The 'failed assimilation of *Technik*' [191] appeared in a variety of more concretely technological forms which were also characterised by the 'double exposure' of *Technik* and primal history. Architecture and its use of modern materials such as iron were an example of this. Iron, Benjamin contended, was a material whose functional efficacy had the power radically to change the scope of building. But 'construction takes on the role of the subconscious'; and the French Second Empire saw in this technology a means for 'renewing' architecture along the lines of ancient Greece.[192] Although architecture was already beginning at this time to 'grow out of art' because of new technical resources,[193] it was only a century later that it finally met the organisational consciousness needed to exploit them. (Benjamin was presumably thinking of the socialist architects of the *Bauhaus*.)[194]

Film and photography were in a similar position. The great advantage of the photograph was its value as information; its ability to reproduce accurately, and in many copies, was not accessible to other media. In comparison with the photograph painting, which like the 'story' carries the traces of its producer's subjectivity,[195] came to seem suspect as a reliable vehicle of information.[196] The photograph meanwhile appeared as a means of extended discovery and control of the world.[197] The only response open to traditionalists was to impugn the value of photography as 'art'. But then, as for iron in architecture or for the *Erlebnis* of the city poet, 'art' was no longer a historically relevant category. It was a jurisdiction the photographer had overthrown.[198] Despite this, the growing popular predilection for photographic portraiture forced the 'traditions' of artiness back into photographic style, first with the paraphernalia of studio props,[199] and later even with an artificial rendering of the 'aura' caused in early photography by primitive technology.[200]

The film, as Benjamin concluded during his visit to Moscow, was an even more powerful basis for retraining the human sensorium. 'With it there really does emerge a new region of consciousness.' In particular, it was a matter of collective self-portraiture and control by the proletarian masses. The film, unlike any preceding medium, was able to abandon illusory individualism and portray the 'architectonic' nature of mass movements.[201] As such, in Benjamin's view, it might emerge as a primary instrument in the developing class consciousness of the proletariat.[202] The vast technology of film was able to achieve what more primitive 'artistic' representations never could – a view of reality entirely devoid of intrusions by the 'artist'.[203] This objectivity, with its devastating reproduction of the mass movement, was a fundamental break in the means of ideological production. And yet, as with photography, this was resisted by reaction, the main technique being to bring in the polarity of 'star' and 'public', thus breaking down the film's potential for representation of the masses themselves.[204]

It is evident that for the intelligentsia this 'growing out of art' poses considerable difficulties. It is an ideological focus of the difficulties facing the petty bourgeoisie generally, a class caught between the owners of the means of production and labour itself, relegated to the increasingly redundant role of administrators. On the ideological level this difficulty is focussed on the problem of the obsolescence of art.

Bogdanov had argued that 'science, prose and poetry' all had their origins equally in myth, the most primitive of mankind's instruments for storing and organising knowledge.[205] In this sense, poetry and the exact sciences shared the same starting point and were still progressing in parallel towards the same goal of enlightened self-control. From that perspective, art and science would both be purged of mythic remnants as they extended their control over the world.

In Benjamin's account, this development is implied by the principle that all human activity, and thus both art and science, take place in the medium of *Technik,* the 'second nature' which humanity creates and to which it must adapt. In primitive societies *Technik* is still entangled in ritual. But historical development is the emancipation of all kinds of *Technik,* from the half-conscious repetition formulae of ritual into the fully conscious realm of practice – specifically, political practice.[206]

Now there is obviously a strong suggestion in Benjamin's argument that 'art' is not a category that has any relevance to contemporary practice. The modalities of pre-industrial art – authority, tradition, aura – are no longer accessible to a world whose 'experience' has changed from *Erfahrung* to *Erlebnis.* In modern social conditions *Erfahrung* can only be produced 'synthetically', as Benjamin remarked in connection with Proust's great novel.[207] Nor was the category of beauty any help in this.[208] Beauty, as we saw in Benjamin's early aesthetics, was an attribute of things that fade and decline. It could be claimed for the fading art of the story-teller, but that was precisely because it was fading and no longer a viable proposition in modern practice. As a practice, art was never in the business of producing beauty, even if beauty might in some remote future be ascribable to a work. And now especially, in an era of technical reproduction, 'beauty has no place'.[209]

What is more, the whole notion of 'art' looked increasingly like another aspect of the reactionary refusal to assimilate modern technology. The basis of the pre-industrial work of art, as we saw, was its individual articulation of communal *Erfahrung,* its 'embeddedness in tradition'.[210] The artist was an ecstatic medium of the general truth, bearer of an authority conferred by the power of tradition speaking through him or her. And the community was the passive recipient of these revelations.

But the whole tendency of modern ideological *Technik,* as Benjamin saw it, was away from this individualistic focus, this celebration of a privileged subjectivity, and into clear and objectively rendered collectivity. The modern person was suspicious of the traces of subjectivity that clung to traditional media. And the 'natural' distance of creative authority no longer played a role in modern ideological technology.[211] Actors in front of the film cameras felt themselves directly accessible to the observing masses, who had an interest in 'controlling' or 'supervising' them (*kontrollieren* means both).[212] and the entire productive relations of film[213] and journalism[214] pressed for collectivist transformation in which individual 'stars' and 'authors' were submerged by the fluid universality of information.

But of course all this was resisted by intellectuals unwilling to give up the authority conferred upon them, as ideological administrators, by traditionalist theory. This could be seen in two areas, in the response of the boffins of culture and in the response of artists themselves. The clearest examples of a direct political mobilisation of traditionalism was in the late nineteenth century with phenomena such as Art Nouveau and *L'art pour l'art.* Both movements used the principles of 'nature' and of the authoritative individual to rescue the autonomous preserve of ritual. Art Nouveau was the response of an art 'besieged in its ivory tower by *Technik*',[215] resisting the advance of a changed environment with the aid of subjective inwardness and symbols of 'natural' purity such as the flower. And the theory of *L'art pour l'art* was among the most crass instances of bourgeois false consciousness, generating as it did the notion of 'cultural history', a purely chimeric sequence with no real content except eternally recurring novelty.[216]

But even more than this, theories such as *L'art pour l'art* threatened to push the ideological formation back again behind even the relative secularisation it had achieved in forms such as the story, and into a realm of outright cult and ritual. *L'art pour l'art* was a 'theology of art', Benjamin claimed.[217] It is true that the work of art with its 'auratic' form of existence never really emancipates itself from 'parasitic' dependence on ritual; but this dependence is re-emphasised in a reactionary way as soon as 'beauty' is brought in to deputise for the original cultic quality. Cult value, the basis of the original totemic object's ritual status, is converted in secular art into 'beauty'.[219] And this becomes ever clearer as bourgeois cultural history turns to the 'worship of beauty as a secularised ritual'.[220] 'It is instructive to see', Benjamin remarked of the cultural historians, 'how the attempt to incorporate film into "art" forces these theorists to interpret cultic elements into it with unprecedented abandon.'[221]

The response of artists themselves showed greater sensitivity towards the changing environment, but in the end a similar reluctance to face up to the social demands of *Technik*. Baudelaire, for example, recognised that the modern poet no longer had an *'auréole'*,[222] a loss which Benjamin evidently understood as the loss of the cultic minister's charismatic authority. This unfrocking of the charismatic minister was made even more explicit in Baudelaire's uncompromising comparison of the writer with the whore.[223] Apollinaire's speculation about the 'murdered poet', similarly, was understood by Benjamin as a vision of the coming general 'pogrom of the lyricists',[224] a drastic formulation of the fact that the social constitution of imperialism made the position of intellectuals more and more difficult – until, that is to say, they woke up to the political dimensions of the problem.[225]

None the less, Baudelaire, and even socialists like Hugo, were unable to penetrate to the political roots of their own position, the problem of the division of labour.[226] This theme is fundamental to

Benjamin's understanding of the reactionary nature of French nineteenth-century intellectual life which, even in its most actively political form, never got beyond the conspiratorial putschism of Blanqui.[227] Benjamin found a positively Klagesian version of double exposure in Victor Hugo's reactionary view of social relations. Faced with the 'impenetrable darkness of the masses' existence',[228] Hugo could see in the urban proletariat nothing more than the natural force of the 'crowd' (*Menge*).[229] Accordingly, he imposed upon it the same animistic vision which in Klages links the individual with the crowd of ancestors. For Hugo, the crowd had the existence of a 'world of spirits'[230] to which he, the poet, ministered. He was one 'genius' in a great assembly of geniuses who were his ancestors;[231] and this vast extent of spirits was organised as his 'public',[232] the passive recipients of his charismatic utterances. As Benjamin asked, 'Can any reliable revolutionary assessment correspond to this view of the suppressed masses as a crowd?'

Baudelaire also was unable to penetrate the 'social illusion' which became manifest in the notion of 'crowd'.[233] In contrast with Hugo's democratic laicism, Baudelaire disliked the crowd even though it fascinated him. And while Hugo sought a spiritual communion with it, Baudelaire confronted it as a 'hero', a lonely individual who, like the fencer, moves through the crowd defending himself against the shocks it inflicts upon him. And the image of this heroic individuality was founded on the same false consciousness as the bourgeois apologia for the division of labour generally. In this instance it was the 'superstition of creativity'.[234] Quoting Marx, Benjamin commented that over-estimation of the 'dignity of labour' led to serious misrepresentation of social relations. Labour could not be effective without concrete means of production, and while that was in the hands of the capitalist, nothing was changed, however much the dignity of the labourer might be celebrated. 'It is all the more dangerous because, in flattering the self-esteem of the producer, it offers excellent protection for the interests of a social order which is hostile towards him.' So the poet's belief that his creative labours are, so to speak, all contained in the confines of his own cranium is just politically naive. Baudelaire's concept of the hero was, in Benjamin's view, one aspect of this glamorisation. His peripatetic existence in hotel rooms, with a minimum of books and equipment, and without access to substantial historical knowledge, was another aspect.[235] Baudelaire's admired street hustler[236] was in danger of being no more than ignorant and helpless. And the 'creative artist' was a ghost so long as he or she had no access to the means of ideological production.

With Baudelaire, in fact, we return once more to the false allegorical consciousness Benjamin identified in the *Trauerspiel* of the Baroque.[237] It is the melancholy of a mind which has evacuated things of sense and meaning, cutting away the ground from under human practice. Baudelaire is suspended within the same tension as the Baroque melancholics. On the one hand, the world of objects is frozen by an allegory in which things mean anything and nothing; and on the other hand, the political intriguers weave their senseless schemes.[238] Baudelaire's poetry was 'putschistic'[239] because, as with Blanqui's professional conspirators,[240] it could never burst the confines of its own intellectualism. Both were crippled by a division of labour which splits the cosmos, a rift which forever thwarted unifying practice.

In Baudelaire this was visible principally in his allegory, where the double exposure of the petty bourgeoisie reached a high point.[241] Just as the utopianism of popular ideology was a blend of modern *Technik* with the 'nature' of primal dreams, so also Baudelaire's notion of the 'modern' was a constant revival of the 'antique'.[242] 'It is precisely the "modern" which always cites primal history.'[243] Benjamin made particular mention of Charles Meryon, an artist much admired by Baudelaire, whose etchings of modern Paris 'brought out the antique countenance of the city without forfeiting a single cobblestone'.[244] And these allegorical visions, as in the Baroque, were heavy with a 'significance' demanding 'interpretation'.[245] But, as in the Baroque, the rich multivalence of allegory's significance crushed the objects it grasped; the city, like the face of nature, was frozen into rigidity,[246] a 'mimesis of death'[247] similar to the Hippocratic death mask produced by the Baroque. And ultimately, even the practising individual, the 'hero', was deprived of a meaningful stage. 'For the modern hero is not a "hero" – he is an actor acting a hero. The heroic "moderne" reveals itself to be a *Trauerspiel* in which the role of the hero may be handed out at random.'[248] Baudelaire's inability to penetrate beyond regard for his own illusory creativity, or to conceive of what social practice might genuinely be, was shown most pitifully in his description of the stones in the barricades of the 1848 uprising as 'magical'. 'It may be conceded that these stones are "magical",' comments Benjamin, 'since Baudelaire's poem has no knowledge of the hands which set them in motion'.[249]

The politicisation of art

But Baudelaire and Hugo were part of a nineteenth-century melancholy now long past. The false consciousness evident in their work and that of other would-be progressives such as Fourier had been appropriated by an ideology of infinitely greater sophistication and menace. Benjamin's 'mortification' of departed Parisians had a very real and urgent purpose – the combating of the ideology of Fascism. Fascism, the militant alliance of the owners of capital with the petty bourgeoisie, could call on enormous resources of philosophical support, precisely because the institution of the 'intelligentsia' was *fundamentally* joined to the existence of the petty bourgeoisie itself. The division of labour represented in the intellectual estate was an ideological summation of the economic situation of the petty bourgeoisie. And to the extent that philosophical resources were concentrated in the hands of this estate, they would all be invested in the petty bourgeoisie's struggle for survival. The mobilisation of the German academic world in 1914 and 1933 was a natural consequence of the circumstances within which that world first developed – as the co-opting of petty bourgeois ideological production by capital from 1870 or so onwards.

The sheer political dimension of what is commonly saluted as modern German philosophy was bitterly apparent to Benjamin, and all the more because he was so aware of the loneliness of the fight. As far as he was concerned, left-wing 'tendency', or superficial obeisances to Marxism, were all more or less dishonest window-dressing unless the essential integration of 'intellectuals' in the petty bourgeoisie was recognised. Before it could be anything else, the struggle of anti-fascist intellectuals had to be institutional and organisational. Starting at the level of theory led straight to left-wing melancholia, the cruellest mockery of any real political engagement. And these were not abstract moral strictures, for Benjamin was surrounded by weaker brethren who adopted the course he knew he must not take. These were, indeed, tough demands, for the requirement that the intellectual should abandon his own class, the petty bourgeoisie, and follow the proletariat was perhaps the modern equivalent of Jesus and the man of good family. 'For the intellectual's road to radical criticism of the social order is the longest, just as the proletarian's is shortest.'[250]

Benjamin's work during the exile was, at bottom, a sustained attempt to mobilise intellectuals against the subtle menace of Fascism. His writings of that time offered a clear summary of the nature of that menace, and also of the means for combating it.

The organisational basis of modern reactionary ideology was the 'phantasmagoria of "cultural history"', in which the bourgeoisie relishes its false consciousness'.[251] Since the end of the last century this phantasmagoria had in Germany been tended by *Lebensphilosophie* and its successors, notably Dilthey and, later, Klages and Jung, 'who has made his commitment to Fascism'.[252] Their concern was to identify '"true" *Erfahrung*', which they sought in all the categories comprehensively elaborated in Klages's cosmology. 'They did not, understandably, start with man's existence in society. They appealed to literature, even more to nature, and in the end their preference was for the mythic age.'

The organisational force of this ideology was its absolutising of the division of labour. Its most direct means towards this end was the 'fetish of the master's name',[253] an obsessive insistence on the cultic opposition between inspired creator and passive community. The arrangement of 'cultural history' around a sequence of artistic geniuses, and the determined dichotomisation of the 'great name' and his 'public' are aspects of this. It received further elaboration in the polarity of a private *'intérieur'*, characterised by Benjamin as the last 'refuge for art',[254] and the disorganised crowds in the city streets outside. This notion of the 'crowd', like the 'public', was a reactionary refusal to take account of the constitution of the masses by economic *class*.[255] In fully developed Fascism, which went to enormous lengths to combat the theory of class struggle with alternative and less dangerous accounts of social grouping,[256] the 'artistic' view of the masses reached grotesque proportions. The crowd on the street is, essentially, no more than a random collection of customers involved in commodity exchange; their class identity is not clear. But the achievement of Fascists with their vast 'collections' (Benjamin refused to call them 'rallies') was to transfigure this random association of customers with the aid of the spurious categories of 'nature': 'They rationalise the coincidence of the market economy, which leads them together in this way, as "fate" in which the "race" comes to itself again.'[257] Earlier theories of the 'public' were simply false consciousness. But in Fascism Benjamin saw a deliberately engineered attempt to disorganise proletarian class organisation by means of competing theories of race, 'estate', and indeed also sex and age (although Benjamin himself did not discuss these other fake forms of 'natural' grouping).

Benjamin's resistance covered all aspects of the reactionary ideological programme. 'Cultural history' was obviously unacceptable as a means of organising resistance. What reactionary ideologists hypostatised as 'culture' was in historical actuality scattered across the whole extent of human practice, and thus inseparable from the political context of that practice.[258] Benjamin proposed a 'new barbarism'.[259] 'For what use is all this educational material to us if *Erfahrung* does not connect us with it?' Apart from the ritualistic petty bourgeoisie, modern people were 'fed up' (*übersatt*) with culture,[260] they wanted to break free from devalued *Erfahrung* and start again at the beginning, making a clean sweep.[261] The best that history could do was to be 'destructive' and rid mankind of the lifeless burden of 'culture'. Reactionary cultural history 'certainly increases the burden of treasures which accumulate on the shoulders of mankind. But it does not give it the strength to shake them off so that it could take them in its hands.'[262] The contemplations of the conserver had to be replaced by the penetrating gaze of political consciousness. Only this could bring to life the powers slumbering in the objects of the past. 'The trick which conquers this world of things – it is more appropriate to speak of a trick than a method – consists in exchanging the historical view of the past for a political one.'[263]

The landscape of culture was obviously being changed by the developments of *Technik*. We have already seen Benjamin's views on film. But the clearest contrast between old and new was for him in architecture. The new building material glass had no aura (according to Benjamin) and it was the enemy of secrecy and property.[264] It had made the secretive subjectivity of the bourgeois *intérieur* impossible. 'Living in a glass house is a revolutionary virtue *par excellence* . . . Discretion about personal things has,

from being an aristocratic virtue, become more and more an affair
of the parvenu petty bourgeoisie.'[265]

But the most serious response to the ideological structures of
Fascism lay in dismantling the division of labour. The notions of
creativity and personality had to be abandoned without remorse.
The intellectual as specialist did his or her duties as commissioned,
unconcerned about the false rewards of name and authorship, and
looking forward to the day when there would be no such thing as a
distinct intellectual 'estate'. The neat elegance of cultured creativity was an illusion:

> Only those who avoid commission and control are that creative.
> Commissioned and controlled work – its model; political and
> technical work – produces dirt and waste, intervenes destructi-
> vely in its materials, has an exploitative attitude towards what it
> has produced, is critical of its conditions and is in everything
> quite the opposite to that of the dilettante who basks in creativ-
> ity.[266]

The revolutionary intellectual's ability to assist the proletariat
depended on his or her willingness to give up the natural estate of
'intellectual', 'artist', or whatever. 'Is not the interruption of his
"artistic career" perhaps an essential part of his [political] function?' Benjamin asked in connection with the politicisation of the
Surrealists.[267] The careers of writers like Breton and Aragon
supplied Benjamin with a basis for reflection on his own political
development, from eroticism to politics, from petty bourgeois
intellectual to revolutionary specialist:

> The petty bourgeois who has resolved to take his libertarian and
> erotic aspirations seriously ceases to present the idyllic aspect
> which Chardonne welcomed. The more resolution and deter-
> mination he brings to those claims, the more certainly he must
> come to politics . . . And at that moment he ceases to be the
> petty bourgeois he once was.[268]

3
The Revolution – Utopia or Plan?

The problem of the *Theses on History*

As we have seen, Benjamin was deeply shocked by the outbreak of the First World War, and especially by the desertion of his youth movement friends to the banners of militarism. August 1914 was followed by a prolonged gap in the production of the previously prolific Benjamin – a silence only broken by the semi-mystical commentary on Hölderlin during that winter.

At the outbreak of the Second World War a similar process took place. Benjamin's horror of war, this time intensified by a conviction that it would result in a gas campaign and the extinction of civilisation,[1] drove him once more to frozen despair. And again, the outbreak of the war was made infinitely worse by his supposed friends' acquiescence in the carnage. Previously, it had been the turncoats of the youth movement. Now, it was the Bolshevik state. As late as 1938, Stalin's Red Armies had represented a hope against the menace of the political future.[2] Benjamin held to this hope until the very end, seemingly even after the arrest of Asja Lacis by the Soviet authorities that year.[3] The breaking point was the act of war itself, the Nazi-Soviet pact of 23 August 1939 which made possible Hitler's assault on Poland a week later. This was the event that finally and abruptly swept from Benjamin's mind any faith in Bolshevism, and that inspired his last work, the famous 'Theses on the Philosophy of History'.[4]

The status of the Theses within Benjamin's work, however, is unclear. They were his last piece of writing (apart from a short review),[5] and have from the beginning been presented as his 'testament',[6] with all the authority and finality associated with such a notion. Even though the text is clearly fragmentary, and Benjamin himself indicated that he did not think it suitable for publication,[7] it has appeared in all the major Benjamin selections from 1955 onwards (unlike other completed writings of the period, such as the first Baudelaire essay and the unpublished *Zeitschrift* reviews). Benjamin's editors have sought to emphasise that the text is the theoretical keystone of the massive 'Arcades' project,[8] and to present it accordingly as the essential distillation of his philosophy. Regular re-publication has helped consolidate its standing among commentators, who almost invariably take the Theses as a starting point.[9] It is probably fair to say that the Theses are still generally accepted as the flagship of Benjamin's theoretical enterprise.

This assessment of the Theses is consistent with the views of Benjamin's literary executors Adorno and Scholem, who, whatever their other differences, were agreed on this point. It is clear, however, that their assessment draws on somewhat doubtful premises. For example, there is the vexed question of continuity. Despite the Theses' seductive status as 'last work', and the undoubted breadth of their theoretical prescriptions, it is by no means clear that they do what it is suggested they do – namely, provide the theoretical completion for Benjamin's preceding writings. In Adorno's editorial policy the Theses were always associated with the so-called 'Theological-Political Fragment', and the two texts have commonly appeared juxtaposed in selections.[10] But although there are undoubtedly continuities between them, the force of this is greatly weakened by the fact that the 'Fragment' is almost certainly a very early text and not, as Adorno maintained, from around 1937.[11] So the suggestion that the Theses are the theoretical complement of the mature work is not supported by their affinity with the 'Fragment'.

Scholem responded to this difficulty by linking the Theses with a fragment that definitely was contemporary, the 'Agesilaus Santander' of 1933.[12] But the theoretical content of this semi-autobiographical fragment is extremely slender, and the 'continuity' that Scholem seeks to demonstrate between it and the Theses[13] cannot really be said to go beyond the level of certain recurrent motifs, and certainly does not establish Benjamin's adherence to the 'mystical tradition'.

At the same time, certain obvious continuities between the mature work and the Theses are ignored by both Adorno and Scholem in their attempts to extricate Benjamin from the class struggle. These are the Theses' direct citations of recent work, in particular the important passage from the Fuchs essay[14] and the critique of social-democratic hypostatisation of 'labour', which is drawn from the first Baudelaire essay.[15] In addition, the Theses' motif of the 'wind' of history,[16] which Scholem links only with the apparently religious 'Santander' fragment, occurs in at least two other places in a very secular context.[17]

But with all these continuities, whether one is disposed to take those of Adorno, Scholem, or dialectical materialism, there remains the underlying problem that the Theses are an idiosyncratic and rather isolated text. Like the Hölderlin commentary written in the first winter of the First World War, the Theses are a meditation inspired by the sudden collapse of valued organisations. Scholem, in fact, was quite clear about the considerable alterations in Benjamin's attitudes at the end of his life. The Theses, he argued, were a reaction to the specific historical event of the Hitler-Stalin pact;[18] the motif of the angel, and Benjamin's thinking generally, had been 'reorientated' *(umfunktioniert);*[19] and the view of secular history expressed in this final text was, in Scholem's assessment, 'melancholic, indeed desperate', and directed its only hopes towards a 'leap into transcendence'.

Benjamin himself commented that the Theses were a response to the new constellation of factors brought about by the war.[20] He fully expected them to be surprising to those familiar with his previous work, and perhaps even confusing *(beirrend).* They were thoughts he had kept concealed 'for some twenty years', not only from others, but even from himself. He was anxious that they should not be published in that form since they would lay themselves wide open to 'enthusiastic misunderstanding'.[21] He had, at a preparatory stage, viewed them as the 'theoretical apparatus for the second Baudelaire essay'; but later on it is clear that Benjamin himself did not see any very direct relation between the Theses and his recent work. The Theses were essentially something distinct, and in important respects a leap back in time to 1919 and 1920, when he had, among other things, probably written the 'Theological-Political Fragment' so prized by Adorno.

It is on this basis, rather than on the somewhat facile assumption that the last text must be the conclusive one, that we should consider the role of the Theses in Benjamin's work generally.

Utopianism and Benjamin's work

The most profound problem posed by the Theses is their apparent utopianism. This is a problem because although both Adorno and Scholem claimed this as a tendency underlying all of Benjamin's work,[22] there are many instances in earlier pieces where utopianism is expressly criticised.[23] And beyond this, it should have emerged from our own commentary that the overall development of Benjamin's thought, from the 'Critique of Violence' onwards, is away from utopianism.

Utopianism may be defined as the view that there is a fundamental discontinuity between the world as we know it and any world that is good for human beings. Utopias are not of our place or of our time. This is indicated by the title of Thomas More's book, and in all other utopian fantasies, from the *New Atlantis* onwards, which are located in different spaces from ours. Such a position almost unavoidably entails a dualistic metaphysics. Utopianism presupposes, if it takes itself seriously, that it can spin a new world from conceptuality alone, free from the empirical givens of the old one. It presupposes that the laws and regularities it attributes to a world in a different space or time can successfully be isolated from the processes within which they appear in this world. It presupposes that the imaginings of the utopianist's intellect are self-contained, and not dependent on material experience of this present condition.

This may have various consequences. Politically, it results in the belief that an individual or group may legitimately, and with some prospect of success, impose enlightenment on the world without regard for prevailing conditions. The 'decisionism' of Carl Schmitt, and the anarchism of Benjamin's 'Critique of Violence', are of this nature.

Philosophically, it results in agnosticism of some kind, the assertion that matter and knowledge never fully coincide. This could be a version of Kantianism, based on the view that the categories of knowledge are the property of the subject, and not of the thing itself. This can then be extended into the idea that it is permissible to speculate on the basis of the categories alone, without having regard for specific material co-ordinates of time or space. Adorno's 'negative dialectics' is a kind of pessimistic inversion of this; for him it was precisely the eternal *failure* of the mind to grasp its object adequately that made it legitimate for the mind to extend itself beyond the brutally empirical. Only in utopianism could the mind break its enslavement to a failed conception of the object, and thus potentially be *more* realistic than in drab delusions of empiricism. It is from this background that Adorno tries to see in Benjamin 'the paradox of the possibility of the impossible'.[24]

In theology, utopianism is an expression of theistic idealism. Within the Christian or Judaic traditions, it is the belief that creation can enter a new life through the redeeming intercession of the Messiah. 'Then I saw a new heaven and a new earth, for the first heaven and the first earth had vanished . . . Then he who sat on the throne said, "Behold! I am making all things new!"'[25] The messianic age is the age when all things are 'redeemed' by entering into the divine truth of themselves, the truth which until that point had been vitiated by the presence of an evil matter. It is the time when the 'idea' and the 'object' finally become identical. For both Adorno and Scholem, Benjamin's technique is precisely this utopian illumination of the empirical object, its representation as it finally will be 'in the condition of redemption'.[26]

Now it is clear that the Theses are not *explicitly* utopian in any of these senses. At a first reading, indeed, there is little to indicate any great divergence from the Bolshevik themes of other mature writings. Certainly the themes of historical materialism,[27] of class struggle[28] and of revolution,[29] are fully in evidence. The overall purpose, it is clear, is to construct a notion of 'history' from which the oppressing class and its historians will no longer be able to draw comfort. The Theses take over from the Fuchs essay the task of uncovering the barbarity that permeates cultural history's 'processes of transmission'.[30]

But there is an obvious widening of the target for Benjamin's criticisms. Benjamin's notes list all the old enemies against whom he had for years directed his attacks: cultural and literary history, 'universal history', empathic history, the 'appreciation'.[31] But these are joined by a whole new category, that of 'progress', and as part of it, specifically, 'the theory of progress in Marx'.[32] Benjamin explains: 'There [in Marx] progress is defined by the development of the forces of production. But human beings, or the proletariat, are part of these. Because of that, the question of the criterion [that is, of progress] is only pushed back a step.' 'Scientific socialism' had relied for its calibration of human affairs on the 'objectivity' of materially quantifiable things: technology, machinery, economic statistics. But, says Benjamin, the quantifiable elements of the 'forces of production' are ultimately inseparable from the human component; and thus 'progress' can still not be defined until there is a criterion for that final and most essential factor. Failure to see this results in a technocratic ideology which is evident in Fascism, but, worse, appears earlier still in socialism.[33]

For readers accustomed to Benjamin's theory of *Technik* this may seem a rather startling change of viewpoint. Not only that, however. To build up his critique of progress Benjamin turns to a set of theoretical resources which had seemed long superseded by his own development. They are concentrated on the theory of *Jetztzeit,* or 'Now-Time', which is the heart of these last theoretical speculations and the principal basis for his commentators' attribution of utopianism. To find affinities to *Jetztzeit* in Benjamin's own work we have to go back many years. One is his early notion of 'topicality' *(Aktualität).* Topicality, as has been pointed out, is used as a technical term by Benjamin.[34] This technical sense, however, is generally confined to the earlier work, and the word is later used mainly in the meaning of 'current interest'. But the word recurs, arguably with the earlier associations, in the Theses.[35]

In Benjamin's earlier theory, topicality was described as 'the reverse of the eternal in history'.[36] This particular turn of phrase occurs in a 1928 letter seeking to placate Hofmannsthal over *One-Way Street,* a book whose sudden political commitments seemed to place Benjamin in a very different light from that which had illuminated his previous concern with eternal ethical verities. This sense of topicality, linked with eternity as reverse and obverse of one coin, indeed has its roots in earlier and for Hofmannsthal more acceptably theological speculations, and especially in the *Announcement of a Journal: Angelus Novus* (1922). In this text, the 'topicality' of Benjamin's proposed journal is expressly contrasted with the 'novelty' of newspapers. 'Novelty' remains on the 'barren surface' of events;[37] the 'genuine topicality' of a journal can only be attained by, if necessary, completely ignoring the misguided expectations of a news-fixated public.[38] A journal that is successful will 'herald the spirit of the age', and its topicality will have a 'historical claim'. The mixture of ephemerality and truth that this implies ('genuine topicality') is compared by Benjamin to the Talmudic legend of countless hosts of angels, created every instant to sing their hymn before God, only to disappear immediately into nothingness.[39] The topical journal, in other words, is completely fresh in the instant of its appearance, only has a genuineness at that one instant, and nevertheless utters its message in the highest courts of history.

Now the question raised by this forceful image is, to put it flippantly, the identity of 'God'. What *is* the central truth around which the ephemeral angels cluster? Or, in secular terms, what is the spirit of the age which an ideal journal can articulate while mere newspapers remain on the surface?

This is not a question that Benjamin ever answers systematically. Rather, it provides a general area of questioning to which he returns spasmodically. The more or less explicit basis of Benjamin's position is that topicality must have a relation to the past, a 'historical claim', which is lacking in mere news. So, from this perspective, although it is unclear what sort of appeals to history may be legitimate in journalism, we can see that historiography itself can be judged on the basis of whether it provides access to any kind of topicality for us now. Indeed, this supplies a touchstone for Benjamin's assessments of other historians. One intellectual historian, for example, is censured for failing to illuminate her material with light shed by the 'white-hot glow of topicality';[40] others are commended for producing substantial works which, however esoteric now, may expect 'sooner or later to be overtaken by topicality'.[41] The link between past and present, the 'best reward' of the historian, is described elsewhere as an 'electrical contact'.[42] Another image for the power emanating from the past is the 'wind of history'. This occurs in the Theses in connection with the 'Angelus Novus', but in earlier comments on historiography Benjamin twice depicts the historian as a sailor setting his or her sails to suit this wind.[43]

Now all this is still somewhat imprecise as a methodology, and does little to explain the link between past and present, or the notions of topicality and eternity as reverse and obverse of one another. In particular, it leaves unclear the relative priority of past and present. Are we looking to the past for an account of the essential nature of the present, as a revelation, so to speak, of our proper fate? Or are we looking to the past as a catalogue of experiment and errors, the aetiology of our present sickness? In the former case, progressing away from our present essence is impossible, and the attempt to do so probably undesirable. In the latter case, movement of some kind is unavoidable, and guided advance, or progress, probably the sensible option. Benjamin's view of history and topicality is suspended between these two views of historicity.

There can be no doubt that Benjamin's early work, perhaps until the *Trauerspiel* book, adhered to the former view. This emerges most explicitly in the celebrated 'Theological-Political Fragment', and in the essay 'Critique of Violence'. Both of these were written in 1921 and were the fruit of Benjamin's first hesitant moves back towards ideas of practical political engagement, and out of the mystical isolation into which the outbreak of the First World War had driven him. These political ideas were still some way from the Bolshevism which he espoused from 1927 or so onwards, after his visit to Moscow. They were much closer to the anarchosyndicalism of Georges Sorel and the utopianism of Ernst Bloch. Neither of these writers can be regarded as orthodox Marxists;[44] and their effect on Benjamin's political commitments was to encourage an enthusiastic activism, nominally sympathetic to Bolshevism[45] but producing views that had little in common with organised socialism.[46] 'Always radical, never consistent' was Benjamin's motto in this early period of political exploration.

Two central principles of Benjamin's early work are given their most explicit formulation in these texts: namely, the critique of secular and temporal processes, and the principle of messianic transformation. The critique of secular processes is focused on the concept of nature and its medium time. The movement of nature in time is, in this early conception, going nowhere. The end of time can never correspond to the goal of history, which is the 'kingdom of God';[47] on the contrary, the goal of history can only be accomplished by the *disappearance* of all natural process. 'For Nature is messianic by reason of its eternal and total transience.'[48] Set against nature is the spiritual world which leads out of time to 'immortality'. The two worlds, of transient nature and immortal spirit, can never be part of the same teleological progression; indeed the 'dynamic' of the 'profane' points in a direction diame-

trically opposed to that of 'messianic intensity'.[49] Obviously this
invalidates almost any sort of goal-oriented practice within the
natural world, such as politics. 'Teleology without a goal at the
end' was Benjamin's characterisation of his view at this time.[50]

But it did leave room for engagement of a sort. One was the
intellectualist messianism we saw in Benjamin's early speculations
about language, 'doctrine' and 'ideas'. Benjamin justified his concern with the interpretation of works of art, by emphasising the
way in which illuminating them in the light of the ideas 'rescued'
them in a way that anticipated the general rescue of nature in the
messianic moment. Mortification of the work of art was parallel
with the other task of humanity, the overcoming of nature. And
interpreting the work of art made it possible for the idea to redeem
creation in the same way that the messianic moment would eventually provide universal redemption. Textual hermeneutics were
therefore concerned with a spiritual realm which in important
respects transcended history itself.[51]

Another form of engagement was a kind of negative politics
which Benjamin characterised as 'Nihilism'.[52] This was negative in
the sense that it systematically rejected pragmatic organisation –
ordinary politics – in favour of the theocracy of a messianic utopia.[53] In his 'Critique of Violence', Benjamin saw secular politics
as merely a cycle of deluded self-interest. The sequence of mu-
tually hostile interest groups, each in turn erecting its own
structures of law, merely consigned humanity to a futile chain of
oppressions.[54] This mythic oppression, an archaic form still underlying the legislative orders imposed even by modern interest
groups, was derived from a primal bondage to the notion of fate.[55]
And like primal fate, the law of the political state was arbitrary
('the law forbids both rich and poor to sleep under bridges'),[56] and
mystifying ('ignorance of the law is no defence').[57] Such legal
systems were a chaotic succession of impositions serving only the
powerful, those who happened to gain supremacy through political
violence.[58] The only way to overcome this directionless cycle was
to break it entirely,[59] and to replace the pernicious instrumenta-
lism of political law by the principle of divine justice.[60, 61] This
would usher in the 'new historical epoch',[62] the de-politicised
messianic utopia. And natural processes, the futile cyclicality of
time, would be replaced by the wholeness of a redeemed cosmos,
creation's *'restitutio in integrum'*.[63]

It is clear that this position is utopian within the terms of our definition. It is politically utopian because it posits absolute discontinuity between the conditions of our present historical existence and those that will follow after messianic transformation. It is theologically utopian because the divine act of creation will happen anew as the old world departs to make way for the new spirit. And it is philosophically utopian because it believes that the existing material world is incommensurate with those ideal forms of knowledge which transcend it and can only find their proper objects after the millenium. The specific instance of this is that pure divine justice, the opponent of mythic legislation, is not immanent in the world, but only appears in 'religious tradition' and 'sacred manifestations'.[64]

This view relies heavily on religious revelation of some kind, and could clearly not sustain the incursions of political interest for very long. On the other hand, it does throw up a classic set of hermeneutic problems which provide a focus for Benjamin's speculations about topicality. We have already dealt with one aspect of this in our discussion of Benjamin's developing conception of practice. The problem of the *sources* of political illumination is a variant of this. The utopian writer must be able to construct a coherent and creditable alternative to the situation that he or she has rejected. If nature and its various processes such as time are rejected, some other site of privileged knowledge must be found to supplant the one that is held to be tainted by creation's degeneration. In his unashamedly theological writings, Benjamin turns to 'doctrine' and 'sacred manifestations'. Later, with the secularisation of his thinking, God is abandoned in favour of other sites of transcendence, such as tradition. Or this, at least, is the implication of those commentators who argue that the heart of Benjamin's hermeneutics is his theory of topicality and the critique of natural time.

Now it cannot be denied that the Theses give some support to this view. Certainly they appear to offer a tighter and more carefuly systematised version of Benjamin's early hermeneutic speculations. It has two elements, a 'constructivist' account of historical hypothesis, and a critique of vulgar tradition.

The Theses, as we have already noted, lay considerable stress on the critique of progress, and to this end they deployed a more explicit and direct analysis of time than in any previous part of

Benjamin's work. Benjamin distinguished between the time cali-
brated by clocks, and that punctuated by calendars.[65] Clock time
was the 'homogeneous and empty time' which was, so to speak,
filled up, like an empty receptacle, by natural processes.[66] It was a
time that continued indefinitely, for ever accommodating, indifferently, events that fell into it. The time marked by calendars,
however, did not just roll on mechanically. Rather, it punctuated
existence with 'days of remembrance', moments that 'gather up'
time into points of concentration.[67] On a day of remembrance, it
might be said, things remembered suddenly become 'topical', and
re-enter existence in the moment of recollection. This, Benjamin
suggested, was the proper character of historical time, and not the
regular ticking of the clock as it levelled all events into an indifferent continuum. It was the sudden pause of impassioned recollection, not the cold advance of infinite progress.

This moment of pause is what Benjamin characterises as 'Now-
Time', and 'Now-Time' is the site of Benjamin's new hermeneutic
principle, namely 'construction'.[68] The problem with naive hermeneutics, naive historiography, was that it resulted in what Benjamin called 'universal history'. Because the naive historian conceived of time as empty and homogeneous, he or she could only
deal with history as though it was a collection of empty time-
containers waiting indifferently to be filled with a 'mass of facts'.
As a result, history written from such a perspective made very
little coherent sense; it was merely a desperate attempt to fill up
the entire past with a seemingly random flood of information.

The constructive historian, on the other hand, had at his or her
disposal a device that would halt the indifferent progress of
history, and present it as a crystalline 'monad'. This monad gath-
ered up the fragments floating down the stream of 'empty' time,
and enveloped them along with time itself.[69] And by virtue of this
ability to envelop time in itself, the monad managed to embrace
the *entire* course of history; in other words, that of the 'present' as
well. So, like the day of remembrance, the historical monad concentrated the mind not merely on something that did once happen,
and had now gone, but on something that happened as part of a
universe which is *still here, now*.

The materialist historian's construction of a monad froze history
into 'crystalline simultaneity' (to use a phrase from the *Trauerspiel*
book),[70] and the elements dispersed across the dimension of time
were reincorporated into a single unit. The unity created by this

was not so much epistemological as political and ethical. Benjamin stressed that this was only possible for the *materialist* historian, because only historians who were on the side of the oppressed and downtrodden were capable of constructing such a monad. They did it in the 'solidarity'[71] of the oppressed of all ages against the oppressors. And only this solidarity in the class struggle was capable of generating an adequate understanding of history. 'The subject of historical knowledge is the struggling, oppressed class itself.'[72]

The other aspect of Benjamin's critique of progress is the problem of tradition, and access to true forms of historical 'construction'. If time as an indifferent continuum was a false basis for understanding history, it would also seem to follow that historical understanding which gradually built up and accumulated with the passage of time was itself misleading. Certainly Benjamin insisted that the point of historical illumination was a momentary one. It was, as he said, a matter of grasping a memory 'as it flashes past in a moment of danger'.[73] The true picture of the past, he emphasised, was something unique and momentary. Each moment of the present had to catch the precise monad of correspondences that included both it and those elements of the past that 'imply' *(meinen)* it. In the notes to the Theses this idea was associated with the notion of the 'dialectical picture', which, in a very different usage from its first appearance,[74] appeared here as the 'involuntary memory of a redeemed humanity.[75] Again it was emphasised that this memory was momentary, 'like a flash of ball lightning which rolls around the whole horizon of the past'.

The opposite of momentary illumination was the persistence of convention, the continuum of a false tradition. Benjamin attacked the historians of conventionality on two fronts. One, taken from the 1937 Fuchs essay, was the front against academic cultural history. In this extract, now incorporated into the seventh thesis, Benjamin emphasised that the cultural monuments celebrated by official history could not be understood outside the context of their origins, a context of oppression and exploitation.[76] Incorporated into the 'tradition' of conventional history, they were no more than booty carried in the triumphal procession of the victors. Just as the cultural object itself was never free from barbarity, 'so neither is the process of handing down by which it has passed from one to the next'.

The attack on cultural history was augmented in the Theses by an attack on the false leaders of Social Democracy, which in this context now meant all those, including the Soviet government, who had capitulated before Fascism.[77] But while the Fuchs essay's comments had originally confined themselves to what might broadly be described as idealist historiography, the Theses' theory of 'Now-time' considerably extended the critique of tradition. The Social Democrats were accused of 'conformism', and Benjamin emphasised how hard, but necessary, it was to generate a view of history that would avoid their crass trust in progress. The people who 'march in step' with time, as Benjamin put it, would never be able to break through to the revolutionary vision of those whose 'visionary gaze' was filled with the mementos of the past.[78] The revolutionary historian, in the Theses' conception, had to break with the measures of his time and the conventions of his associates, and 'brush history against the grain'.[79] And the only sane account of the present moment was one which recognised that it was, always and inevitably, a 'state of emergency' (*Ausnahmezustand*). So, on the one side, the rise of Fascism, against all the predictions of the believers in progress, was nothing to be surprised at. And on the other side, there was no reason to suppose that the present *ever* preserved a reliable normality. With that in mind, the revolutionary recognised that the only chance was to work for the 'real state of emergency', the break with history that would finally interrupt the unending sequence of exploitation and brutality. Social Democracy had failed in this task. It had to be supplanted by a political vision which realised that the task ahead was infinitely more radical than had been supposed.

The theoretical context

Such was the character of Benjamin's supposed political testament; a return, at least, to the pessimistic chiliasm of Georges Sorel, augmented by a complex transposition of historical materialism. There can be no doubt that Benjamin did intend a very radical critique of the philosophical basis of Bolshevism, and that he realised that the heart of it was in his treatment of time. Thesis XVII states decisively the monadic theory of time, whereby temporal extension is 'internal', a 'valuable but tasteless' moment in the phenomenal appearance of the monad.[80] Progress, causal sequence, and all other regularities derived from absolute time, are abandoned.[81] Benjamin himself pointed to Thesis XVII as of particular interest, and even as a 'hidden' methodological account of his previous work.[82] It should be clear from what has been discussed in earlier sections that this statement is not easy to assimilate.

In trying to do this we must look in two further directions. In the first place, it is necessary to identify the theoretical context of Benjamin's 'critique of progress'. Theoretical utterances do not bloom in lonely isolation; they take their place, wittingly or otherwise, in the pre-established choruses of organised opinion. As Benjamin himself repeatedly stressed, the critique of literary transmission is an integral part of literary criticism itself; no book can be considered outside the stream that it enters, and that brings it to the notice of the modern reader.[83] This is a consideration that overrides any notion of the intentions of the individual writer, or demands that his or her oeuvre should be seen as a seamless totality.

And because of this, we can also look to the remainder of Benjamin's work for instruments of critical appraisal to bring to this last piece. If it turns out that there genuinely is a theoretical hiatus between segments of his work, then it is important to clarify this without imagining that it would somehow reflect on his merit. Otherwise, Benjamin will stay forever under what Adorno characterised as the 'nimbus of the sophisticated man of letters'.[84]

The utopianism that Benjamin embraced in the early work, and that arguably carried over into the final texts, was explicitly related to the thought of Sorel and Bloch. Sorel's pessimistic attitude to progress, and his belief that the revolution was an epistemological as well as a political break, were undoubtedly important influences, as was Bloch's Judaic and messianic socialism. But these thinkers did not concern Benjamin for long. Apart from them, there were others about whom he was less open, but who provided a more fundamental set of reference points, and who serve to locate his theories rather more precisely in the general framework of European debate.

The first of these was Franz von Baader (1765-1841), an eccentric philosopher and occultist whose collected works were an early and prized element in Benjamin's library.[85] Baader's view of history, which interested the young Benjamin greatly,[86] was idealistic, and based on a Christian eschatology. Baader saw time as a 'dualism' between successive time and eternity.[87] Successive time was the time of evolution and continuous development, and distinct from the absolute simultaneity of eternity. In his eschatology, things would appear in individual fragments along the course of successive time, but only in an 'abstract' or 'masked' character.[88] The end of time, the moment of redemption, would release these fragments into their universal truth. And only then would things have an authentic 'present', in the perfect simultaneity of eternity. Meanwhile, during the course of history itself, this redemptive wholeness would remain concealed, 'within' *(inner)* time as opposed to 'in' *(in)* it. And because of this, the word 'remember' *(erinnern)* could be seen to have 'a deeper significance than is usually given to it'. It was, in fact, the process of searching out, by mystic contemplation or simply by history, the fragments of future wholeness which had so far emerged in time.[89] The second coming of Christ was the moment at which successive time and material existence would cease, and the fragments which had so far manifested themselves 'masked', would become part of the completed ideal 'formation', the ultimate timelessness of absolute present.

There are obvious themes in Benjamin's utopian writings that could be linked with these speculations of Baader's, notably perhaps the scepticism towards 'successive' time, the opposition to it of a transcendent present containing the integrated ideal truth (Benjamin's 'monad'), and the emphasis on pious remembrance. At the same time, however, it must be recognised that Baader was not a figure whom the Benjamin of 1925 to 1939 would have regarded as a safe theoretical authority. Baader, although a Lutheran, was associated with Roman Catholic revivalism – a phenomenon that claimed among others the subject of Benjamin's doctoral dissertation (Friedrich Schlegel, a contemporary of Baader's), and towards which he was always extremely suspicious. Baader addressed many of his writings to the Catholic Franz Josef Molitor, author of a book, *The Philosophy of Tradition,* much esteemed by Scholem. In a way, it was apt that Benjamin's concern with Baader, which may well have been encouraged by Scholem, should have terminated on one level at least with the sale of the collected works to the Hebrew University in Jerusalem, a sale engineered by Scholem in 1934.[90] Benjamin himself commented in 1931 that Baader's work should be seen as a warning rather than a guide.[91]

The second thinker whose influence can clearly be discerned in the Theses is Klages. We have already discussed Klages's theories, and here we need only point to the element in the Theses that would seem to reflect them. It is Benjamin's use of the 'picture', specifically the 'dialectical picture'. It will be remembered that Klages introduced the 'picture' as a way of underlining his hostility to conceptual theories of knowledge. The traditional categories of epistemology – 'universals' 'forms' 'ideas' and the like – were all regarded by Klages as abstractions, incursions by a degenerate intellect into the primal integrity of the 'soul'. Pictures were a way of representing knowledge as something independent of language and the conceptual apparatus of the mind; 'sayable things' were opposed to 'unsayable pictures', the more fundamental level of knowledge.[92] And knowing by means of 'pictures' was quite different from knowing by means of the intellect; while intellect operated by means of conceptualised identity, analytical continuity, the picture was something that flashed momentarily[93] in an 'ecstatic vision'.[94] And, said Klages with reference to anamnesis, or remembrance, it was this ecstatic vision that 'in contrast to the act of perception [that is, intellectual knowing] is directed to the . . . reality of the past'.[95] And, finally, the 'pictures' that are recovered in the past by this act of 'ecstatic vision' are not, so to speak, inertly available; they only respond to the 'polar touch of a receptive soul'.[96]

All of this is rendered in the fifth thesis, where Benjamin notes that what we receive from the past is a picture, that it is momentary (that is, remote from the empty time of conceptual vision), and that it is only recoverable by those who recognise that they are 'implied' by it (Klages's 'polar touch').

Rather than comment at once on Benjamin's use of Klages, we may first consider the work of a contemporary who was also heavily influenced by Klages (a fact generally ignored by his commentators), namely Martin Heidegger. The latter sections of Heidegger's *Being and Time,* which appeared in 1927, are in important respects a systematisation of the cosmology of Klages and the George circle generally. Benjamin was familiar with Heidegger's book.

Heidegger's theory of history may be divided into three elements: metaphysical, epistemological and methodological. Metaphysically, it is based on a critique of empty or absolute time. Time is not, says Heidegger, a succession of momentary realities, and neither is a stretch of time like an empty framework into which realities accumulate.[97] Time is not a channel within which things become briefly real before relapsing again into the unreality of the past. 'Being' is entirely real, regardless of the sequentialities of time; being *includes* the dimension of temporal extension as part of its own self. Although time is a condition for existences, it is not like a stage on which only one thing can appear, or 'be real', at any one time. An existence is a total unity which has time as part of itself. Seeing only one part of this unity at any one moment is like seeing only one side of an object whose other sides are concealed. It is a condition of three-dimensional being that this should be the case, and that you cannot see everything at once. Equally, it is part of an existence to 'stretch' itself out temporally; but that does not mean that an existence is not in a certain sense always all there and completely real. (This is an attempt to explain Heidegger's argument without falling into the religious terminology which would in the long run be inevitable. The position of people like Klages was much more honest in its mysticism.)

Within and along the extensions of its temporality an existence also has the chance to know itself, to travel to the extremes of its past, present and future. Heidegger calls this the 'ecstatikon of temporality'. *Ecstatikos* is a Greek adjective meaning 'inclined to depart from'. Heidegger associates it with 'ecstasy', and interprets the whole complex as the inclination or propensity to 'go out of oneself', or perhaps 'out of one's mind'. This, he says, is the character of authentic existence in relation to time. Past, present and future are the 'ecstasies' of temporality; they are the modes in which an existence 'goes out of itself', is thrown into temporal extension. Knowledge, in this sense, is not the processing of phenomena through the (Kantian) 'aesthetic form' of time; it is the going-out-of-itself into phenomenality of an existence.[98] (All of this is considerably easier to understand in Klages's account of cultic ecstasy.)[99]

As the use of the term 'ecstasy' implies, the kind of knowledge associated with these excursions across time is rather different from the calculating reasonableness of normal science. In particular, its action within time is different. It is – and here again Heidegger takes over a component of Klages's scheme – the action of an instant (the *Augenblick*). For Heidegger, the instant is the site of 'decision'; and he makes use of another play on words *(entschlossen, erschlossen)* to emphasise that the moment of decision is also the moment of 'openness' – openness to the full extent of existence carried in the ecstasies of past, present and future.[100]

This raises the question of what kind of thing it is that is 'stretched out' in time, that 'goes out of itself' in the 'ecstasies' of temporality, and that has to be 'open', or 'decisive', in relation to itself. In Heidegger's perspective, knowledge is identical with the reality of the known, so in a sense this is not an epistemological question. It is not something external which some assumed subject comes to know: it is a form of authentic self-discovery.

The thing that decisiveness decides on, and openness is open to, is 'fate'.[101] The instant of decision and openness is the instant of fate; the instant that captures in itself all the existence that is ecstatically phenomenal in time. The existence that ecstatically flashes through the dimensions of time appears as fate. As before, the difficulty of expressing this in a way that makes sense is mainly a reflection of Heidegger's ultimately rather absurd project of converting mythic imagery into a philosophical system. When Heidegger talks of fate, he ultimately means what is usually understood by fate – the sort of thing that is read off in horoscopes, and that describes how any particular individual will come to the world of experience and, finally, leave it in death. Knowledge and acceptance of this fate is what Heidegger means by the terminological pair decision and openess *(entschlossen/erschlossen)*. A decisive person is someone who grasps fate as it comes to him or her in the instant of openness. And grasping fate properly (authentically, *eigentlich*) also involves accepting its ultimate limit, the limit of death which is always and inevitably written into it. The guarantee of the wholeness of a fate is precisely that it has a term; it is one closed and particular scheme for one individual, his or her own 'being unto death'. This terminality is emphasised by Heidegger in his notion of the future. Future (one of the 'ecstasies' of temporality) is not, in his view, an abstract stretch of empty time waiting to be filled up. It is finite and complete. The ecstasy into the future comes across a boundary, an end, just the same as it does, obviously, in the past.[102] Birth and death are written equally in the stars.

Whether the hypnotic punning of Heidegger's ontology is any more than a rather strenuous kind of poetry is an open question. For our purposes, however, it does eventually emerge in a specific set of methodological propositions, constituting for Heidegger the basis of any future science of history.

The object of history,[103] it emerges from Heidegger's reading of the finitude of being, is fate, either individual *(Schicksal)* or collective *(Geschick)*.[104] (It is worth noting the overtones of 'mission' – sent by a deity? – in the German word *Geschick.)* In order to do this successfully, it is necessary to abandon what Heidegger repeatedly attacks as the 'vulgar understanding of Being'. The vulgar understanding is what Heidegger stigmatises as 'reasonableness' *(Verständigkeit),*[105] concern with the merely available world of objects, belief in the abstract and empty nature of time, and inability to grasp temporality in an authentic manner. In particular, the vulgar interpretation of time cannot break away from its impoverished conception of the present.[106] Unable to grasp the decisive instant of fate, to choose its *Schicksal* openly, it concerns itself only with the drab abstraction of its view of the present. Lost in the meaningless habits of the collective, its past is no more for it than 'unrecognisable left-overs'; the height of its historical consciousness is the search for 'the modern'.

Authentic historical consciousness, on the other hand, bursts this unworthy obeisance to a misunderstood present. In the instant of decisiveness it 'rids today of the present', expanding existence into the ecstasies of temporality, consciousness of the unity of past, present and future. 'Authentic historicity understands history as the "return" of the possible and knows that the possibility will only return if existence is open for it in the fateful instant of decisive repetition.' Authentic existence is the decisive grasping of the handed-down possibilities of the past,[107] and their implementation for the individual's own forward-looking 'being unto death'.

The methodological counterpart to the totality of being is the hermeneutic technique's 'circularity of understanding'.[108] Time is not, in Heidegger's view, a sequence of events offering themselves indifferently to the knowing subject. Existence is essentially historical, which means that *an* existence contains within itself the whole extension of itself throughout time; it has a unity, its fate, which transcends the fragmentary form in which it may seem to appear in phenomenal time. In order to describe the methodology for a conceptual appropriation of this, Heidegger uses the old argument against hermeneutic understanding, but in a way that turns it to his own advantage. The argument was that a belief in the uniqueness of each historical epoch precluded the understanding of other epochs by any particular one. It had no equipment to engineer such an understanding, since its conceptuality was isolated on the planet of its own uniqueness. This is a variant of the translatability problem: how, in a world constituted by languages, and in the absence of any neutral control, could any language claim to have translated another language exhaustively into its own?

From Heidegger's point of view, this neatly illustrates his own position. He is expressly opposed to the neutral control – abstract and empty time – and the 'problem' of the circularity of understanding therefore resolves itself into a positive and accurate account. The purpose of history is the recovery of one's *own* fate (*Eigentlichkeit*, 'authenticity', means 'ownishness'); what happens as the world 'goes on' after death, or beyond our existence, or whenever, is an abstract and unhistorical question.[109] Hermeneutics is like Ariadne's thread: the purpose of it is to get back to where you started from, having ascertained the nature of your surroundings. Heidegger calls it a 'leading thread . . . made fast to the place from which it originates and to which it returns'.[110]

The vulgar understanding of being reaches a view of history that Heidegger classifies as 'world history'.[111] It is the viewpoint that has no 'authentic' anchor point and no hermeneutic thread; it understands history simply as the arrival and passing away of indifferent objects. History becomes a huge exhibition of unrelated artefacts. 'World history' is the scientific correlative of the amorphous human collective. Ultimately, it is the intellectual manifestation of the bankrupt ethics of modernity with its inability to decide for 'being unto death'. According to Heidegger, 'being lost in the collective and the world-historical' is part of the 'flight from death'.[112]

In contrast to this, says Heidegger, the properly 'existential' interpretation of history appears to be 'violent'; it is a struggle to wrest authentic understanding from the grip of the inauthentic.[113] The instrument used in this is 'phenomenological construction',[114] the blunt weapon of a revolutionary transformation. 'Construction' is a conceptual account of the structure of Being,[115] an intellectual version of what in practice only appears as fate in the instant of decisive openness. 'Construction', we might say, is the casting of the horoscope. It is the understanding generated by going out and coming back along the hermeneutic thread.

The affinities between Heidegger's position and the hermeneutics sketched in Benjamin's Theses are obvious. Heidegger, like Benjamin, takes over Klages's conception of the instant and momentary perception of fundamental truths inaccessible to contemplative rationality. Heidegger and Benjamin, or at least the Benjamin of the Theses, share the same sceptical attitude towards time. On this basis, both Benjamin and Heidegger build a constructive theory of historical interpretation which is to yield time-transcending unities of essence. Heidegger calls these unities 'fate', and sees them constituted in the moment of decision which 'responds' to the appropriate moment in the past, and having appropriated this moment as its rightful 'heritage', carries it on in the finitude of its 'being unto death'.[116] Benjamin, less religious but hardly less mysterious, calls them 'monads' which crystallise at the moment of remembrance in response to the call of that section of the past that 'implies' it. And finally both thinkers share the same scorn for the unthinking collective with its feeble conception of temporality. Benjamin calls it conformism and rejects its production of 'universal history'. Heidegger calls it *das Man*[117] and spurns its 'world history'.

Materialism and 'hermeneutics'

It would seem, then, to be unnecessary to follow Benjamin's tip about the concealed dwarf of theology in order to make sense of the mysteries of the Theses.[118] Even if there are Judaic motifs secreted in the text, they evidently do not play a very crucial role in it. Nor is it especially necessary to turn to Benjamin's own earlier work for enlightenment. The real theoretical context of the Theses, which they do to some extent share with the earlier work, is the philosophy of the George circle and its successors. In this instance, Heidegger's philosophy of history as expressed in *Sein und Zeit* may be seen, like some of Benjamin's work, as a philosophical systematisation of what had been pioneered by thinkers like Klages.

This has not so far been seen as a problem by Benjamin's commentators, either because, like Adorno, they probably preferred this influence to orthodox historical materialism, or else because they were themselves sympathetic to the 'hermeneutic' tradition which has derived so much from Heidegger. It is probably the case that the historical and ideological dimensions of modern hermeneutic theory, whose most distinguished postwar representatives have been Gadamer and Habermas, have not been all that thoroughly explored.[119] Certainly there are immense differences in political orientation between Gadamer and Habermas. But it is still true that even Habermas and his followers, who would prefer to call their theory 'critique of ideology', share certain problematic features with earlier thinkers. These are a persistent scepticism about what is dismissed as 'positivist' or ('objectivist') historiography – that is to say, the possibility of a neutral account of events *tout simple*; and the supposition that consciousness, so to speak, swims at the centre of its own universe of meaning, and has no immediate access to other universes.[120] The aim of 'critique of ideology', in those terms, is ultimately the same as Heidegger's: to shake off the grip of conformity or ideology, and to attain a clearer vision of the potential offered in our particular universe of meaning. The political terminology is different; the theoretical structure very much the same. And, despite Habermas's claims,[121] the disadvantages of both positions are very similar; their relation to pragmatic and *rational* political intervention is very indirect.[122]

Habermas himself was somewhat sceptical about the value of Benjamin's hermeneutics, which he felt to be insufficiently political and too conservative.[123] Other commentators have asserted, probably with justice, that Benjamin's Theses can well be associated with the programme of 'critique of ideology'. Peter Bürger and Jeanne-Marie Gagnebin would be examples of this.

But these critics, like many writing on Benjamin, have perhaps been too hasty in assimilating a difficult oeuvre to a position more familiar to them, and not sufficiently careful in acquiring the same sensitivity for the pedigree of ideas that Benjamin himself had. As is constantly pointed out, Benjamin esteemed the work of many thinkers, and among them were persons who could not possibly be considered politically acceptable to him personally. Carl Schmitt and Ludwig Klages are examples often given. But this does not mean that Benjamin picked up intellectual trinkets like a jackdaw, heedless of where they came from and what their normal function was. His judgements on the political function of ideas – the mechanisms of ideology – are the pillars of his critical structure. He knew perfectly well that Klages was an anti-Semite and near Fascist, and, what is more important, he wove Klages's ideas brilliantly into his own critique of that position. In another example, the judgement on Baader quoted earlier is not simply a casual warning against theosophical enthusiasm; it is made in the specific context of contemporary attempts to create a new political 'myth'.[124] One need only recall the title of Rosenberg's textbook of Nazi philosophy, *The Myth of the Twentieth Century*, to realise how 'topical' Benjamin's concern with theoretical pedigree and ideological transmission was.

In the case of Heidegger, Benjamin was clearly aware of the philosopher's general ideological orientation without, however, ever fully systematising the differences between them. This was perhaps a fateful omission. The mentions of Heidegger, both in the early period and during work on the 'Arcades' complex, reveal a persistent antipathy; but Benjamin always draws back from his projected attempts at a full critique. In 1919, Benjamin roundly dismissed Heidegger's early essay on the difference between historical and mechanical time, but without elaborating his own objections.[125] Benjamin's reading of the Duns Scotus dissertation seems to have begun with outraged rejection,[126] but then retreated into a grudging concession that Heidegger had indeed rendered 'the essentials' of the scholastic position (and thereby made Benjamin's own researches in that area redundant).[127] In the later period, Benjamin again found Heidegger across the path of his own work, and insistently sought to distance himself from what 'Heidegger's school' were now doing in literary studies.[128] He was dismayed and disgusted when he found that the Moscow journal, *Internationale Literatur*, had associated his position with Heidegger's.[129] At the same time, however, the projected critical confrontation between his and Heidegger's 'very different' views on history came to naught,[130] as did the plan to 'demolish' Heidegger in a reading group with Brecht.[131] So, the theoretical enterprise that would perhaps have served more than any other to situate Benjamin's oeuvre never came about; and the bizarre recantations and back-trackings of the Theses were left to confuse his commentators. In what respect were the views of Benjamin and Heidegger on history 'very different'? Certainly the Theses give us little help in answering such a question. Indeed, taken at face value, they would seem to force on us the conclusion that Benjamin was never more than a Heideggerian in left-wing clothes, and one who finally re-entered the fold when it became clear that Bolshevism had failed. Must we conclude this? It seems to be the only answer if we do accord to the Theses the status which they have traditionally received. But it hardly seems the sort of answer that Adorno or Scholem would have relished. Perhaps we should turn once more to Benjamin's historical materialism and his work under the allegedly 'catastrophic' influence of Brecht.[132]

There are, if we may summarise what has been said, two principal components to Benjamin's theoretical stance in the Theses, one philosophical and one political. The philosophical component is scepticism, first towards time as an absolute and objective component of all events, and second towards the 'causal chain' of regular and objective sequences within time. The Theses' tactic in the first instance is to develop a critique of progress, positing time as 'internal' to the essential reality and crystalline simultaneity of the 'monad'. From that point of view, time is a mode of appearance, but not of essence. In the second instance, the Theses posit a theory of 'construction' in opposition to causality. According to this argument, historiography is not based on observation and induction, but on the magical flash of the 'dialectical picture', the sudden redemptive memory which emerges complete at the instant of danger.

The second element, the political one, is messianic utopianism. The basis of this is the contention that present existence is more or less totally lost to truth and goodness, and that only the most radical transformation of the world can save humanity. Political transformation, in the sense of organisational and institutional advance, is in the end not enough. Experience itself has to be altered. This is the basis for the Theses' reinterpretation of revolution. Revolution is not to be seen, in a Marxian way, as the locomotive of world history – in other words, the instrument of significant advance. Instead, it is to be seen as 'grabbing the emergency cord',[133] which would have as its consequence the 'messianic cessation of events happening'.[134]

Every component of this position is open to more or less direct refutation from the work of Benjamin's maturity. The most convincing refutation is probably that of the *Trauerspiel* book, but since pp.103–52 have already followed the course of Benjamin's development from an early religious transcendentism to a political theory of practice, we shall not repeat it here. Instead, we will look to the hermeneutic principles stated or implied in his expressly materialist writings.

The first topic is Benjamin's sceptical attitude towards 'empty time'. His replacement for this, it will be recalled, is the notion of 'Now-Time', the simultaneity of the monad. There are, it is true, parts of earlier work that seem to foreshadow this collapsing of all history into a kind of supercharged present; the remarks about the 'electrical contact' between present and past, and the need for a 'white-hot topicality' in the historian's work might suggest this. But this does not mean that Benjamin generally thought history should be lifted off its hinges and burnt in a fire of messianic ecstasy. Most of his earlier remarks about 'topicality' were no more than the relatively trivial methodological precept that the historian must avoid allowing his or her work to lapse into antiquarianism, 'the museal'.[135] And the remedy for this, as Benjamin in fact had made clear in the essay where Thesis VII first appeared, was not 'brushing history against the grain',[136] but simply making sure that cultural artefacts were properly contextualised economically and politically![137]

Beyond this, it is overwhelmingly clear in Benjamin's work that inductive history, the spadework of empirical and philological research, was a central concern.[138] Although he stipulated that historical writing should reflect an awareness of present-day interests and circumstances,[139] he repeatedly warned against sacrificing historical accuracy to the imagined needs of the contemporary world. The myth-builders of nationalistic literary history were his prime targets. 'There is a type which is now not uncommon among younger university teachers: the academic who thinks he is promoting a "renewal" by obscuring the boundaries between his subject and journalism. He sails in with urbanity and elegance, only to cut a most pathetic figure with his scholarly apparatus.'[140] History had no need of 'overheated topicality';[141] and its common accompaniment, the 'misty distances of the past,'[142] were equally redundant. Real scholarship would be overtaken by 'topicality' in due course, whatever its apparent relation to the immediate present.[143] Benjamin's direct reproach to the historians of the George school – writers who *did* systematically adhere to the kind of hermeneutic theory we have discussed – was that they produced 'exorcism of history'.[144] Complete respect for the objectivity of the course of history, and extreme suspicion of any over-valuation of the hermeneutic standpoint: these were the components of Benjamin's own work. Writings like the first Baudelaire essay and the examinations of cultural technology were outstanding examples of this approach – very different from the 'sacred groves with temples of timeless poets' produced by the hermeneuticists.[145]

The same thing may be discerned in his attitude towards historical regularity and the causal chain. In the Theses, Benjamin produced the theory of 'construction' and the dialectical picture, the instantaneous vision of the past which dispenses with conceptual analysis or theory. In the earlier work, it is quite clear which side Benjamin stands on. Faced with Kommerell's lyrical descriptions of the past, Benjamin comments that, as far as he is concerned, 'we have to declare our allegiance . . . to theory, which abandons the magic circle of vision (*Schau*). There may be timeless pictures, but there are certainly no timeless theories.'[146] And as far as Kommerell's hagiography of Hölderlin was concerned, 'Hölderlin was not the sort of person to be resurrected, and this country, to whose seers visions appear over corpses, is not his.'[147]

In opposition to such uncontrolled visions Benjamin turned to the straightforward explanations of theoretical analysis and causal determination. It was quite clear to him that individual historical events, such as cultural phenomena, were connected to the historical process by relations of determination and function.[148] A satisfactory account of cultural events was one that related them to other more generalised objects, such as economic, environmental and ethnic conditions.[149] This was not to be a naive reduction of culture to what Benjamin termed 'pragmatic' history (in this he was probably thinking of writers such as Ranke and especially Mehring).[150] But an isolated history of culture alone, however 'dialectical', was equally unacceptable; cultural events were 'scattered' across the whole range of historical practice, and could only be recovered with the aid of a full-scale materialist analysis and its focus on 'genuine, i.e. political experience'.[151] History is only lifted above mere sedimentation of events once it reaches the level of the political; this is perhaps particularly the case with cultural history, which may otherwise be a 'fetish', the worship of meaningless trophies. And it is historical materialism, in particular, that makes it possible to raise the past in this manner, revealing the 'interior of history'.[152] Historians without this strong theory can only come up with 'fortuitous' facts; historical materialism reveals the 'secret constellations' of history. It does this by 'seeking out the concrete and changing forces in an epoch's relations of production which, without their knowledge, determine the behaviour both of the powerful and of the masses'.

The other difficult element in Benjamin's Theses is political messianism, the utopianism we saw in early anarcho-syndicalist writings, such as the 'Critique of Violence'. Again, it is the *Trauerspiel* book that provides the most conclusive answers; if, as Scholem said, the Theses were an attempt to leap into transcendence, then the book's critique of ethical transcendence supplies a full rebuttal. But outside these more philosophical topics, the more directly political implications of the Theses' messianism are also answered in Benjamin's mature materialist writing. In particular, the notion of total transformation, of radical messianic upheaval, is contradicted. Benjamin's theory of *Technik*, the alteration of the relations of production through organisational advance, clearly excludes sudden mass illumination. Its motif is universality of education and technical expertise, not the moral and epistemological Armageddon implied by the advent of a Messiah. Benjamin endorsed Brecht's view of communism: 'Communism is not radical.'[153] It was capitalism and its Fascist ideologists who were clamouring for the totality of 'renewal'; communism only favoured discreet 'innovation', the rational encouragement of an underlying historical process. Fascism, one might say, engineers revolutions as a cultural event; but real revolution from below is the organic climax of processes in humanity's 'second nature'. And so communism procedes with the 'step by step of a healthy common sense, which is the opposite of radicalism.'[154]

The great monographic essays of the 1930s, on Kraus, Kafka and Baudelaire, were concerned precisely with this problem – the inability of individualistic intellectuals to submit to pragmatic political discipline, and their tendency to slide away instead into mysticism or anarchism. Kraus's lifelong battle against the press and the corrupt condition of public letters was, despite its inherent justice, ultimately invalidated by what he chose to set against it. This was a kind of pessimistic Catholic eschatology. The world was a place of natural hierarchies,[155] which, however, could look forward to no salvation, and certainly no historical development, but only to the immolation of the world by a demented technology.[156] The weakness of Kraus's position, even from his own moral perspective, was that he was, in the end, prepared to believe in his *own* authority,[157] and to put his faith in the impotent radicalism of the 'personality'.[158] His vision was blocked by the illusions of individual 'creativity', and never penetrated to the historical realities of 'commissioned and controlled labour, with its model, the political and the technical'.[159]

Kafka, as well, was not proof against 'the temptations of mysticism'.[160] The entire quasi-religious structure of his work, in which the world confronted him with the aspect of impenetrable fate, was nothing but a wall preventing him from seeing the true nature of what he was describing. 'In every case it revolves around the question of the organisation of life and work in the human community. This concerned Kafka all the more frequently as it became more opaque to him.'[161] Kafka's writings, unwittingly, are a portrait of human beings at the point when alienation has gone further than ever before, but also when the possibilities offered by a revolutionary technology are greatest. Kafka's desperate study of the riddles of 'fate' are like the bafflement of a person who cannot recognise his or her own voice in a recording. Is the breakthrough possible? 'He would be able to understand himself, but how gigantic the effort would be! For it is a storm which blows from forgetting.'[162] (It is interesting to note that here it is precisely technological *progress* that helps defeat the 'wind of history'!)

And finally, as we have already considered in detail, the first Baudelaire essay shows the poet as a person unable to see to the centre of his historical circumstances. He was able to confront the bleak existence of writing for the market place, and brilliantly to describe the alienation of the urban intelligentsia, but not to see the relation between such subjective circumstances and the changing forms of social organisation. Baudelaire, like the political revolutionaries among his contemporaries, was condemned to the fantasy existence of a conspirator, a histrionic hero of the mind. And it is precisely such people, the conspirators and heroes with their worship of 'decisiveness', who could never come to terms with the wearisome demands of actual progress. The fortieth section of *Zentralpark* makes this connection, and Benjamin's judgement on it, completely clear.[163]

The difficulty with Benjamin's work is that it does not resolve itself into another science, another way of doing cultural history. For Engels, Ludwig Feuerbach was the end of classical German philosophy, and, to all intents and purposes, the end of philosophy altogether. Academics who followed careless phrases by Engels, or Lenin, and have resuscitated 'Marxist philosophy', 'dialectical materialism', and the like, are abusing the intentions of their mentor.[164] The same can be said of Benjamin's work and its attempted appropriation by the literary criticism industry. The result has been that the parts of his work that do still seem to support such notions, like the Theses, have been eagerly taken up, while other parts have been ignored, or dismissed as derivative and Brechtian. The whole process has been worsened by misunderstandings of the complex theoretical background of Benjamin's work, and cloudy perceptions of the relations between different texts.

But Benjamin does not, even in the Theses, see an intellectual future spent among the lotus groves of hermeneutics. His account of intellectual practice, or at least of revolutionary intellectual practice, is ascetic in the extreme. The problem with intellectual institutions is that, in a variant of Parkinson's Law, they expand their objects of study to fit the resources available. In philosophical and artistic areas, this can easily become caught up in a reciprocity between financial support and ideological complaisance. The most sophisticated version of this is philosophical scepticism: the generalised invalidation of pragmatic intervention by intellectuals, coupled with the construction of objects of study whose mysterious heights can be scaled only by the intellectuals in that particular institution. Cultural history is one such object. Progressive criticism can best respond to this with simple 'destruction': discrediting of an unscientific historiography erected only on fantasies of contemporary relevance; and refutation of the 'titles of origin' drawn up by enthusiastic myth-builders on the basis of such disreputable evidence.[165] This applies equally to all histories that grow from an 'overheated topicality', whether of the left or of the right. And it should view all magical reminiscences, be they of 'fate' or of the 'dialectical picture', with extreme suspicion.

The present day is indeed important, but not as something to be heralded by uncontrolled historical fantasy. In fact, the day of the effective deed, of organisation and intervention, is distinctly grey and uninspiring. Benjamin calls it 'shabby' (*dürftig*).[166] But then the task of an intellectual in the modern day, beset by real and immediate political dangers, is not to look for cultural ornamentation. Sheer survival is the first priority; and intellectual practice must be adjusted to meet that need. The high technology of advanced militarism must be matched by the political reorganisation of the intellectual avant-garde. With their work 'humanity can prepare itself to outlive culture, if need be'.[167]

Benjamin's image of the progressive intellectual is that of the petroleum engineer, 'applying his expertise at precisely calculated points in the desert of the present day'.[168] The political resources that may yet save us lie deep, and their access is obstructed. But to get at them we need general education, not the subtleties of the arcane; organisation, not imagination. We must survive culture, if need be.

Notes and References

NOTE. References to Benjamin's own writings are in two parts: first the German, then the English translation. The two are divided by an oblique /. If nothing appears after the German reference, it means that no translation is available in the major English Benjamin selections. I have, however, offered short English titles for all the complete pieces cited (these may sometimes appear in the text itself). Most of the works with only a German reference are either letters (all the Br references) or fragments from the critical apparatus at the back of the German collected works. For the meaning of the asterisk * against certain references see the introduction, p.10.

Abbreviations

German sources

I-IV = Walter Benjamin, *Gesammelte Schriften* (Frankfurt: Suhrkamp, 1977ff); Br = Walter Benjamin, *Briefe* (Frankfurt: Suhrkamp, 1966); B/S = Walter Benjamin, Gershom Scholem, *Briefwechsel 1933–1940* (Frankfurt: Suhrkamp, 1980); Illum = Walter Benjamin, *Illuminationen. Ausgewählte Schriften* (Frankfurt: Suhrkamp, 1980); BC = Walter Benjamin, *Berliner Chronik* (Frankfurt: Suhrkamp, 1980); MT = Walter Benjamin, *Moskauer Tagebuch* (Frankfurt: Suhrkamp, 1980); VuB = *Versuche über Brecht*, second revised and expanded edition (Frankfurt: Suhrkamp, 1978).

English sources

Ill = Walter Benjamin, *Illuminations*, trans. Harry Zohn (London: Fontana, 1973); Origin = *The Origin of German Tragic Drama*, trans. John Osborne (London: New Left Books, 1977); 1-Way St = *One-Way Street and Other Writings*, trans. Edmund Jephcott and Kingsley Shorter (London: New Left Books, 1979); Und Brecht = *Understanding Brecht*, trans. Anna Bostock (London: New Left Books, 1973); Baudelaire = *Charles Baudelaire: A Lyric Poet in the Era of High Capitalism*, trans. Harry Zohn (London: New Left Books, 1973); NGC = *New German Critique*, no. 17 (Spring 1979) special Walter Benjamin issue.

Introduction

1. The *Gesammelte Schriften* are edited by Hermann Schweppenhäuser and Adorno's student Rolf Tiedemann, 'with the assistance of Theodor Adorno and Gershom Scholem'.
2. Bibliographies of secondary literature on Benjamin may be found in NGC, and in *Text und Kritik* no. 31/32, 2nd extended edition (Munich, 1979).
3. Werner Fuld, *Walter Benjamin zwischen den Stühlen* (Munich: Hanser, 1979) 16.
4. Terry Eagleton, *Walter Benjamin, or Towards a Revolutionary Criticism* (London: Verso, 1981) Preface. There are of course numerous full-length studies of Benjamin available in German, generally of a specialist nature. On a less analytical level, Gershom Scholem's memoir *Walter Benjamin – die Geschichte einer Freundschaft* (Frankfurt: Suhrkamp, 1975) is interesting and very readable.
5. The controversy is described in the *Text und Kritik* bibliography. It should be mentioned that the Frankfurt 'Benjamin Archiv', at present at the disposal of the editors of the collected works, is not to be made public until the edition is complete.
6. *New German Critique*, 31.
7. II 540/Und Brecht 44.
8. See, for example, Kautsky's remarkable *Foundations of Christianity* (New York: International Publishers, 1925).
9. Fuld, *Walter Benjamin zwischen den Stühlen*, 234.
10. Br 425.
11. Br 523.
12. IV 397/1-Way St 157.
13. II 366/1-Way St 289.
14. III 281/'Left-Wing Melancholy'.
15. *Philosophisches Wörterbuch* (Leipzig: VEB Verlag, 1975) 422.

I   Benjamin's life

1. Fuld, *Walter Benjamin zwischen den Stühlen*, 20.
2. Asja Lacis, *Revolutionär im Beruf* (Munich: Rogner und Bernhard, 1971) 42.
3. Ibid, 49.
4. Ibid, 63f.
5. Br 619.
6. Br 292.
7. Br 339.
8. Fuld, *Walter Benjamin zwischen den Stühlen*, 21.
9. Lacis, *Revolutionär im Beruf*, 49.
10. Br 409.
11. Scholem, *Walter Benjamin*, 160.
12. Ibid, 70.
13. Br 292.
14. Fuld, *Walter Benjamin zwischen den Stühlen*, 79.
15. Scholem, *Walter Benjamin*, 20ff; B/S 128ff.
16. Scholem, *Walter Benjamin*, 168.
17. B/S 127.
18. B/S 164.
19. B/S 38.
20. II 1351, 1354.
21. Lacis, *Revolutionär im Beruf*, 72.
22. B/S 218; Br 797.
23. III 290/'Literary History and Literary Science'.
24. III 223, 287, 209/Book reviews in 1929, 1930, 1931.

II Context and background

1. The early years

1. George Steiner, Introduction to Walter Benjamin, *The Origin of German Tragic Drama*, trans. John Osborne (London: New Left Books, 1977) 24.
2. T. Adorno, *Über Walter Benjamin* (Frankfurt: Suhrkamp, 1970) 97.
3. II 849.
4. II 873; Br 63; compare also Br 127.
5. II 826.
6. II 827ff.
7. II 828.
8. II 831, 846.
9. Br 48.
10. II 825, 844.
11. II 867, 869; BC 34/1-Way St 305.
12. II 845, 876.
13. II 49ff/'Moral Instruction'.
14. II 836.
15. II 839.
16. II 871.
17. II 879.
18. Br 119.
19. Br 83.
20. Br 121.
21. Br 106.
22. Br 121.
23. Br 86.
24. Br 92; II 46/'Romanticism'.
25. Scholem, *Walter Benjamin*, 122.
26. Ibid, 235.
27. BC 56/1-Way St 316.
28. Compare II 46; the essay 'Erotische Erziehung', etc.
29. Br 47ff.
30. Br 67ff.
31. II 84ff.
32. Br 857.
33. Br 115, 119.
34. Br 59.
35. Br 121ff.
36. If his response to Scholem's comments on George's 'Der Krieg' (Br 156).
37. B/S 128ff.
38. III 394.
39. BC 24/1-Way St 300.
40. III 393.
41. III 394.
42. III 398.
43. BC 41/1-Way St 308.
44. BC 27/1-Way St 302.
45. BC 24ff/1-Way St 301.
46. II 824.
47. C. E. McClelland, *State, Society and University in Germany 1700-1914* (Cambridge University Press, 1980) 240.
48. Scholem, *Walter Benjamin*, 108.
49. Br 236.
50. Br 221.
51. Br 295.
52. Br 319.
53. I 868.
54. Br 293.
55. Br 250.
56. Br 241.
57. I 870.
58. I 872.
59. Br 339.
60. For example, Br 316.
61. Br 373, 399.
62. Br 250.
63. Br 169.
64. Br 382.
65. Br 344.
66. Br 119.
67. See, for example, the collection *Aufrufe und Reden deutscher Professoren im Ersten Weltkrieg* (Stuttgart: Reclam, 1975).
68. Br 121ff.
69. But see his article 'Vom Weltbürger zum Grossbürger' IV 815–63.

70. See J. F. Roberts, 'The Progressive Role of the Opposition', in *The Times Higher Education Supplement* 11 September 1981.
71. Compare Lukács on the historical development of Germany in *Die Zerstörung der Vernunft* (Darmstadt: Luchterhand, 1973) 37–83.
72. See McClelland, *State, Society and University in Germany 1700–1914.*
73. See R. Samuel and R. H. Thomas, *Education and Society in Modern Germany* (London: Routledge, 1949) 117.
74. See the discussion in F. K. Ringer, *The Decline of the German Mandarins: The German Academic Community 1890–1933* (Cambridge, Mass.: Harvard University Press, 1969).
75. Br 375.
76. Br 376.
77. I 900ff.
78. Br 400.
79. For discussions of Zionism see Jochanan Bloch, *Judentum in der Krise* (Gottingen: Vandenhoeck, 1966); H. -H. Knütter, *Die Juden und die deutsche Linke in der Weimarer Republik* (Düsseldorf: Droste, 1971); Werner E. Mosse (ed.), *Juden im Wilhelminischen Deutschland* (Tübingen: J. C. B. Mohr, 1976); Stephen M. Poppel, *Zionism in Germany* (Philadelphia: Jewish Publication Society 1976).
80. Hermann Cohen, *Jüdische Schriften* (Berlin: Schwetschke, 1924) Introduction to vol. I (by Franz Rosenzweig), xxx.
81. 'Ever more clearly we can discern the logic which brought this war into being.' (*Jüdische Schriften*, II, 290).
82. Hermann Cohen, *Die Religion der Vernunft aus den Quellen des Judentums* (Frankfurt, 1929).
83. See Gershom Scholem, *Von Berlin nach Jerusalem. Jugenderinnerungen* (Frankfurt: Suhrkamp, 1977) 74.
84. Martin Buber, *Drei Reden über das Judentum*, in *Der Jude und sein Judentum* (Köln: Melzer, 1963) 15.
85. Ibid, 13.
86. Ibid 14.
87. Scholem, *Benjamin*, 87.
88. Ibid, 148.
89. Br 125ff.
90. Scholem, *Benjamin*, 14.
91. See also Benjamin on Buber and National Socialist terminology, B/S 228.
92. VuB 158/Und Brecht 110.
93. Scholem, *Jugenderinnerungen*, 73.
94. Ibid, 66ff.
95. Scholem's specialist writings were generally written in Hebrew after his move to Jerusalem. See also B/S 75.
96. *Major Trends in Jewish Mysticism*, first published in 1941, was the book which established Scholem's international standing.
97. II 244/'Proposal for the magazine *Angelus Novus*'.
98. Scholem, *Benjamin*, 162ff.
99. Ibid, 172.
100. Ibid, 174.
101. Br 463.
102. Scholem, *Benjamin*, 191.
103. Br 311.
104. Lacis, *Revolutionär*, 104.

2. *Socialism and the writer*

1. II 76/'Life of Students'.
2. BC 69/1-Way St 322.
3. II 858.
4. II 847.
5. MT 211.
6. Scholem, *Benjamin*, 154.
7. Fuld, *Benjamin*, 155; Lacis, *Revolutionär*, 41.
8. Lacis, *Revolutionär*, 41.
9. Br 374.
10. Br 370.
11. Scholem, *Benjamin*, 34.
12. Ibid, 101, 104.
13. Br 217 etc.
14. On the problem of continuity see Ulrike Hörster-Philipps, 'Grosskapital, Weimarer Republik und Faschismus', in R. Kühnl, G Hardach (eds), *Die Zerstörung der Weimarer Republik* (Cologne: Pahl-Rugenstein, 1977).
15. See E. H. Carr, *A History of Soviet Russia*, vol 7 (London: Macmillan, 1964) 98ff.
16. F. Deppe, Georg Fülberth, Jürgen Harrer (eds), *Geschichte der deutschen Gewerkschaftsbewegung* (Cologne: Pahl-Rugenstein, 1978) 178ff. 178ff.
17. Br. 368.
18. Scholem, *Benjamin*, 151.
19. Br 382.
20. Lacis, *Revolutionär*, 52.
21. Br 417.
22. Br 437.
23. Br 425.
24. Br 425.
25. Br 426.
26. Br 425, 430.
27. Br 382.
28. MT 106.
29. MT 108.
30. MT 107, 123.
31. MT 162.
32. MT 82.
33. MT 107.
34. MT 109.
35. See also Br 373ff.
36. Br 531.
37. Helga Gallas, *Marxistische Literaturtheorie* (Frankfurt: Roter Stern, 1978) 45ff.
38. MT 50.
39. Bertolt Brecht, *Tagebücher und autobiographische Aufzeichnungen* (Frankfurt: Suhrkamp, 1978) 217.
40. MT 210.
41. MT 57, 117.
42. MT 33.
43. Br 531.
44. B/S 87.
45. B/S 75.
46. B/S 33ff.
47. MT 108.
48. MT 109.
49. Br 319.
50. Fuld, *Benjamin*, 140; Br 381, 471.
51. See Hugo von Hofmannsthal, Willy Haas, *Briefwechsel*, 1968.
52. Br 380; Scholem, *Benjamin*, 159.
53. Scholem, *Benjamin*, 159.
54. IV 1053.
55. IV 815–62/'From Citizen of the World to High Bourgeois'.
56. IV 796–802/'Revue or Theatre'.
57. IV 307–16/1-Way St 167–76.
58. MT 108.
59. Br 381, 462.
60. B/S 33.
61. Scholem, *Benjamin*, 196.
62. *Die Linkskurve*, I, no. 1 (August 1929), 24.
63. Walter Fähnders, Martin Rector, *Literatur im Klassenkampf* (Frankfurt: Fischer, 1974) 21ff.
64. See Gallas, *Literaturtheorie*, and W. Fähnders, M. Rector,

Linksradikalismus und Literatur (Reinbek: Rowohlt, 1974) II, 207ff.

65. Lacis, *Revolutionär*, 58ff.
66. See, for example, Br 715ff; VuB 138ff.
67. Gallas, *Literaturtheorie*, 184.
68. I 1027; III 677.
69. Lacis, *Revolutionär*, 72.
70. Br 747.
71. Lacis, *Revolutionär*, 77; and see Scholem, *Benjamin*, 263.
72. Br 530.
73. Rolf Tiedemann, *Studien zur Philosophie Walter Benjamins* (Frankfurt: Suhrkamp, 1973) 112.
74. Br 605.
75. For example, Br 594, 663.
76. Lacis, *Revolutionär*, 49.
77. Br 502.
78. B/S 119ff.
79. B/S 130.
80. Br 596.
81. Br 778.
82. Brecht, *Arbeitsjournal* (Frankfurt: Suhrkamp, 1977) I (1938–42), 14.
83. Compare Brecht's letters to Benjamin in Bertolt Brecht, *Briefe* (Frankfurt: Suhrkamp, 1981).
84. Brecht, *Schriften zur Politik und Gesellschaft* (Frankfurt: Suhrkamp, 1977) 370.
85. Br 663.
86. Br 710.
87. Br 778.
88. Brecht, *Arbeitsjournal*, I, 301.
89. *Introduction to Critical Theory* (London: Hutchinson, 1980) 399.
90. *Text und Kritik,* Sonderband T h e o d o r W. A d o r n o (Munich, 1977) 5.
91. Br 380; II 1440; IV 1053.
92. II 1508.
93. Br 475.
94. Br 724; T. Adorno, W. Krenek, *Briefwechsel* (Frankfurt: Suhrkamp, 1976) 20.
95. II 1508.
96. II 1509.
97. Br 561; II 1509.
98. Martin Jay, *The Dialectical Imagination; A History of the Frankfurt School and the Institute of Social Research 1923–50* (London: Heinemann, 1973) 29, 31, 37, 39.
99. II 1512.
100. II 1514 (in 1934); III 674ff.(in 1935); I 999 (in 1936); II 1345 (in 1937); for 1938 and after see below.
101. Despite this, it should be noted that in 1932 Horkheimer had apparently refused a request from Adorno that Benjamin be given another chance to take the Habilitation (*Text und Kritik: Adorno*, 14).
102. II 1318; Lacis, *Revolutionär,* 72ff.
103. II 1185; 1319ff.
104. I 1018.
105. I 1019.
106. II 1342ff.
107. II 1351ff.
108. II 1354.
109. Br 744.
110. I 872.
111. Jay, *Imagination,* 23; *Über Walter Benjamin,* ed. S. Unseld (Frankfurt: Suhrkamp, 1968) 10; Scholem, *Benjamin,* 199; Br 663.
112. II 1508.
113. Br 558.
114. Adorno/Krenek, *Briefwechsel,* 43.
115. Ibid, 44. Adorno received a grant from the 'Academic Assistance Council' to go to Oxford, but his parents also continued to support him. *(Text*

und Kritik: Adorno, 22ff).
116. See Adorno/Krenek, *Briefwechsel*, 105.
117. Ibid, 125; II 1347.
118. Adorno/Krenek, *Briefwechsel*, 126.
119. Br 558.
120. See Adorno/Krenek, *Briefwechsel*.
121. Ibid, 85; see also Fuld, *Benjamin*, 227.
122. II 1508.
123. II 1173.
124. Br 638ff.
125. I 986. The first Baudelaire essay too was not sent to Adorno but to Horkheimer – see Br 773.
126. III 698; II 1397.
127. III 702.
128. II 1184.
129. II 1185.
130. Scholem, *Benjamin*, 270ff.
131. Br 810.
132. *Über Walter Benjamin*, 134.
133. Scholem thought not. See B/S 284ff, 288.
134. Br 568, 570.
135. I 1226.
136. Br 685.
137. II 1349.
138. Rolf Tiedemann's position on this has apparently changed: compare his Afterword in the first *Versuche über Brecht* (Frankfurt: Suhrkamp, 1966) with that of the second edition of 1978.
139. II 1186.
140. The most recent is Werner Fuld; see his *Benjamin*, 15.
141. See his comments on the 'Eduard Fuchs' commission.

3. The intellectual background

1. One of the strengths of traditional German intellectual history was its recognition of (a) the cyclicality and (b) the historical relativity of metaphysical systems. See, for example, Adolf v. Harnack, *History of Dogma*, trans. William McGilchrist (London: Williams & Norgate, 1899) VII, 7, on Nominalism; and a parallel discussion in G. Ficker, H. Hermelink, *Handbuch der Kirchengeschichte*, II (Das Mittelalter) (Tübingen: J. C. B. Mohr, 1929) 196ff.
2. See J. F. Roberts, *Ideology and the University* (Cambridge: Broadsheet, 1978).
3. Leopold von Ranke, *Die grossen Mächte* (Leipzig: Insel n.d. (1916)) 4.
4. Christofer Zöckler, *Dilthey und die Hermeneutik* (Stuttgart: Metzler, 1975) 235.
5. Ibid, 244.
6. G. Lukács, *Die Zerstörung der Vernunft* (Darmstadt: Luchterhand, 1974) II, 99.
7. *Logos,* II, 2 (1911) 132.
8. Heinrich Rickert, *Kulturwissenschaft und Naturwissenschaft* (Tübingen: J. C. B. Mohr, 1910) 10.
9. Lukács, *Zerstörung,* III, 19.
10. Ibid, II, 9.
11. *Logos,* II, 1 (1911) 30.
12. Rickert, *Kulturwissenschaft,* 98.
13. Georg Simmel, *Philosophie des Geldes* (Leipzig: Duncker & Humblot, 1907) Preface, viii.
14. Wilhelm Dilthey, *Einleitung in die Geisteswissenschaften* (Leipzig: Duncker & Humblot, 1922) I, xix.
15. Ibid, xvii.
16. Ibid, 6.
17. Ibid, 97.
18. Gunter Reiss (ed.),

*Materialien zur Ideologiege-
schichte der deutschen Liter-
aturwissenschaft* (Tübingen:
Niemeyer, 1973) I, 57.
19. Ibid, 65.
20. Ibid, 58.
21. Ibid, 57.
22. Wilhelm Dilthey, *Das Erlebnis
und die Dichtung* (Leipzig:
Teubner, 1922) 13.
23. Ibid, 11.
24. Dilthey, *Geisteswissenschaften,* 6
25. See the cited texts by Zöckler
and Lukács, and Werner
Krauss, 'Literaturgeschichte
als geschichtlicher Auftrag' in
Studien und Aufsätze (Berlin:
Rütten & Loening, 1959).
26. Ranke, *Mächte,* 4.
27. See, for example, Rickert in
Logos II, 2, 132; in *Kulturwissenschaft,* 10; Husserl in *Logos,* I, 1, 293 and 340; Carl
Schmitt, *Politische Theologie*
(Munich: Duncker & Humb-
lot, 1934) Preface.
28. Emil Lask, *Gesammelte Schriften* (Tübingen: J. C. B. Mohr,
1923) II, 25.
29. Gillian Rose, *Hegel Contra
Sociology* (London: Athlone,
1981) 9.
30. Martin Heidegger, *Gesamtausgabe* (Frankfurt: Kloster-
mann, 1978) I, 55.
31. See below,113–15.
32. Rickert, *Der Gegenstand der
Erkenntnis* (Tübingen: J. C.
B. Mohr, 1928) 6th edition,
208.
33. Ibid, 212.
34. Ibid, 199.
35. Kant, *Kritik der reinen Vernunft,* B 55.
36. Ibid, B 105.
37. Ibid, B 52; B 146ff.
38. Rickert, *Gegenstand,* 184.
39. Ibid, 186.
40. Ibid.
41. Ibid, 185.
42. Ibid, 200.
43. Ibid, 198.
44. Ibid, 201.
45. Ibid, 200ff.
46. Ibid, 197.
47. Rose's first chapter contains
an illuminating discussion of
this difficult position.
48. Rickert, *Gegenstand,* 196.
49. Ibid, 199.
50. Ibid, 201.
51. Ibid, 195, 452.
52. Ibid, 199.
53. Ibid, 195.
54. Ibid, 196, 198.
55. Ibid, 194.
56. *Kulturwissenschaft und
Naturwissenschaft,* already
cited.
57. Lask, *Schriften,* II, 5ff.
58. In *Logos,* I, 1 (1910), 324.
59. See Reiss, *Ideologiegeschichte,*
I, 60.
60. Husserl, in the article cited,
326.
61. Rickert, *Gegenstand,* xvii.
62. In the article cited, 313.
63. Ibid, 333.
64. *Gesamtausgabe,* I, 225 note.
65. Ibid, 263.
66. For example, in *Kulturwissenschaft,* 16, 54.
67. Lask, *Schriften,* II, 287.
68. *Gesamtausgabe,* I, 266.
69. Compare, in this connection,
Heidegger's use of the slogan
in *Sein und Zeit* (Tübingen:
Niemeyer, 1976) 27 and 34.
70. Heidegger's Habilitation was
on Scotus; both Lask and
Husserl cite Scholasticism in
terms which clearly allude to
Scotism (Lask, *Schriften,* II,
201, 216; Husserl, in the article cited above, 305).
71. Edmund Husserl, *Ideas,*
trans. Boyce Gibson (Lon-
don: Allen & Unwin, 1969)

54.
72. *Sein und Zeit,* 38.
73. Lask, *Schriften,* II, 288.
74. Heidegger, *Gesamtausgabe,* I, 272ff.
75. *Sein und Zeit,* 32.
76. *Logos,* I, 1, 341.
77. Ibid, 305.
78. Heidegger, *Gesamtausgabe,* I, 255.
79. See *Selections from Medieval Philosophers,* ed. R. McKeon (New York: Scribner, 1930) II, 430.
80. Heidegger, *Gesamtausgabe,* I, 260.
81. Ibid, 263.
82. *Sein und Zeit,* 33.
83. Ibid, 30.
84. Ibid, 34.
85. Ibid, 32.
86. Ibid, 32ff.
87. Compare *Kritik der reinen Vernunft,* B 102.
88. *Sein und Zeit,* 33.
89. Ibid, 29.
90. Ibid, 32.
91. Ibid, 34.
92. *Logos,* I, 1, 305.
93. Ibid, 335ff.
94. H. -G. Gadamer, *Wahrheit und Methode* (Tübingen: J. C. B. Mohr, 1960) 450.
95. Ernst Bloch, *Geist der Utopie* (Gesamtausgabe, vol. 16) (Frankfurt: Suhrkamp, 1971) 398.
96. Ibid, 397.
97. Ibid, 398.
98. Ibid, 399.
99. Ibid, 404.
100. Ibid, 402.
101. Ibid, 405.
102. Georg Lukács, *History and Class Consciousness,* trans. Rodney Livingstone (London: Merlin, 1971) xviii.
103. Ibid, xvii.
104. Ibid, xxiv.
105. Georg Lukács, *Lenin: A Study in the Unity of his Thought* (London: New Left Books, 1970) 79.
106. V. I. Lenin, *What is to be Done?* (Peking: Foreign Languages Press, 1975) 92.
107. Ibid, 93.
108. Lukács, *Lenin,* 26.
109. In the historical materialism which developed after he had completed the book on German *Trauerspiel* in Spring 1925.
110. Lukács, *History and Class Consciousness,* xvii.
111. Lukács, *Lenin,* 43.
112. Lukács, *History and Class Consciousness,* 299.
113. A. Bogdanov, *Allgemeine Organisationslehre* (Berlin: Organisation, 1926) 86.
114. Ibid, 70.
115. Ibid, 44.
116. Lenin, *Selected Works* (Moscow: Progress Publishers, 1975) II, 308.
117. Bogdanov, *Organisationslehre,* 52.
118. Ibid, 55.
119. Lenin, *Selected Works,* II, 308.
120. Bogdanov, *Organisationslehre,* 10.
121. Ibid, 31ff.
122. Ibid, 28.
123. Ibid, 58.
124. Ibid, 81.
125. Ibid, 54.
126. Lenin, *Selected Works,* II, 273.
127. Bogdanov, *Organisationslehre,* 38ff, 85.
128. Ibid, 56.
129. Lenin, *What is to be Done?,* 47.
130. Lenin, *Selected Works,* II, 661.
131. Bogdanov,

Organisationslehre, 42.
132. See the essay by Henri Deluy in A. Bogdanov, *La Science, L'Art et la Classe Ouvrière* (Paris: Maspero, 1977).
133. Bogdanov, *Organisationslehre,* 80.

III   Benjamin's work

1.   From ethics to politics

1. Stefan George, *Gedichte,* ed. Boehringer (Stuttgart: Reclam, 1958) 33.
2. See Michael Winkler, *George-Kreis* (Stuttgart: Metzler, 1972) 32ff.
3. Br 112.
4. Scholem, *Benjamin,* 30.
5. Br 515.
6. I 608/Baudelaire 110.
7. Ludwig Klages, *Vom kosmogonischen Eros* (Bonn: Bouvier, 1963) 98.
8. Ibid 100.
9. Ibid, 92.
10. Ibid, 97.
11. Ibid, 112.
12. For example, in Ludwig Klages, *Der Geist als Widersacher der Seele* (= Sämtliche Werke, vols 1 and 2) (Bonn: Bouvier, 1969) I, 844.
13. Klages, *Eros,* 132.
14. Ibid, 63.
15. Ibid, 68.
16. Ibid, 62.
17. Ibid, 109ff.
18. Ibid, 127.
19. Ibid, 128.
20. Ibid, 129.
21. Ibid, 61.
22. See *Philosophisches Wörterbuch,* 11th edition (Leipzig: VEB Verlag Enzyklopädie, 1975) 539.
23. Klages, *Eros,* 131.

24. II 124/'Two Poems by Friedrich Hölderlin'.
25. II 126/Ibid.
26. II 125/Ibid.
27. This distinction is central to the *Wahlverwandtschaften* essay; compare I 189.
28. Scholem, *Benjamin,* 73.
29. See Benjamin's comments on tradition and the Talmud in Br 146.
30. I   149/*Wahlverwandtschaften* essay.
31. I 148/Ibid.
32. II 141/1-Way St 108. Benjamin's early texts on language are perhaps the most opaque part of his entire oeuvre, not least because of their uncharacteristic eclecticism. I would suggest that Benjamin derived some of his early ideas on language from the scholastic doctrine of hylomorphism. (For one account, see Copleston's *History of Philosophy* (New York: Doubleday, 1962) vol. 2/2, 48ff.) Benjamin's notion of the increasing linguisticality of 'spiritual essence', with divine language at the summit, may be compared with the scholastic opposition of *'materia prima'* and the divine *'actus purus',* and the hierarchical scale of being which extended between these. Benjamin had a declared interest in scholastic philosophy at this period (II 146; Br 230, 246), possibly under the influence of Scholem, who did his own doctorate with the Catholic church historian Clemens Bäumker. (II 931; Scholem, *Benjamin,* 145). But these notions were among the first to be abandoned by the mature Benja-

min, and I have therefore not thought it wise to burden my account with a more systematic account of the background to the hierarchies of language.

33. II 161/'On the Programme of a Future Philosophy'.
34. II 142/1-Way St 109.
35. II 149/1-Way St 115. It is significant, in connection with the similarity between this theory and the scholastic notion of God as *'actus purus'*, that Benjamin calls God's creativity 'actuality'. (II 149/1-Way St 116).
36. II 148/1-Way St 115.
37. II 144/1-Way St 112.
38. II 149/1-Way St 116.
39. II 144/1-Way St 111.
40. II 147/1-Way St 113ff.
41. II 149/1-Way St 116.
42. Genesis 31.
43. II 152/1-Way St 119.
44. II 153ff/1-Way St 120.
45. II 150/1-Way St 117.
46. II 155/1-Way St 121. Benjamin's idea of the magical language of Nature, and its present silence, may be found also in Novalis. See *'Die Lehrlinge zu Sais'*, in W. Rehm (ed.), *Novalis* (Frankfurt: Fischer, 1956) esp. 47.
47. Compare *Philosophisches Wörterbuch*, 561; also Br 235.
48. II 145/1-Way St 112*.
49. *Sein und Zeit*, 33.
50. II 147/1-Way St 114.
51. II 166ff/'On the Programme of a Future Philosophy'.
52. I 148/'Goethes Wahlverwandtschaften'.
53. I 214ff/Origin 34ff.
54. Ibid.
55. Hegel is credited, in the *Trauerspiel* book, with having produced the 'sketch for a description of the world'. (I 212/Origin 32). See Tiedemann's book for a discussion of Benjamin in relation to Hegel.

56. I 217/Origin 37.
57. I 216/Origin 36.
58. I 217/Origin 37.
59. I 47.
60. I 218/Origin 38.
61. I 217/Origin 37.
62. I 228/Origin 48.
63. I 227/Origin 46.
64. I 218/Origin 38.
65. I 227/Origin 47.
66. I 218/Origin 38.
67. I 208/Origin 28.
68. I 210/Origin 30.
69. I 212/Origin 32.
70. I 208/Origin 28.
71. Scholem, *Benjamin*, 173.
72. I 148, 154/'Goethes Wahlverwandtschaften'.
73. I 216ff/Origin 36ff.
74. II 156/1-Way St 123.
75. II 157/1-Way St 123.
76. II 156/1-Way St 122.
77. This was an important and explicit part of Cohen's aesthetic thought. See also I 284/Origin 105.
78. IV 19/I11 80.
79. IV 21/I11 81ff.
80. IV 16/I11. 76ff.
81. IV 21/I11 82.
82. IV 17/I11 77.
83. IV 15/I11 76.
84. II 242/'Announcement of the magazine *Angelus Novus*'.
85. See I 62ff/'Romantic Art Criticism'.
86. Br 341.
87. Winkler, *George-Kreis*, 67.
88. Friedrich Gundolf, *Goethe* (Berlin: Bondi, 1930) 21.
89. Ibid, 23.
90. Ibid, 27.
91. Ibid, 6.

92. Ibid, 25.
93. Ibid, 1.
94. I 133/'Goethes Wahlverwandtschaften'.
95. I 159/Ibid.
96. I 135/Ibid.
97. I 166/Ibid.
98. I 152/Ibid.
99. I 150/Ibid.
100. I 154/Ibid.
101. I 151/Ibid.
102. I 154/Ibid.
103. I 164/Ibid.
104. I 158/Ibid.
105. I 171, 189/Ibid.
106. I 135/Ibid.
107. I 177/Ibid.
108. I 169/Ibid.
109. I 163/Ibid.
110. Br 83.
111. Br 152, 159, 166, 181.
112. II 178/1-Way St 130.
113. For example, Harnack, *History of Dogma*, VII, 53; Hermann Cohen, *Jüdische Schriften* (Berlin: Schwetschke, 1924) II, 256.
114. Scholem, *Benjamin*, 78ff.
115. Scholem, *Major Trends in Jewish Mysticism* (New York: Schocken, 1954) 36.
116. *Jüdische Schriften*, I, 304; II, 256.
117. Cohen, *Die Religion der Vernunft aus den Quellen des Judentums* (Frankfurt:, 1929) 12.
118. See *Jüdische Schriften*, II, 291; *Religion der Vernunft*, 391.
119. *Jüdische Schriften*, II, 254.
120. Ibid, 256.
121. Ibid, 254.
122. *Religion der Vernunft*, 66.
123. Romans 3.
124. See Van A. Harvey, *A Handbook of Theological Terms* (London: Allen & Unwin, 1966) 123.
125. II 198/1-Way St 149ff.
126. II 199/1-Way St 150.
127. II 202/1-Way St 153.
128. II 203/1-Way St 154.
129. Harvey, *Handbook*, 216.
130. *Jüdische Schriften*, II, 245.
131. *Religion der Vernunft*, 391, 394.
132. I 163/Goethes Wahlverwandtschaften'.
133. I 163, 175, 189/Ibid.
134. I 134/Ibid.
135. I 139/Ibid.
136. Br 245.
137. *Jüdische Schriften*, II, 250.
138. Ibid, 290.
139. Ibid, I, 141ff.
140. I 184/'Goethes Wahlverwandtschaften'.
141. Ibid.
142. I 188/Ibid.
143. I 192/Ibid.
144. I 194/Ibid.
145. I 193/Ibid.
146. Ibid.
147. I 194/Ibid.
148. I 200/Ibid.
149. I 198/Ibid.
150. *Vom kosmogonischen Eros*, 138.
151. I 163, etc./'Goethes Wahlverwandtschaften'.
152. I 154, 157/Ibid.
153. I 157, 184/Ibid; also II 201/1-Way St 152.
154. I 200/Ibid.
155. Ibid.
156. G. W. F. Hegel, *Phänomenologie des Geistes* (Frankfurt: Ullstein, 1973) 122.
157. Ibid, 123.
158. Ibid, 129.
159. Ibid, 129.
160. Ibid, 131.
161. Ibid, 122.
162. I 212/Origin 32.
163. I 242, 253, 257, 267, 268, 319/Origin 61, etc.
164. I 317/Origin 138.

165. I 390/Origin 216.
166. I 200, 292/Origin 113.
167. I 283ff etc./Origin 104ff.
168. I 289/Origin 110.
169. I 294/Origin 115.
170. I 285/Origin 106ff.
171. I 295/Origin 116.
172. I 287ff/Origin 108ff.
173. I 294/Origin 115.
174. I 282/Origin 103ff.
175. I 297/Origin 118; see also I 200.
176. I 293/Origin 113.
177. I297/Origin 118.
178. I 288, 298/Origin 109, 118.
179. I 296/Origin 117.
180. I 296, 298/Origin 117, 119.
181. I 298/Origin 119.
182. I 242ff, 299/Origin 63, 120.
183. I 298/Origin 119.
184. I 243/Origin 62.
185. I 229, 236/Origin 48, 56.
186. I 299, 363/Origin 119, 187*.
187. I 267/Origin 88.
188. I 260/Origin 81.
189. I 259/Origin 80.
190. I 308/Origin 129.
191. I 309/Origin 130.
192. I 317/Origin 138.
193. I 246/Origin 66.
194. I 263/Origin 84.
195. I 318/Origin 139.
196. Ibid.
197. I 320/Origin 142.
198. I 260/Origin 81.
199. I 208/Origin 28*.
200. I 246/Origin 66.
201. I 318/Origin 139.
202. I 260/Origin 81.
203. I 320/Origin 142.
204. I 319/Origin 140.
205. I 400/Origin 226.
206. I 337/Origin 160.
207. I 336/Origin 160.
208. I 337/Origin 160.
209. I 180ff/'Goethes Wahlver-wandtschaften'.
210. I 339/Origin 162.
211. I 336/Origin 160.
212. I 350ff/Origin 174ff.
213. I 343/Origin 166.
214. I 342/Origin 165.
215. I 351/Origin 176.
216. I 354/Origin 178.
217. I 373/Origin 197.
218. I 337/Origin 160ff.
219. I 342/Origin 165.
220. I 337/Origin 160.
221. I 342ff/Origin 166.
222. I 352/Origin 176*.
223. I 351/Origin 175.
224. I 352/Origin 176.
225. I 353/Origin 177ff.
226. I 355/Origin 179.
227. I 358/Origin 182.
228. Ibid.
229. I 357/Origin 182.
230. I 358/Origin 182.
231. I 356/Origin 180*.
232. I409/Origin 235.
233. I 351/Origin 175.
234. I 376/Origin 201.
235. I 378ff/Origin 204.
236. I 377/Origin 201.
237. Ibid.
238. I 378/Origin 202.
239. I 376/Origin 200ff.
240. I 351, 381/Origin 175, 207.
241. I 350/Origin 175.
242. I 383/Origin 209.
243. Ibid.
244. I 381/Origin 207.
245. I 382/Origin 208.
246. I 381/Origin 207.
247. I 383/Origin 209.
248. Ibid.
249. I 351/Origin 175.
250. I 376ff, 389/Origin 200, 215.
251. I 387/Origin 213.
252. II 178ff/1-Way St 131.
253. I 326/Origin 149.
254. I 329/Origin 151.
255. I 321/Origin 142.
256. I 327/Origin 149.
257. I 332/Origin 155.
258. I 275/Origin 97.
259. I 333/Origin 156.
260. Hegel, *Phänomenologie,* 187.

261. II 153ff/1-Way St 119.
262. I 217/Origin 37.
263. IV 21/Ill 82.
264. I 351/Origin 175.
265. I 384/Origin 210.
266. I 407/Origin 233.
267. I 403/Origin 230.
268. I 404/Origin 230.
269. I 405ff/Origin 232.
270. I 406/Origin 232.
271. I 701/Ill 263.
272. I 319/Origin 140.
273. I 320/Origin 141ff.
274. I 347/Origin 170.
275. I 299/Origin 120.
276. I 343/Origin 166.
277. I 236/Origin 56.
278. I 234/Origin 54.
279. I 236/Origin 56.

2. Historical materialism

1. Br 392.
2. Br 387.
3. Br 384.
4. Br 374.
5. Br 373.
6. Br 455.
7. Br 531.
8. Br 523.
9. See Friedrich Engels's essay, *Ludwig Feuerbach and the End of Classical German Philosophy.*
10. III 290/'Literary History and Literary Science'.
11. I 695/Ill 257*.
12. III 491/'Paris Letter I'.
13. II 474/1-Way St 357.
14. III 490/'Paris Letter I'.
15. III 44/Reviews, 1926 and 1935.
16. III 490ff/'Paris Letter I'.
17. III 491/Ibid.
18. IV 85/1-Way St 45.
19. II 701.
20. III 490/'Paris Letter I'.
21. IV 148/1-Way St 104.
22. I 469; III 238/Ill 244; NGC 120.
23. I 468/Ill 243.
24. II 800; III 250/'The French Writer'; NGC 128.
25. II 475/1-Way St 358.
26. II 494/1-Way St 376.
27. II 778/'The French Writer'.
28. III 240/NGC 121.
29. III 238/NGC 120; Bogdanov, *La Science*, 231.
30. III 250/NGC 128.
31. I 343/Origin 166.
32. III 247/NGC 126.
33. II 688/Und Brecht 90*.
34. III 492ff/'Paris Letter I'.
35. II 694/Und Brecht 96.
36. III 493/'Paris Letter I'.
37. Bogdanov, *La Science*, 218; *Allgemeine Organisationslehre*, 28.
38. II 213/1-Way St 163.
39. III 209, 223, 287/Reviews, 1929, 1930, 1931.
40. III 287/'Literary History and Literary Science'.
41. II 467/1-Way St 351.
42. MEW 3, 26ff.
43. Illum 180/Baudelaire 172.
44. III 258ff/'Against a Masterpiece'.
45. II 691/Und Brecht 93.
46. II 686/Und Brecht 88.
47. II 693/Und Brecht 95.
48. III 351/'The Error of Activism'.
49. II 777/'The French Writer'.
50. III 350/'The Error of Activism'.
51. III 175/1929 review.
52. II 690/Und Brecht 91.
53. III 176/1929 review.
54. III 352/'The Error of Activism'.
55. III 351/Ibid.
56. II 690/Und Brecht 92*.
57. Compare Raimund Rämisch, 'Der berufsständische Gedanke als Episode in der NS-Politik', *Zs für Politik*, IV, no. 3 (1957) 265-6.

58. II 691/Und Brecht 93.
59. II 701/Und Brecht 102.
60. III 225/'An Outsider Makes his Presence Felt'.
61. I 1161.
62. II 800/'The French Writer'.
63. For example, *Selected Works,* 2, 661.
64. III 208/1929 review.
65. III 203/1929 review.
66. II 794/'The French Writer'.
67. II 701/Ibid.
68. II 688/Und Brecht 90.
69. III 352/'The Error of Activism'.
70. II 802/'The French Writer'.
71. III 350/'The Error of Activism'.
72. III 482/'Paris Letter I'.
73. IV 595/'A Russian Debate in German'.
74. III 283/'Left-Wing Melancholy'.
75. III 351/'The Error of Activism'.
76. III 446/Und Brecht 81.
77. II 696/Und Brecht 98.
78. III 280/'Left-Wing Melancholy'.
79. III 184/1929 Review.
80. II 696/Und Brecht 98.
81. IV 108/1-Way St 67.
82. II 472/1-Way St 355. See also Bertolt Brecht, *Über Politik auf dem Theater* (Frankfurt: Suhrkamp, 1971) 26ff.
83. I 452/'The Work of Art in the Age of Mechanical Reproduction' – first version only!
84. I 569/Baudelaire 66.
85. I 567/Baudelaire 64.
86. I 568/Baudelaire 66.
87. I 565/Baudelaire 62ff.
88. II 801/'The French Writer'.
89. III 288/'Literary History and Literary Science'.
90. Ibid.
91. III 208/1929 review.
92. III 283 'Left-Wing Melancholy'.
93. See Illum 180/Baudelaire 172.
94. III 289/'Literary History and Literary Science'.
95. III 192ff/1929 review.
96. III 285/'Literary History and Literary Science'.
97. III 289/Ibid.
98. I 696/Ill 258.
99. I 700/Ill 262*.
100. Illum 184/Baudelaire 176.
101. II 432/Ill 134.
102. I 701/Ill 263.
103. III 203/1929 review.
104. I 561/Baudelaire 58ff.
105. II 367/1-Way St 290.
106. III 223/'An Outsider Makes his Presence Felt'.
107. See below, final chapter.
108. See Gillian Rose, *The Melancholy Science,* (London: Macmillan, 1978); and David Held, *Introduction to Critical Theory* (London: Hutchinson, 1981).
109. Adorno acknowledged that Benjamin found this, at least, 'suspiciously idealist'. (Adorno *et al., Der Positivismusstreit in der deutschen Soziologie* (Darmstadt: Luchterhand, 1972) 50.)
110. I 1095/Ernst Bloch *et al., Aesthetics and Politics* (London: New Left Books, 1977) 128.
111. I 1096/Ibid 129ff.
112. I 1107.
113. Leo Löwenthal, *Mitmachen wollte ich nie* (Frankfurt: Suhrkamp, 1980) 79.
114. I 1105/*Aesthetics and Politics,* 138.
115. I 451, 456.
116. I 1032.
117. I 1107.
118. I 1098/*Aesthetics and Politics,* 131.
119. I 1097/Ibid, 130.
120. I 1103/Ibid, 136.

121. III 574/Review of Stern-
berger.
122. III 573/Ibid.
123. III 582ff/Review of *Ency-
clopédie Francaise.*
124. Compare Jacques Lacan on
the 'Fort, da' game, in *Écrits*
(Paris: Seuil, 1966) I, 203ff.
125. See III 131/1928 review.
126. I 561/Baudelaire 59.
127. I 1107.
128. III 130/1928 review.
129. III 203/1929 review.
130. II 214, 298, 302; III 356,
574/'Experience and Po-
verty', 1-Way St 228, etc.
131. III 131/1928 review.
132. I 609ff/Baudelaire 111ff.
133. I 612/Baudelaire 114.
134. II 442/Ill 87.
135. II 440/Ill 85.
136. II 442/Ill 87.
137. II 448/Ill 92.
138. I 611/Baudelaire 113.
139. II 444/Ill 89.
140. II 364/1-Way St 286.
141. II 343/1-Way St 266.
142. III 131ff/1928 review.
143. I 611/Baudelaire 113.
144. I 701/Ill 263.
145. Sigmund Freud 'Jenseits des
Lustprinzips' in *Gesammelte
Werke* (London: S. Fischer,
1940-) vol. 13.
146. Ibid, 41.
147. Ibid, 41.
148. I 440, 647/Ill 224, Baudelaire
148.
149. III 131/1928 review.
150. For example, III 145/1928 review.
151. For example, I 639/Baude-
laire 141.
152. II 450/Ill 94.
153. II 376/1-Way St 248.
154. I 438/Ill 223.
155. II 453/Ill 98.
156. II 460/Ill 104.

157. II 450/Ill 94.
158. II 451ff/Ill 96.
159. II 457/Ill 102.
160. II 339/1-Way St 263.
161. II 463/Ill 107.
162. II 352/1-Way St 275.
163. II 458/Ill 103.
164. II 442/Ill 87.
165. II 364/1-Way St 286.
166. II 340/1-Way St 263.
167. See the correspondence between Benjamin and Scholem
over the Kafka essay, re-
printed in B/S.
168. Scholem, *Benjamin,* 213.
169. II 420/Ill 122.
170. II 427/Ill 128.
171. B/S 174ff.
172. II 297/1-Way St 227.
173. For example, Illum 184/Bau-
delaire 176.
174. III 101ff/1928 review.
175. I 559/Baudelaire 56.
176. II 297/1-Way St 227.
177. I 562/Baudelaire 59.
178. II 299/1-Way St 229.
179. II 297/1-Way St 227.
180. II 299/1-Way St 229.
181. Illum 180/Baudelaire 171.
182. I 612ff/Baudelaire 114ff.
183. I 630; also III 583n./Baude-
laire 132; 1940 review.
184. I 630ff/Baudelaire 132ff.
185. I 614/Baudelaire 116.
186. I 556ff/Baudelaire 53.
187. For example, III 220, etc./'An
Outsider Makes his Presence
Felt'.
188. II 216ff/'Experience and Poverty'.
189. Illum 172/Baudelaire 159.
190. Illum 175/Baudelaire 165.
191. II 475/1-Way St 358.
192. Illum 170ff/Baudelaire 158.
193. Illum 173/Baudelaire 161.
194. Illum 171/Baudelaire 159.
195. II 447/Ill 92.
196. Illum 174/Baudelaire 162.

197. Ibid; also II 371/1-Way St 243.
198. II 369/1-Way St 241.
199. II 375/1-Way St 246ff.
200. II 377/1-Way St 248.
201. II 752ff/'Reply to Oscar A. H. Schmitz'.
202. I 456/'The Work of Art in the Age of Mechanical Reproduction' – first version only!
203. I 458/Ill 235.
204. I 451ff/Ill 233.
205. Bogdanov, *La Science,* 220.
206. I 444ff/'The Work of Art in the Age of Mechanical Reproduction' – first version only! also I 442/Ill 226.
207. I 609/Baudelaire 111.
208. I 453/Ill 232.
209. I 646/Baudelaire 147.
210. I 441/Ill 225.
211. I 458/Ill 235.
212. I 451/'The Work of Art in the Age of Mechanical Reproduction' – first version only!
213. I 442: 'The film is an acquisition by a collective'. ('Reproduction' essay, first version only). The remains of the original passage appear in footnote 7 of the later version (Ill 246).
214. I 455/Ill 234.
215. Illum 213/Baudelaire 168.
216. Illum 180ff/Baudelaire 172.
217. I 441/Ill 226.
218. I 442/Ill 226.
219. I 638/Baudelaire 140.
220. I 441/Ill 226.
221. I 448/Ill 229.
222. I 651/Baudelaire 152ff.
223. I 536/Baudelaire 34.
224. I 583/Baudelaire 80.
225. II 777ff/'The French Writer'.
226. I 513/Baudelaire 11.
227. I 604/Baudelaire 106.
228. I 567/Baudelaire 64.
229. I 564/Baudelaire 62.
230. I 565/Baudelaire 63.
231. I 566/Baudelaire 63.
232. I 567/Baudelaire 64.
233. I 569/Baudelaire 66*.
234. I 574/Baudelaire 71.
235. I 573ff/Baudelaire 70.
236. I 582/Baudelaire 78ff.
237. Illum 179/Baudelaire 170.
238. I 519/Baudelaire 17.
239. I 603/Baudelaire 100.
240. I 515/Baudelaire 13.
241. I 591/Baudelaire 87.
242. I 593/Baudelaire 90.
243. Illum 180/Baudelaire 171.
244. I 590/Baudelaire 87.
245. I 591/Baudelaire 87.
246. I 585/Baudelaire 82.
247. I 587/Baudelaire 83.
248. I 600/Baudelaire 97.
249. I 517/Baudelaire 15.
250. II 802/'The French Writer'.
251. Illum 180/Baudelaire 171.
252. I 608/Baudelaire 110.
253. II 503/1-Way St 384.
254. Illum 178/Baudelaire 168.
255. I 565, 618; II 472/Baudelaire 63, etc.
256. See I 1185.
257. I 565/Baudelaire 63.
258. II 477/1-Way St 360.
259. II 215/'Experience and Poverty'.
260. II 218/Ibid.
261. II 215/Ibid.
262. II 478/1-Way St 361.
263. II 300/1-Way St 230.
264. II 217/'Experience and Poverty'.
265. II 298/1-Way St 228.
266. II 366/1-Way St 289.
267. II 309/1-Way St 238.
268. II 802/'The French Writer'.

3. The revolution – utopia or plan?

1. Scholem, *Benjamin,* 279.
2. VuB 167ff/Und Brecht 117.

3. Lacis, *Revolutionär*, 74.
4. Scholem, *Benjamin*, 274ff.
5. I 1227.
6. I 1224.
7. I 1223.
8. I 1224.
9. See P. Bulthaup (ed.) *Materialien zu Benjamins Thesen 'Über den Begriff der Geschichte'* (Frankfurt: Suhrkamp, 1975); also the writings of Peter Bürger on Benjamin, etc.
10. For example, in the 1955 *Schriften*, and the 1980 *Illuminationen*.
11. II 946ff.
12. S. Unseld (ed.), *Zur Aktualität Walter Benjamins* (Frankfurt: Suhrkamp, 1972) 87ff.
13. Ibid, 89.
14. I 696; II 476ff/Ill 258; 1-Way St 359.
15. I 699; I 574/Ill 260ff; Baudelaire 71.
16. I 697ff/Ill 259ff.
17. III 96; I 674; and see II 436/1928 review; 'Zentralpark'; Ill 138.
18. *Zur Aktualität*, 129.
19. Ibid, 134.
20. I 1223.
21. I 1226ff.
22. Theodor Adorno, *Gesammelte Schriften* (Frankfurt: Suhrkamp, 1977) 10/1, 250ff; Scholem in *Zur Aktualität*, 131.
23. For example, Illum 172, 176ff/Baudelaire 160, 166.
24. *Gesammelte Schriften*, 10/1, 252.
25. Revelation 21.
26. Adorno, *Gesammelte Schriften;* and see Scholem, *Zur Aktualität*, 131.
27. I 696/Ill 258.

28. I 694/Ill 256.
29. I 701/Ill 263.
30. I 696/Ill 258.
31. I 1238.
32. I 1239.
33. I 699/Ill 260ff.
34. See P. Gebhardt *et al.* (eds), *Walter Benjamin – Zeitgenosse der Moderne* (Kronberg: Scriptor, 1976) 126ff.
35. I 701/Ill 263.
36. Br 459.
37. II 242/'Announcement of a Journal'.
38. II 241/Ibid.
39. II 246/Ibid.
40. III 97/1928 review.
41. III 366/1932 review.
42. III 193/1929 review.
43. III 96; I 674/1928 review; 'Zentralpark'.
44. See Leszek Kolakowski, *Main Currents of Marxism* (Oxford: Clarendon, 1978) 2, 149ff; 3, 421ff.
45. II 191/1-Way St 143.
46. Br 425.
47. II 203/1-Way St 155.
48. II 204/1-Way St 156.
49. II 203/1-Way St 155.
50. Br 247.
51. Br 322ff.
52. II 204/1-Way St 156.
53. II 203/1Way St 155.
54. II 202/1-Way St 153.
55. II 187/1-Way St 139.
56. II 198/1-Way St 149ff.
57. II 199/1-Way St 150.
58. II 198/1-Way St 149.
59. II 202/1-Way St 153.
60. II 203/1-Way St 154.
61. II 198/1-Way St 149.
62. II 202/1-Way St 153.
63. II 204/1-Way St 156.
64. II 200/1-Way St 151.
65. I 701ff/Ill 263ff.
66. I 701/Ill 263.
67. I 701/Ill 263. *'Zeitraffer'*, lite-

rally 'time-gatherer', is the mode in which a projector 'speeds up' the film.
68. Ibid.
69. I 703/Ill 265. The same motif occurs in the *Trauerspiel* book – see I 218.
70. I 218/Origin 38.
71. I 1233.
72. I 700/Ill 262.
73. I 695/Ill 257.
74. Illum 180/Baudelaire 171.
75. I 1233.
76. I 696/Ill 258.
77. I 698/Ill 260.
78. I 1235.
79. I 697/Ill 259.
80. I 702ff/Ill 265.
81. I 704/Ill 265.
82. I 1226.
83. See III 290/'Literary History and Literary Science'. Also H. M. Enzensberger (ed.), *Kursbuch* (Frankfurt: Suhrkamp, March 1970) 20, 1ff.
84. *Gesammelte Schriften*, 10/1, 241.
85. Scholem, *Benjamin*, 33.
86. Br 139.
87. Franz von Baader, *Sämtliche Werke* (Leipzig: Bethmann, 1851-60) 4, 357n.
88. Ibid, 293 and footnote.
89. Ibid, 356ff.
90. See B/S 147.
91. III 308.
92. *Vom kosmogonischen Eros*, 100.
93. Ibid, 109ff.
94. Ibid, 112.
95. Ibid, 131.
96. Ibid, 112.
97. *Sein und Zeit*, 374.
98. Ibid, 328ff.
99. *Vom kosmogonischen Eros*, 63.
100. *Sein und Zeit*, 328.
101. Ibid, 386.
102. Ibid, 329ff.
103. Ibid, 375.
104. Ibid, 386.
105. Ibid, 315.
106. Ibid, 391.
107. Ibid, 384.
108. Ibid, 314. It should of course be emphasised that this is what is now commonly understood by 'hermeneutics', but that there are other perfectly legitimate hermeneutic traditions which have nothing to do with the work of Heidegger, Gadamer or Habermas.
109. Ibid, 330.
110. Ibid, 38.
111. Ibid, 389.
112. Ibid, 390.
113. Ibid, 311.
114. Ibid, 375.
115. Ibid, 312.
116. Ibid, 386.
117. Ibid, 390.
118. I 693/Ill 255.
119. But see Zöckler, *Dilthey und die Hermeneutik*, on Dilthey.
120. See Held, *Introduction to Critical Theory*, 310ff.
121. For example in *Zur Aktualität Walter Benjamins*, 212.
122. See Held, *Introduction*, 398ff.
123. See the essay in *Zur Aktualität*, now translated in *New German Critique* no. 17 (Spring 1979).
124. III 308/1931 review.
125. Br 129ff.
126. Br 246.
127. Br 252.
128. Br 524.
129. Br 771; and see Fuld, *Benjamin*, 274.
130. Br 506.
131. Br 514.
132. *Über Walter Benjamin* (Frankfurt: Suhrkamp, 1968), 52.
133. I 1232.

134. I 703/Ill 264.
135. III 288/'Literary History and Literary Science'.
136. I 697/Ill 259.
137. II 476ff/1-Way St 359ff.
138. See III 288/'Literary History'.
139. III 259/'Against a Masterpiece'.
140. III 301/1931 review.
141. III 264/1930 review.
142. II 514/Und Brecht 36.
143. III 366/1932 review.
144. III 289/'Literary History and Literary Science'.
145. Ibid.
146. III 258/'Against a Masterpiece'.
147. III 259/Ibid.
148. See III 301ff/1931 review.
149. III 192ff/1929 review.
150. See III 263; II 477/1930 review; 1-Way St 360.
151. II 477.
152. II 263/1930 review.
153. II 511/Und Brecht 33.
154. II 513/Und Brecht 36.
155. II 339/1-Way St 263.
156. II 340ff/1-Way St 264.
157. II 344ff/1-Way St 268.
158. II 364/1-Way St 286.
159. II 366/1-Way St 289.
160. II 422/Ill 124.
161. II 420/Ill 122ff.
162. II 436/Ill 138.
163. I 687.
164. See W. F. Haug, 'Wider den bloss verbalen Materialismus', in *Das Argument* no. 92 (October 1975).
165. III 255/'Against a Masterpiece'.
166. III 259/Ibid.
167. II 219/'Experience and Poverty'.
168. II 506/Und Brecht 27.

Index